Latinx

Latinx

The New Force in American Politics and Culture

Ed Morales

VERSO
London • New York

First published by Verso 2018

Unless otherwise indicated, illustrations are in the public domain. Every effort has been made to identify copyright holders for the illustrations reproduced here. But if any oversight has been made, author and publisher will emend the text in the next edition. Thanks to Adál for kind permission to use the photographs on p. 129.

1 3 5 7 9 10 8 6 4 2

Verso
UK: 6 Meard Street, London W1F 0EG
US: 20 Jay Street, Suite 1010, Brooklyn, NY 11201

versobooks.com

Verso is the imprint of New Left Books

ISBN-13: 978-1-78478-319-8
ISBN-13: 978-1-78478-320-4 (US EBK)
ISBN-13: 978-1-78478-321-1 (UK EBK)

British Library Cataloguing in Publication Data
A catalogue record for this book is available from the British Library

Library of Congress Cataloging-in-Publication Data

Names: Morales, Ed, 1956– author.
Title: Latinx : the new force in American politics and culture / by Ed Morales.
Description: London ; Brooklyn, N.Y. : Verso, 2018. | Includes bibliographical references and index. |
Identifiers: LCCN 2018008770 (print) | LCCN 2018015986 (ebook) | ISBN 9781784783198 (United States E book) | ISBN 9781784783211 (United Kingdom E book) | ISBN 9781784783198 (hardback) | ISBN 9781784783198 (US ebook) | ISBN 9781784783211 (UK ebook)
Subjects: LCSH: Hispanic Americans—Politics and government—21st century. | Hispanic Americans—Social conditions—21st century. | Hispanic Americans—Ethinc identity. | Cultural pluralism—United States. | United States—Ethnic relations. | BISAC: SOCIAL SCIENCE / Ethnic Studies / Hispanic American Studies. | SOCIAL SCIENCE / Anthropology / Cultural.
Classification: LCC E184.S75 (ebook) | LCC E184.S75 M666 2018 (print) | DDC 973/.046872—dc23
LC record available at https://lccn.loc.gov/2018008770

Typeset in Fournier by MJ&N Gavan, Truro, Cornwall
Printed in the US by Maple Press

For my father

Contents

Introduction

After several years of debate about America's progress on its racial question, the election of Donald Trump has brought white supremacy into the mainstream. Replacing coded dog whistles with an authoritarian bullhorn, he has openly declared undocumented Mexican and Central American immigrants to be violent threats to the American people and, indirectly, to the integrity of American identity. While Trumpian white supremacy still features anti-black racism at its core, as well as a large dose of Islamophobia, its intensified scapegoating of the undocumented has disrupted the black-white binary that has anchored race discourse throughout American history. Latinx, neither just black or white and eternally considered outsiders despite our 500-year presence in this hemisphere, are poised to signal a crucial turn in this debate.

Conversations about race in the United States have always been plagued by the unresolved trauma of Europe's colonization of the Americas and the resulting legacy of slavery. The United States, along with most of the Western world, has long roiled in an identity crisis stemming from the unfinished business of race and the slow decentering of the white, male, Western subject. Could

America's identity begin to include people of color, women, and LGBT people?

With the election of President Barack Obama in 2008, two contradictory narratives emerged: one of a post-racial society in which racism was "withering away" with the emergence of elites of color, and the other arguing that white supremacy and overt racism had been obscured by what sociologist Eduardo Bonilla-Silva calls "racialized social systems." The latter narrative pointed to a structural racism evident in racist micro-aggressions and in "dog whistle politics," a set of coded signals transmitted to America's eroding white majority assuring them that they were still in charge. Trump's emergence signaled the crash and burn of post-racial ideology, while at the same time foregrounding new racial scapegoats and blurring the neat boundaries of black-white opposition.

Latinx is a book about a growing group of Americans who are injecting a different idea about race into the American race debate. It will attempt to demonstrate that Anglo- and Latin America are two versions of the idea of "America," with two very different articulations about race. In Anglo-America, race is considered through a binary in which white and black are strictly defined opposites. In Latin America, while the racial binary still resonates, it is complicated by a tangled caste system that openly acknowledges several categories of mixed-race people and different ideas about how to assimilate them.

I don't intend to argue for the superiority of one of these ideologies or forms of social organization—they're both seriously flawed and represent competing traditions of Western modernism. But I believe that the Latinx view of race, inherited from nation-building ideologies that lionized race-mixing in Latin America, poses narratives that challenge and resist Anglo-American paradigms. While these ideologies have not ended racism and in some ways have even reinforced it in Latin America, they have the potential to explode binary contradictions. The convergence of Anglo- and Latin American ideas about race may point the way towards more nuanced ideologies, and possibly significant social change.

By titling this book *Latinx*, I'm attempting, like the mostly young folks that are embracing this label, to engage with several threads of thinking about identity and naming, recognizing and evaluating the potential of such a label's elasticity and ability to evade categorization. I'm drawing attention to the Latinx people as one of the primary destabilizers of American—and by extension, Western—identity. Often erased from America's founding narrative, Latinx—in all our previous guises—have always been present as a crucial counter-narrative, a people that live in a world of many worlds, possessing an identity of multiple identities.

What's in a Name?

The advent of the term *Latinx* is the most recent iteration of a naming debate grounded in the politics of race and ethnicity. For several decades the term *Latino* was the progressive choice over *Hispanic*; according to G. Cristina Mora's *Making Hispanics*, the latter was pressed into service by the Nixon administration in the 1970s, an apolitical attempt at an antidote to the "unrest" created by increasing activism in Latinx communities inspired by the African American civil rights movement. As he did with African Americans, Nixon promoted Hispanic entrepreneurship by appointing a Mexican American as the head of the Small Business Administration. *Hispanic* became a "pan-ethnic" category whose development was fostered by data researchers such as the Census Bureau, political "entrepreneurs" of both liberal and conservative stripes, and media marketers, who ultimately created the vast Spanish-language media.

Hispanic overtly identified Latinx with Spanish cultural, racial, and ethnic origins. Yet *Latino* carried with it the notion that Latin American migrants to the United States were not merely hyphenated Europeans, but products of the mixed-race societies and cultures south of the border who freely acknowledged that they were not "white." It has over the years become more widely accepted among liberals, while *Hispanic* still carries a strong weight among conservatives—including many who are Latinx.

Still, as *Latino* became the preferred choice of those who wanted to identify as multiracial, gender politics quickly emerged in the politics of labeling. Spanish is a Romance language in which all nouns are assigned a gendered identity (ordinary objects such as shoes, automobiles, and computers, for example, are male or female); therefore the Latino population necessarily consists of Latinos (male) and Latinas (female). As racial identity began intersecting with gender and sexual preference, *Latino* became *Latino/a*, then *Latina/o* to move "o" out of the privileged position. After the universalization of digital communication, it briefly became *Latin@* among Latino/a student unions and nonprofit organizations and in academic articles and books (*Latino/a Condition: A Critical Reader*, published in 2012, became *Contemporary Latin@ Media Production* in 2015).

For all of *Latinx*'s space-age quirkiness, the term has a technocratic emptiness to it that can make it hard to warm up to. It feels like a mathematician's null set, and many are unsure of how to pronounce it. But even amid ongoing debate around the term on campuses and in the media, the growing movement to embrace *Latinx* highlights how it dispenses with the problem of prioritizing male or female by negating that binary. The real power of the term and its true meaning, however, erupts with its final syllable. After years of Latin lovers, Latin looks, Latin music, and Latin America, the word describes something that is not as much Latin—a word originally coined by the French to brand non-English- and Dutch-speaking colonies with a different flavor—as it is an alternative America, the unexpected X factor in America's race debate.

Who or What Are Latinx, and What Is the Nature of Our Doing?

Latinx intends to describe the in-between space in which Latinx live, which allows us to cross racial boundaries more easily and construct identities, or self-images, that include a wide variety of racial, national, and even gender-based identifications. Rather than simply creating a new shade of person somewhere between black and white, this in-between space has the potential to reveal the blackness and indigenousness often erased in Latin America by mixed-race utopian ideologies, but kept alive through oscillating tendencies toward tolerance and repression. Many premodern roots and traditions remained intact while others, fragmented by Spanish colonialism, always threatened to reemerge, and new hybrid identities, like the syncretic religions of the Afro-Caribbean, took hold.

While mixed-race culture in Latin America evolved with the help of Catholic doctrine, Spanish law, and twentieth-century nation-building ideologies, the development of racial identity in the United States has been significantly different. Because of the United States' unique racial ideology of hypodescent—one drop of black blood makes you black—with no official recognition of "mixed-ness" in state ideology, media, or "common sense" discourse, the hybrid and mestizaje elements of American culture remain obscured. Yet the widespread creation in the United States of hybrid and hyphenated identities such as Nuyorican, Chicano, Dominican-York, Tejano, and Miami Cuban has created space for excluded identities to assert themselves.

For Latinx in the United States, this relatively new process of creating hybrid identities dates back to the end of the Mexican-American War and the absorption of the Southwest territories in 1848. While the hegemony of the black-white racial binary has effectively rendered a true understanding of the Latinx experience unintelligible in the standard narrative of American history, the pattern of racial discrimination has had the paradoxical effect of encouraging a stronger assertion of African and indigenous identities. This became particularly clear in the 1970s when Puerto Ricans in New York formed the Young Lords, a militant political group modeled on the Black Panthers, and Chicanos of California and the Southwest organized around an indigenous identity connected to an imaginary homeland called Aztlán.

In a nation built on profit extracted from slavery, the legacy of Jim Crow, the exploitation of imported Asian workers, and guest worker bracero arrangements with migrant Mexican labor, Latinx can play a pivotal role in uncovering the uncomfortable truths of America's dark past as well as the fallacy of "non-racist" societies prevalent in the countries from which our parents emigrated. While the one-drop rule was metaphorically reversed in Latin America, allowing a majority to believe that we were white, this whiteness has not transferred smoothly to the States, revealing not only US racism but also aspects of racial identity formation that had been papered over in the home countries. The messy conversation about racial identity, multiracial identification, passing, and potential inter-ethnic alliances has already begun.

Yet the possibility looms of a shift in the United States towards what some have called a tri-racial system of whites, blacks, and an unnamed in-between category, presumably for those of mixed-race or not-quite-white identities, in which, as Eduardo Bonilla-Silva argues, increasing numbers of non-European people will be granted honorary white status. One of the challenges of observing the Trump era will be to monitor how the extension of class privileges to non-whites that began in neoliberal Obama-world may actually continue, despite the seemingly overt white supremacist rhetoric embodied by Trump. The fact that as many as 29 percent of Latinx voted for Trump indicates that these privileges may be extended to people of color who accept the language of xenophobia and intolerance as a path to the restoration of American "greatness."

What Is Race for Latinx?

There is a long and unresolved argument about what race is, what racism is, and when and where it started. Historians have traced anti-black racism to antiquity, although it has not always been used to justify slavery. Regardless of when and how the idea of race began, it seems to be the product of a distrust and/or condemnation based on distance, whether in religious beliefs, physical location, or phenotypical appearance. Some historians and religious scholars believe that the biblical story of Ham—the son of Noah banished to reign over Africa because he laughed at his father's nakedness—was revived in the nineteenth century and sparked the ill-conceived "race science" that defined five racial categories. Foucault, on the other hand, argued that racist thinking emerged from the civil wars of the medieval era among the nobility and was merely translated in the formation of the European state. And the decolonial school, particularly followers of Argentine-Mexican philosopher Enrique Dussel, proposed that the Spanish Catholic re-conquest of Iberia after almost 800 years of gradually receding Islamic occupation transformed religious differences into ones based on "race."

As the twenty-first century unfolds in America, we are still grappling with racial division, which the election of Trump appears to have made even more explicit. Trumpian authoritarianism shuns difference and promotes intolerance to protect white supremacy and "make America great again." But despite Latinx being "racialized" or branded as "non-white," it's not clear how they fit into the new authoritarianism. Through centuries of racial mixing, Latinx in some senses constitute our own race, albeit one that includes Northern, Southern, Eastern, Western, and Mediterranean Europeans; Northern and sub-Saharan Africans; Muslims and Jews; Semites from the Middle East; Asians from East Asia; and their descendants called Native Americans.

The word that is often used to denote that Latinx are a "collective" race, itself a mixture of races, is *raza*: Spanish for race. This use of *raza* became popular in the early twentieth century to describe mixed-race society in Mexico, largely driven by the publication of an essay by postrevolutionary Mexican minister of culture José Vasconcelos. Titled *La Raza Cósmica*, or "The Cosmic Race," the essay argued that

Latin America's mixed-race societies augured a kind of racial tran-
scendence that would end racial categorization and liberate humanity.
Vasconcelos's treatise formalized a social process of race-mixing
called *mestiẓaje*, a system of social ranking based on permutations of
sexual unions (sometimes coerced, sometimes allowed by the relax-
ing of laws against intermarriage) between Spaniards, indigenous
people, members of the African diaspora, and Asian migrants.

Vasconcelos's cosmic raza, which grew into an ideology that had
parallel versions in several other Latin American countries—was the
twentieth-century reimagining of a centuries-old, inherently racist
caste system through which a peculiar and somewhat tainted brand
of Spanish whiteness devalued, diminished, and erased the presence and importance of indigenous Americans and those of African
descent. Membership in la raza was ostensibly open to everyone, but
was ultimately a mechanism for gradual whitening over generations.
African and indigenous presence in politics, culture, and sports was
embraced, but only to the extent that it prioritized universalized
national identities and minimized cultural particularities.

As Latinx became a part of the fabric of Anglo-America through
both the absorption of the Southwest territories in the mid-nineteenth
century and gradual migration from the Caribbean and South
America in the early twentieth, *raẓa* became part of local vocabu-
laries. While not entirely universal among Latinx—some preferred
Hispano, others *Latino*—*raẓa* began to be primarily used in the
United States by Mexican immigrants. Faced with racism in their
new country, they used the term to unite different Latin American
national identities into one progressive force and collective "brown"
identity, one that would give voice to marginalized people of color
erased by mestizaje.

There's an irony here that can only be explained by viewing
the migration of Latinx to the United States as a kind of dialectical process, in which one view about race collides with another and
creates something new. The same mestizaje ideology that worked to

sublimate indigenous and African identity in Latin America became a resource for Latinx to claim racial difference as their identity in the black-white race binary of the United States. This is central to the Latinx factor, and explains why *raza* matters in America. It also explains why the choice by the National Council of La Raza to change their name in 2017 to UnidosUS—fearing that Latinx would be marginalized by the Trump version of white supremacy—was a panicky attempt to blunt the racial awareness of the label *raza*.

Although *raza* has been primarily used by Mexican Americans, who make up about 62 percent of all US Latinx, other Latinx groups have drawn on variations of the term to identify themselves, particularly when confronted by the binary choice of black or white. The word at once carries the legacy of the Spanish idea of race and how it was transferred to the New World, but it has a kind of pliancy that makes it a recognizable concept among Latinx. I use it here mainly to make the structure and inherent fiction of America's race narrative visible.

The Language of Latinx: Where I'm Writing From

As I undertake the task of writing about why *raza* matters, my first challenge is to find the proper language to describe it. As America finds itself in the throes of unending racial conflict and tries to untangle both the meaning of race and the systemic inequality produced by it, the object of inquiry often seems to slip away, harder to grasp by any measure of interpretation by the sciences or humanities. Now recognized as a social construction and not a matter of biology—despite DNA analyses becoming increasingly popular with the Ancestry.com crowd—the slipperiness of race becomes more evident even as overt racist feelings, attitudes, and, increasingly, violence grow.

I also want to avoid the perception that by saying, "*Raza* matters," I'm making some kind of rejoinder to "Black lives matter." Nothing could be further from the truth. The best place for *raza* to find meaning is within the "collective black" of the United States and the developed world. This notion of "collective black," developed by sociologist Eduardo Bonilla-Silva to highlight the common racial and social class interests of African Americans and other racialized groups, is reminiscent of the "black" label devised in England to unify Afro-Caribbean and Asian communities, expressing that even though they were not culturally, ethnically, or physically the same, they were seen and treated similarly by the dominant culture. That's why, throughout the course of this book, I argue for the importance of Latinx and African Americans forming alliances, rather than competing through contesting testimonies of marginalization. Latinx share a variant of the double consciousness of African Americans that Du Bois famously evoked, their experience distinguished more by historical and geographical differences than racial ones.

By the same token, the history of black, Native, and Asian American people in the United States has also been marked by mixture, and in many ways the imposition of the binary lens prevents them from having insight into this aspect of their identity formation. While the oppressive weight of racism based on phenotypical perception is undoubtedly the dominant narrative, the history of the Americas is unavoidably hybrid, in the daily lives as well as the cultural legacies of blacks, Natives, and Asian Americans. Foregrounding the mixed-race reality of Latinx may, ultimately, have a liberating effect on groups that don't always view themselves that way.

My raza-speak flows from my location, or where I'm writing from. My starting point is a place of radical exteriority, playing the tried-and-true outsider game of counter-discourse. My experience is that of a racialized person living in a US mega-city, who has a somewhat ambiguous phenotypical appearance, who in daily life speaks a mixture of two European languages that themselves are mixtures of many world languages, who embraces the collective black urban space of my upbringing in New York, and who holds within me memories of Africanness and indigenousness that I'm constantly bringing to light, even as medieval and Greco-Roman cultural politics ebb and flow in the background.

I could begin with a story, like Cornel West does in his book *Race Matters*, about the bitter memory of feeling at the top of my game in New York City, only to be reminded of how I can never escape my racial identity by cab drivers in Midtown Manhattan who turn down my hails as if I were an ambassador from a leper colony. What if I were to say that at various points in time, depending on where I was hailing the cab, what I was wearing, and how the sunlight was hitting my skin, the chances of the cab stopping for me hovered between 40 and 60 percent. What if I were to say that I feel, in a society ruled by a binary perception of race, that I am judged more by my performance than by my appearance, even though the latter might still be enough to classify me as "other."

I recall an incident when two Latinx policemen stopped me at West 125th Street and Broadway, just around the corner from the campus of Columbia University, where I am a lecturer, and insisted that I was carrying a knife and that I show it to them immediately. I'd come to campus to get a couple of books out of the library, and because I wasn't teaching that day I was wearing a backward baseball cap, worn-out jeans, and a long-sleeved T-shirt, attire that made me either look "ghetto" or resemble a criminal suspect which, for these policemen, who were employing the controversial stop-and-frisk approach of postmodern urban policing, justified my questioning. They looked at me with insistent eyes, convinced that I was carrying a weapon and that this was going to be a long afternoon, evening, and perhaps several days for me, ostensibly sitting in a local precinct waiting to be processed.

Consider the ambivalence that passed between us in this charade. Although I come from a working-class background, could not be considered a "white" Latinx by mere appearance, and have at times actively chosen to identify as black, at least for political or cultural reasons, I've avoided street fights and petty crime for the most part, have never carried a weapon, and live a rather pedestrian life built around teaching, writing, and attending cultural events.

The policemen, on the other hand, were signaled by my unkempt appearance and perhaps a furtive movement of my hand toward a keychain holder protruding from my right front pocket, a plastic Puerto Rican flag in the shape of an island. They were operating in the context of 125th Street; in Morningside Heights, a neighborhood on the gentrified West Side of Manhattan, the street is a racial and class dividing line of sorts, a border zone to be patrolled. Both Latinx with complexions similar to mine, they no doubt categorized me as "black," as they probably wouldn't have stopped me if they thought I was "white." At the same time, they were probably involved in complex internal negotiations about their own "whiteness" and "blackness."

Did they recognize me as someone from their own racialized upbringing, or did they identify as white and see me as a threat? In enacting the colonial narrative of racial identity, were they both feeling "black" and "white" simultaneously? They looked blankly at my university ID, reluctantly questioned me for a few more minutes, then decided I was not who they were looking for and did not pose a threat. It was difficult to tell whether their lack of emotion indicated frustration at the waste of time or indifference as they went through the motions with another faceless suspect. It was a Fanon *en español* moment, and whatever black or white masks we were wearing had dissolved into an uncertainty of racial identity, despite the fact that the reason for the stop was racially charged.

The Stories of Latinx Past, Present, and Future

Latinx begins with Chapter 1, "The Spanish Triangle," describing the partial origins of our constantly changing identity in Spain, which struggled to reconstitute itself as a universal Christian nation after a nomadic branch of Islam encountered the post-Roman fragments of

Iberia. Despite centuries of *convivencia*, or a tenuous "living together" arrangement between Christians, Jews, and Muslims, exclusion based on religion shifted to one based on race. This ultimately became the root of the modern conception of race, as Spain's racial politics allowed for genocide, slavery, indoctrination, and acculturation. The unique model of race and class hierarchy formed in Latin America remains influential to this day through centuries of strife, miscegenation, and race-based trial and error.

The saga continues with Chapter 2, "Mestizaje vs. the Hypo-American Dream," which describes how mestizaje, in ideology and practice, became the cultural legacy that accompanied Latinx on their migration north to the United States, characterizing racial mixedness both as a path towards whiteness and as a source of strength, the basis of a Latin American exceptionalism. A precursor to the forces of globalization waxing poetic on "hybridity," Latin America's view of race seems to represent the borderless future. But despite being an ideology of the powerful that preserves white supremacy, mestizaje differs from globalized notions of hybridity because it represents an "organic" form of cultural mixing achieved through centuries of interracial procreation and intra-societal cultural negotiation. Mestizaje itself is built on the stories of everyday people, narratives in transition, as Afro-Latinx and pro-indigenous movements continue to grow in Latin America and push back against the white supremacy inherent in it.

This chapter next examines how mixed-race realities have been obscured in culture and ideology during the gestation of the United States, a necessary part of establishing the black-white racial binary. Rather than arising simply from the opposition between Anglo Protestantism and Latin American Catholicism, the imposition of the binary through hypodescent was designed to maintain slavery as a driver of capital accumulation. The tension between the black-white binary and mixed-race realities produced a marginal space that spurred the creation of new hybrid identities for Latinx in the United States.

Chapter 3, "The Second Conquista: Mestizaje on the Down-Low," tells the story of Latinx arrival in the United States through both migration and absorption of territory thanks to nineteenth-century Manifest Destiny, laying the groundwork for a new set of nomadic cultural identities. These were inflected both by Latinx's Latin American origins and efforts to remake their new homes in their own image. Such nomadic identity formation is evident in the hybrid living spaces of the Southwest borderlands, the Caribbean transformation in Northern cities such as New York, Boston, and Chicago, and the establishment of Miami as the northernmost capital city of Latin America. It also leaves a significant cultural footprint, generating artistic touchstones from salsa to bilingual literature to the concept of intersectionality as developed by Kimberlé Crenshaw that has deeply informed the feminist and LGBT movements. I argue in this chapter that Latinx's cultural inclination to view the world through multiple perspectives has given them a central role in US cultural creativity.

In Chapter 4, "Raza Interrupted," I describe the parallel histories of the formation of Nuyorican and Chicanx identities, contemporaneous with and inspired by the African American recontextualizations of the civil rights era. A new kind of nationalism, crafted around identifications with racial difference, helped create hybrid cultural and political practices that at once tried to strip away the racism of Latin American mestizaje, yet still struggled with feminism and gay activism in parallel fashion to the New Left movement of America's 1960s.

What follows are narratives that grapple with how two facets of Latinx reality—English-Spanish bilingualism and mixed-race identities—have an innate potential to resist the restrictions of normalized American identity. Chapter 5, "Border Thinking 101: Can La Raza Speak?," explains that Latinx self-perception and how they are perceived are fundamental to assessing twenty-first-century America, as such narratives break down phenotypical determinism and the rigidly polarized conceptions of racial experience. The transgressive potential of Latinx viewpoints stems from "border thinking," a notion rooted in the work of Mexican American writer Gloria Anzaldúa, who was intent on disrupting the divide between a boundaried self and the reality of multiple subject positions. Her work, as well as that of the many writers influenced by her, begins with the argument that Latinx can be perceived differently in terms of race at varying moments of the day, even when they gather as family units, which creates a radical exteriority to the false notions of unity at the center of Trumpist white supremacy.

My discussion of border thinking is done in conversation with W. E. B. Du Bois's "double consciousness," a mind-state that not only parallels Latinx consciousness but in practice fuses with it, particularly in urban areas where blacks and Latinx mix.

Chapter 6, "Our Raza, Ourselves: A Racial Reenvisioning of Twenty-First-Century Latinx," tries to move the mestizaje ideal from the Latin American project of race erasure to the need for Latinx assertion of racial difference and ultimate bonding with African Americans and other racial minorities, theorizing about the potential political strength of the "collective black."

Once the personal internal border is breached and the new racially diverse subject is crystallized through bilingual oral and written expression, music, theater, and visual arts, as well as the always necessary quotidian interactions on the streets, Latinx reality can manifest itself as a political phenomenon. As Chapter 7, "Towards a New Raza Politics: Class Awareness and Hemispheric Vision," argues, merely inhabiting and performing the de-centered identity of Latinx becomes a political act, one that can render the binary, two-party political debate dysfunctional and irrelevant and substitute a class-based, hemispheric-visioned politics that constantly centers exploitation of the Global South in the discussion.

In Chapter 8, "Media, Marketing, and the Invisible Soul of Latinidad," I describe the contradictory reality of how Latinx are excluded from some media narratives and highly targeted by marketers at the same time. As the subjects of a commodifying effort by media and marketing forces, politically aware Latinx—from Providence, Rhode Island, punk rockers Downtown Boys and L.A. folkloric Mexican fusionists Las Cafeteras to socialist firebrands such as Rosa Clemente and Immortal Technique—see through the false set of homogenizing traditions invented for them to appeal to global consumers.

All of these tendencies—the border thinking of multiple subjects contained within a single individual, the code-switching of bilingualism, the assertion of racial difference, the ability to participate in local politics while fighting against worldwide wealth inequality and worker exploitation, and the potential to remain elusive to the targeting forces of media marketing—can be nurtured in unique urban spaces, whose postwar multicultural essence mirrors the multifaceted Latinx experience itself.

Chapter 9, "The Latinx Urban Space and Identity," focuses on the merging and cross-fertilizing of multiracial cultures that is best accomplished in cities, particularly in opposition to neoliberal projects that ironically intend to reduce them to cultural artifacts. It is in these urban spaces that Latinx best achieve their necessary integration into the collective black, which includes people of color, women, sexual minorities, and anyone alienated from the binary order that has remained constant from colonialism to neoliberalism. Urban spaces allow for the creation of oral, textual, and visual languages that Latinx are central to devising, and reclaiming these spaces can be seen as one of the first key moments in a broader resistance.

The argument made by Audre Lorde with her famous invocation to use new tools to dismantle the master's house is the subject of *Latinx*'s Chapter 10, "Dismantling the Master's House: The Latinx Imaginary and Neoliberal Multiculturalism." At this crucial historical juncture, Latinx have the challenge of interpreting and acting on their future as they are offered new ideologies of inclusion, acculturation strategies that are neoliberal updates of the mestizaje ideology they inherited from Latin America. Even as the old white supremacist order is temporarily revived by the Trump presidency, false neoliberal narratives of racial inclusion will tempt many people of color into believing that racial inequality is finally eroding in twenty-first-century America. Latinx will have to decide how their identity will survive in the context of new syncretic symbols of inclusion forming the basis of a revisionist history, which may have the same results as in Mexico, when the government put indigenous heroes and symbols on their paper currency.

In conclusion, the Epilogue argues that both overtly and under the radar, a conscious movement of Latinx and other people of color struggling to define themselves outside of whiteness is emerging. Rather than finding new paths to assimilation, they are discovering the other that exists within themselves, the one previously relegated to unconscious dreams of Iberia, Africa, Aztlán, and the Moors transferred to the New World. They are finding that the "otro yo," the inner dialogue between indigenous and diasporic utterance and African origins and the media-reified urban Latino reality, is becoming foregrounded by practices such as hip-hop, jazz, and plena, folkloric retellings of syncretic religion, and work songs. These are counter-narratives that are forms of resistance.

The social contract that underpins the American nation hinges on forgetting. For almost two centuries the project seemed as if it might succeed, but of late, we have been besieged by a flood of memories. The emergence of Black Lives Matter is inexorably tied to the many atrocities and genocides that have occurred in the Americas and have not been properly addressed. Latinx have brought many memories with them as well, some forgotten in their native lands but all kept alive through a common language of translating traditions. Latinx can play a crucial role by translating and transcending the rigid rhetoric that is splitting the left: the conflict between racial and sexual identity politics and class-based politics. From their words and actions arise a real-time image of what is happening in communities across the country to the targeted, reviled, and rejected. It's a voice of indigenous blackness, both those who identify as such and those who live in their embrace, struggling to think differently, living in the space where the self cannot silence them.

1

The Spanish Triangle

The often-invoked reason that politically progressive Latinx prefer *Latin* over *Hispanic* is that the latter seeks to identify us with Spain, embracing European whiteness and acceptability over our African and indigenous DNA. But while today Spaniards seem white and European, Iberia has always been the darkest corner of Europe. Having shifted from almost 800 years of Islamic occupation to initiating the conquest of the New World, Spain lives at the crossroads of European identity, straddling the space between colonized and colonizer.

The process through which Spain made itself white through the expulsion of the Jews and Moors has always been haunted by the legacy of its "appropriated" dark side. The techniques by which the country used race and culture as forms of social control persist today in Latin America and in Latinx America. When Stuart Hall muses on a twentieth-century "globalized" subject permeated by the new rules of transnationalism, postcolonialism, and the advent of widespread digital information technology—"fragmented, multiple, unstable, and decentered"—he may well be talking about Spain (and by extension, Iberia) at the end of the fifteenth century.

It is from Spain that we get the word *raza*, the clear forerunner to the current conception of race which embodies the transition from its use as a classification tool for plants and animals to one for human beings. *Raza* was key to Spaniards' self-definition when Spain became a nation-state, a Christianizing, whitening process that required the expulsion of two long-entrenched religious groups, Islam and Judaism, newly defining Spanishness by racial rather than religious purity.

The Islamic presence in Spain had begun in the eighth century and peaked near the beginning of the millennium, after which caliphate control gradually receded southward. Jews, Muslims, and Christians had coexisted for centuries under "an uneasy and anxious arrangement that often erupted into persecution, cruelty, and war," as Ivan Hannaford argues. In the early 1200s, Christian rulers and clerics began to demand verifiable proof of the lineages of converted Jews and Muslims to determine their authenticity as Spaniards. The fever for blood purity climaxed with the Inquisition that began in the mid-fifteenth century, with its expulsion and conversion of Jews and Muslims in Iberia just as the conquest of the New World was beginning. Spain's national identity was defined: it was not only Christian, but "white."

Although this Spanish nation-building project took place long before Europe emerged from the feudal era into the modern one, neither Spain nor its Iberian neighbor Portugal were central to the formation of capitalism and the Enlightenment, and thus their processes are often seen more as prehistory than modern history. But the concepts of race and racism clearly began before slavery in the American colonies and the imposition of the black-white binary. Spanish racism was indeed driven by anti-black racism but not exclusively.

Despite employing walled cities or "barrios" to separate Christians, Jews, and Muslims, Spain's state of *convivencia* tolerated cultural fusion through hybrid languages like Mozarabic and the translation of Arabic texts into neighboring Romance languages, creating a multicultural society that echoed the combination of ethnic groups in the Roman Empire. While this made Spain relatively "enlightened" compared to the rest of Western Europe, which was still in the Dark Ages, the pitfalls of convivencia and the Roman Catholic Church's growing intolerance of Jews began to turn the tide in the early thirteenth century. At the same time, as they began to recoup territory lost to Muslim invaders, Spanish Christians began to consolidate their religious rule by exposing previously tolerated outsiders.

This is where the notion of raza begins, forming the basis of modern racism. Formerly used to classify wines, plants, horses, and the emblematic bulls of Spain, *raza* came to describe lineage and thereby impute desirability or undesirability to a citizen. It came into more widespread use to distinguish *conversos* and *moriscos*—Jews and Muslims who agreed to convert to Catholicism—from old-line, "pure-blood" Catholics. *Buena raza* and *mala raza* (good and bad race) were phrases used to describe inevitable biological afflictions that derived from common sense discourse about the nature of the social order. Spanish history scholar David Nirenberg quotes the early fifteenth-century book *Arcipreste de Talvera*, by Alfonso Martínez de Toledo, asserting a naturalness to race and the characteristics associated with it. Martínez describes a converso who held office in Toledo: "Thus you will see every day in the places where you live, that the good man of good raza or lineage, no matter how powerful or how rich, will always return to the villainy from which he descends." Nirenberg also cites Sebastián de Covarrubias, who in the early seventeenth century made the connection between the original use of raza to categorize animals and its negative implications for humans. Once used for horses, which should be "marked by a brand so that they can be recognized," it had then evolved to describe human lineages "negatively, as in having some race of Moor or Jew." These examples illustrate that raza in Spain was not necessarily associated with color, particular since there were no stark phenotypical differences between many Christians, Jews, and Muslims. Since it was hard to tell by physical appearance who was a true "old Christian," the negative "natural" qualities of a suspected convert needed to be revealed by investigating lineage (*linaje*) or caste (*casta*) and bloodlines.

As Ramón Grosfoguel describes it, the "re-conquest" of Spain was a "universalizing project" that rolled back Islamic resistance in their remaining region of strength in Southern Iberia, known as Al-Ándalus (Andalucía), where multiple identities and spiritualties were allowed to exist. The Spanish royal families of the northern province of Aragón wanted to create an uninterrupted correspondence between Catholic identity and their territory, swallowing up the peninsula with the Christian faith. In doing so, using religious critiques that had been building over centuries and that condemned Islam and Judaism as the "wrong religions," the Spanish crown offered Jews and Muslims the choice of expulsion or conversion. In employing their own Inquisition, separate from the Vatican's, the Spanish quest for religious and racial purity merged with the creation of an absolutist state.

Nelson Maldonado-Torres argues that as Spain's discomfort with the Islamic caliphate increased, contemporary religious thinkers began to develop the idea that non-Christian believers were lacking in humanity because of their beliefs. This reflected the Roman Empire's distrust of "pagans," but was directed at a long-present resident population and used to encourage widespread conversion to Catholicism under threat of expulsion. One of the important precedents for this thinking, writes Maldonado-Torres, was, ironically, *The Guide for the Perplexed*, written by Maimonides, a Sephardic Jew who was fluent in Arabic and who lived in Córdoba, Spain, in the twelfth century. In one passage he writes that "people who ... have no religion ... are irrational beings ... below mankind, but above monkeys, since they have the form and shape of a man and a mental faculty above that of a monkey." Maimonides was arguing against

Islamic theology, but eventually his argument was used against Jews and all non-Christians in Spain.

Hannaford imputes the emergence of racism in Spain to the post-Roman tensions between the role of the state and the church in society. "Racism was created out of an attempt to have political solutions in a church-state dialogue about diversity," he writes, "because those who considered themselves to have ultimate authority and natural rights to power found it threatened by those they did not perceive to be part of their religion or in-group, and the outsiders were determined through biological lineage."

Conversion efforts produced a large-scale culture of "passing," in which some of the ostensibly converted remained deeply hidden, secretly practicing their faith. Many former Muslims and Jews were convincing enough as converted Christian moriscos that they began to ascend in Spanish society to the extent that their growing power necessitated a reinvigoration of the Inquisition nearly 100 years later. In sixteenth- and seventeenth-century Spain, in a manner evoking the conquest and designation of indigenous people as subhuman, Muslims were denounced as non-human and attacks on the undesirability of their bodies and appearance became common in oral and textual expressions. Ignacio de las Casas, a Jesuit morisco, wrote at the beginning of the sixteenth century:

> The Christians have developed a hatred of them so deep that they do not even want to see them, and since that is not possible they take their revenge by insulting them, calling them "dog of a Moor," and visiting on them every grave and frequent outrage that they can get away with.

The original policy of conversion, which evolved into a witch hunt for pure blood, created a kind of cognitive dissonance for Christian Spaniards, who had integrated much of Islamic culture into their own and continued to appropriate it subliminally even as they rejected actual Muslims. In her book *Exotic Nation: Maurophilia and the Construction of Early Modern Spain,* Barbara Fuchs makes the case that Moorish culture was fetishized even after their expulsion through *mudéjar* (hybrid Spanish–Moorish) architecture, *caballería* (horsemanship), derived from Moorish tradition, forms of dress and the practice of sitting on the floor on pillows, and *juegas de cañas,* Moorish jousting games. The concept of the "good moor," which is found in several literary and poetic texts, draws a distinction between light and dark Moors and suggests that some may be successfully converted and not necessarily excised.

The concealed presence of former Muslims in society also made Spain's "pure" whiteness in reality a kind of "off-whiteness," one perpetually susceptible to racialization in Europe, through the infamous Black Legend writings of the nineteenth century, and then Anglo-America. During the second Inquisition in the sixteenth century, all Spaniards were forced to prove their pure Christian lineage and were in effect under suspicion at any point in time to be "passing" for Christian. Citing Etienne Balibar's theory that "fictive ethnicity" helped construct a nation-state, Fuchs suggests that passing was accomplished through a "border-crossing transvestism" in which changing forms of dressing disguised not only gender but national, racial, and ethnic identity as well. She quotes Covarrubias, writing at the height of anxiety over blood purity, suggesting as much. Even though he doesn't directly address religious passing, it seems to be embedded in his observation.

> All nations have had their own dress, which distinguishes them from others, and many have preserved their costume for a long time. In this regard, Spaniards have been noted as fickle, because we change habit and dress with such ease. And so a fellow who was mad or pretended to be, running around in rags with a cut of material over his shoulder, when asked why he did not have clothes made from it, would answer that he was waiting to see where fashion would end up.

The carnival of passing that is said to have occurred in the sixteenth and seventeenth centuries is even referenced in *Don Quixote*, considered to be the first modern novel, where several sequences conflate Moorish/Christian passing with male/female passing. Fuchs describes a sequence in the novel in which a Spanish viceroy interrogates an apparently Moorish captain of an invading corsair who stands before him with a noose around his neck, who appears "so beautiful, so brave, so humble":

> "Tell me, captain, are you of the Turkish nation or a Moor or a renegade?"
>
> To which the lad answered, in the self-same Spanish tongue, "I am neither of the Turkish nation nor a Moor nor a renegade."
>
> "Then what are you?" countered the viceroy.
>
> "A Christian woman," answered the young man.
>
> "A woman and a Christian and in such an outfit and in such straits? That is a thing rather to be marveled at than to be believed."

In a few lines of dialogue, says Fuchs, the captain reveals "herself simultaneously as a transvestite and as an excluded Christian forced out of Spain into an uncomfortable allegiance with its enemies." In this way, "passing reminds us that, along with repressive categories, there have always existed sophisticated strategies for escaping categorization" and that "narratives of national or religious cohesion are surprisingly vulnerable to creative imitation."

As Spain was transformed by its expulsion or conversion of Jews and Moors, it was also competing with Portugal, hunting for gold, conquering the Americas, and encountering those continents' inhabitants. The process of Iberian colonization was shaped by the shift from religious exclusion to one based on race, reinforced by the presence of a new, completely exterior other. When Columbus, whom Sued-Badillo claims was a converted Jew, arrived in Hispaniola in 1492, he was motivated to find justifications to enslave the local inhabitants to make the extraction of gold easier. In a text attributed to Columbus and dated to his first encounter with the indigenous population on October 12, 1492, he writes:

> They all go naked as their mothers bore them ... I supposed and still suppose that they come from the mainland to capture them for slaves. They should be good servants and very intelligent, for I have observed that they soon repeat anything that is said to them, and I believe that they would easily be made Christians, for they appeared to me to have no religion.

Maldonado-Torres asserts that Columbus's continued observation that the inhabitants of the Caribbean islands had no religion—not just the "wrong religion"—laid the grounds for the dehumanization of indigenous people and later African slaves that would be the basis for modern racism. While allowing for their "intelligence," which here does not necessarily indicate humanity, Columbus is at once declaring their fitness for slavery and for the Christianizing process that had fostered national unity in Spain.

Sylvia Wynter observes that Columbus saw the world through Spain's religious categories, with Christians at the apex, Muslims and Jews as "infidels," and idolaters, who were pagans and non-believers. But, Wynter argues, Columbus considered the indigenous population not as idolaters but as akin to "the Aristotelean concept of the natural slave." In this way, the conquest of the New World and its transformation of the world economy fused Spain's religious mission to a political-economic one, where the moral guidelines shaping interactions with this new non-human escaped the boundaries of religious debate.

The correct view of the indigenous people was also the subject of debate between two clergymen, Gines Sepulveda and Bartolomé de las Casas, in the mid-sixteenth century. Sepulveda argued that indigenous people were without religion or "soul," essentially uncivilized, and by virtue of natural law should be enslaved and subjugated by a superior moral force, writing in his *Treatise on the Just Cause of the War Against the Indians*:

> It will always be just and in conformity with natural law that such [barbaric] peoples be subjected to the empire of princes and nations that are *more cultured and humane,* so that by their virtues and the prudence of their laws, they abandon barbarism and are subdued by a more humane life and the cult of virtue.

A significant element of his argument was that the indigenous were idolaters because they practiced human sacrifice. He felt the Spanish crown must intervene not only because it was just, but to save the indigenous from themselves by putting an end to the "great injury" of "the many innocent mortals that these barbarians sacrificed every year."

De las Casas, on the other hand, was the first to allow that indigenous people were human. "Are they not men?" he asked. "Do they not have rational souls? Are you not obligated to love them as you love yourselves?" He argued that the indigenous people's moral-religious view of the world included sacrificing humans, and that they should be taken seriously as reasoning beings. The Spaniards were then morally responsible for crafting a compelling argument that would convert the indigenous people to Christianity.

Enrique Dussel cites de las Casas's intervention as the first critique of modernism. According to Dussel, the Jesuit friar was arguing "the first anti-discourse of Modernity." He, at once refuting "the claim of superiority of Western culture," grants the "Other" the "universal claim of his truth"; and "demonstrates the falseness of the last possible cause justifying the violence of the conquest, that of saving the victims of human sacrifice, as being against natural law and unjust from all points of view."

Despite de las Casas's appeals, Sepulveda's exclusionism helped solidify Spain's intolerance at home, which culminated in the fascist Franco state of the twentieth century. But de las Casas's argument

would heavily influence Spanish policy in the New World toward
indigenous people, ending their widespread enslavement in favor of
a heavy-handed acculturation process, and set into motion the dominance of the nascent Atlantic slave trade of sub-Saharan Africans.

The Indigenous Reprieve and the Condemning of Blackness

Ramón Grosfoguel observes that the outcome of the fifteenth-
century Sepulveda–de las Casas debate changed the fate of indigenous
people in the Americas from literal enslavement to colonial subject-
hood through conversion to Christianity and the highly exploitative
encomienda system. The two sides of the argument, he argues, were
predecessors to the two contemporary views of racism, biological
and cultural. Cultural racism asserts that the subject of racism is not
less than human, but in need of acculturation to the rational normalcy of the West. The insistence on American norms (including, for
example, a pro-business economic system, exclusive use of English,
and embrace of pop cultural models) and the need for conversion
to them, while "humanistic" in a sense, does not go far enough to
acknowledge "difference" and the validity of the cultural traditions
and religious practices of marginalized groups.

At the dawn of the colonization project, Spain and its neighbor
Portugal needed to look no further for a group to be enslaved than the
emerging slave trade on the West Coast of Africa. Historian James
Sweet argues that Spaniards and Portuguese inherited the historical
roots of racist views toward sub-Saharan Africans through their intimate connection with Islamic customs, culture, and practices. Muslim
practices of enslavement appear to have anticipated the binary ultimately in place in the United States, dividing slaves between field and
house work according to skin color. Lighter-skinned slaves, often
from Northern Africa and called Saracens, were favored over the
darker-skinned, called Mauros. These designations were also used

to identify invading armies led by North African Berbers and Arabs, and free Moors and sub-Saharan Africans.

Sweet finds a similar distinction between military foes of Spain in the thirteenth century: the lighter-skinned North African Almohads, who conquered from Northern Africa, and the darker-skinned sub-Saharan Almoravids, who attacked from the East. The Almohads, although enemies and Islamic infidels, were considered to be less barbarous than the Almoravids and therefore deserving of more respect. The Almohad rule of the twelfth century fostered the most cultural crossover, particularly between Sufi Islam and Jewish Kabbalah—a key moment in the development of European mysticism.

Turning to Africa for slave labor, the Spanish established a new form of white supremacy and anti-black racism in the New World that left room for some ambiguity thanks to interracial mixing and

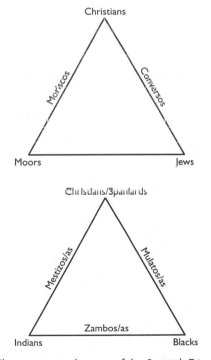

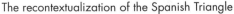

The recontextualization of the Spanish Triangle

categorization. In an attempt to locate himself in the dynamic of Latin American/Latinx identity, semiotician Walter Mignolo devised a triangular template that described not only the transfer of Spanish national identity to the New World, but the shift from systems of domination derived from religious identification to systems determined by race. The first triangle shows the hierarchical positions occupied by Christians, Moors, and Jews at the end of the Moorish occupation in the late fifteenth century, as well as the "hybrid" groups of moriscos and conversos.

The second triangle suggests that this model was transferred to the New World. Christians are at the top, but they are now reconstructed as the new, purified post-Inquisition Spain, with Indians (Native Americans) and blacks in the same positions as Moors and Jews, and hybrids known as mestizo/as and mulato/as on the triangle sides. The difference between indigenous people of the New World and imported Africans was measured by race rather than religion, given that their religions were polytheistic and earth-based and therefore considered invalid.

Mignolo calls this the colonial "racial matrix" that is "the historical foundation of racism as we know it today." But his triangle model shows why the United States was formed by a different kind of racial matrix. Those colonies were settled by Europeans from countries whose only religious difference was often just sectarian, rather than a country like Spain that had created a tenuous balance between three of the world's major monotheistic religions over eight centuries. The United States developed a racial matrix based on strict separation of races, rather than adopting the relatively fluid models of Iberian colonization, which engaged in a kind of exponential racial variation through both forced and negotiated miscegenation.

The sides of the Spanish Triangle and the model's ability to create fluidity of identity in order to reinforce the supremacy of its apex are key to understanding how the model promotes white or "off-white" supremacy while nurturing a subversive dynamic of race-mixing that plays at the edge of the model's self-destruction, because of the potential to reinfuse it with racial difference. This third, mixing space suggests the simultaneous presence of both *mestizos*, a term mostly used to describe intersections between Spaniards/Iberians and indigenous Americans, and *mulatos*, used to describe intersections between Spaniards/Iberians and African-descended people.

Mestizos and mulatos parallel Spain's hierarchical "others," including the Mauros and Saracens, Almohads and Almoravids, Moors and Jews, moriscos and conversos. The way in which categories are integrated into the matrix is a precursor to the twentieth-century liberal whiteness hinted at by Roland Barthes in his *Mythologies* when he refers to the rhetorical figure of "inoculation." Through an "inoculation" of modest doses of "dissimilarity," the white liberal can grow toward a tolerance of difference without threatening its supremacist assumptions and while strengthening its hold on power by demonstrating a humanistic magnanimity open to outside influence.

The Latin American version of the "colonial matrix" mechanism appears to be increasingly coming into play in the current US race debate. While the black and white binary is still very strong, playing a determining role in race discourse, the emergence of neoliberalism and its deference to inclusivity has created a space for new conflict and dialogue about race. These are more subtle conflicts about, for example, cultural appropriation and racial micro-aggressions.

Social media is in a constant buzz over the casting of superheroes in the now-ubiquitous comic-book-fantasy-scifi movie genre. Whether it's Scarlett Johansson or Tilda Swinton "whitewashing" roles originally written for Asians, Matt Damon starring in a movie about the Great Wall of China, or Iggy Azalea appropriating rap music through the reshaping of her body in the manner of Nicki Minaj, a torrent of derision and disapproval arises from people of color. They seem dumbfounded that mainstream Americans can shamelessly hunger for black, Latinx, and Asian cultural forms while excluding them from their origin, and from representation in general.

The #OscarsSoWhite hashtag, which had a tangible effect on reform in the practices of the Academy of Motion Picture Arts and Sciences, was a response to cultural erasure by Hollywood.

The daily anxiety surrounding micro-aggressions is captured in a series of short videos by Franchesca Ramsey on MTV called *Decoded*. In these and other media creations, made by outlets like Fusion and BuzzFeed, the seemingly unconscious racist attitudes and beliefs harbored by conservative and liberal whites alike are revealed, along with the detailed reasons for why they cause harm. Movies like *Dear White People* fluctuate between addressing subtle slights and overt offenses, like campus parties where white students engage in cross-dressing based on negative stereotypes. "Whitesplaining" is also a focus of some of this discourse, in which liberal whites are shown to believe they know quite a bit about racism and are well-equipped to explain it to its targets. Latinx, who are often featured on Fusion, are also busily producing similar media artifacts.

While contemporary negotiations and conflicts in America have evolved, the dynamic can bring to mind the way in which the Spanish, according to Barbara Fuchs, romanticized their Moorish past after either violently expelling them or allowing them to convert to Christianity. This process involved incorporating them into the off-white Spanish racial identity, which was echoed in the way Latin Americans embraced indigenous people only through the whitening process of mestizaje. These days even fashion magazines such as *Vogue* seem to be pushing their measure of beauty in an off-white direction, with fashion models such as the Russian Irina Shayk (who is commonly mistaken as Brazilian) dominating the tabloids.

In similar fashion, through both popular culture and the growing acceptance of urban hip-hop culture, white Americans have developed a strong affinity for certain aspects of African American culture even as mass incarceration and police brutality toward unarmed black men mushroom. In an America where hip-hop has finally supplanted rock music as the dominant pop music genre, it seems hard to understand the shift toward openly racist taunting and behavior in the age of Trump. Yet it does make sense if you view it through the lens of early modern Spain, which wanted everything about their pseudo-Arabic dress, dance, and horseplay without the actual Muslim people, and their religion, present.

How *Casta* Became a Model for Class—and Race—Mobility

The concept of caste, or in Spanish, *casta*, began with the stability that convivencia allowed during the Muslim occupation. By segregating Christians, Moors, and Jews, and allowing minimal or no conversion between the members of each faith, the caliphate—itself a mixture of converted North African Berbers and Arabs from the Middle East—created a semi-peaceful society that also allowed them to collect taxes from non-Muslims.

In the New World, the new system would result in the tortured duality that marked both the conflict and efficient collaboration between the Spanish state and the church. Again the dynamic here is dialectical, a society generating state identity by addressing internal conflict through both tolerance and exclusion. While medieval Spain prosecuted fewer heretics than other European countries, its expulsion of groups it had tolerated for years revealed the limits of its open-mindedness. Franco's fascist regime in the twentieth century also undertook a nationalizing project along with the reassertion of purity, betraying a strong affinity with Nazism.

The race paradigm the Spanish set up in the New World transposed the strange inclusion/exclusion principle that governed their love-hate relationship with Muslims and, to a lesser extent, Jews, onto the incestuous population of mestizos created by their interactions with the Americas' indigenous people, ostensibly salvageable through forced conversion to Catholicism. This conflictive dynamic was recently illustrated with shocking clarity through the 2015 conferring of sainthood on Juniper Serra, a notorious eighteenth-century Catholic missionary who oversaw a mass conversion of Native Americans in California by Pope Francis. Native American activists claimed, according to a report in the *Guardian*, that upon Serra's arrival in 1769, natives were "ravaged by European diseases" like syphilis, and those brought into missions "were not allowed to leave, and if they tried they were shackled and severely beaten." They also said labor was coerced, they were fed poorly and packed tightly into close living quarters, and their rebellions were brutally repressed. Serro was seen as a founding father of California, and his actions were very much the modus operandi of the Catholic Church's civilizing mission in Latin America, with its philosophical roots in de las Casas's arguments. This structure of racism is at the center of my understanding of how Latinx's view of race differs from and interacts with the debate about race in America. Rather than a stark Manichean contrast between black and white, good and evil, self and other, there's a lot of gray area surrounding what in the end is still a white supremacist system.

Mestizaje: The All-Inclusive Ideology of Exclusion

Mestizaje, which can refer to the general process of race-mixing in Latin America as well as the product of that race-mixing, is the legacy of Spain's contradictory angst over religion and race, transmitted to the New World. As Mignolo and others have described it, celebrating mestizaje was a way of creating the idea of Latin America as a region of Catholic tolerance and postcolonial national unity. Its history reflects the many strands of Iberian reality, as well as the sometimes overtly violent, sometimes peacefully negotiated nature of the process.

The classic origin story of mestizaje involves the Spanish conqueror of Mexico, Hernán Cortés, who encountered an indigenous woman, referred to as La Malinche, and made her a slave, his translator, and his mistress. This pairing set up the betrayals that surround the historical phenomenon of mestizaje: translation, in which power is ceded in language to create a zone of understanding, and procreation, which produces mixed-race offspring. While Malinche's children were quickly shipped back to Spain to become indoctrinated in privilege and Malinche's translation of various tribal languages resulted, in the long arc of history, in the supremacy of Castilian Spanish, this union was paradigmatic for progenitors of mestizaje for centuries to come.

The word *mestizaje* describes the transfer of Spain's raza, linaje, and casta concepts of social organization to the New World. It was popularized in the early twentieth century in Mexico following the 1910 Revolution, which emphasized land reform and its implications for indigenous communities. Later in the century, particularly in Vasconcelos's positive assertion of it in his essay *La Raza Cósmica,* Octavio Paz's more bleak appraisal in *The Labyrinth of Solitude,* and the revolutionary recontextualization of it in the work of Gloria Anzaldúa, the term has become an archetypal way of describing Mexican identity formation.

The story of La Malinche had the effect of imbuing all mestizo unions with the metaphorical character of conquest and subordination through intermarriage and racial mixture. A significant strand of Latin American misogyny evolved as a response to La Malinche's "betrayal," which evoked the emasculation of indigenous men through the conquering privilege of Spaniards. These indigenous men had little hope in continuing their influence outside of a model of intermarriage that would make their offspring white enough to move higher in the casta hierarchy.

María Elena Martínez's ambitious book *Genealogical Fictions: Limpieza de Sangre, Religion, and Gender in Colonial Mexico* connects the tumultuous centuries before and after the Age of Exploration with the construction of race and caste in Mexico. The development of these systems in Mexico parallels those in other parts of Latin

America, and the fact that Mexican Americans make up about 62 percent of all Latinos in the United States makes the construction of mestizaje there crucial to the way we can view its influence here.

The elaborate casta system implemented by the Spanish in Latin America took intermarriage into account and established rules for the racial status of children who resulted from it, with the ultimate status afforded to white Spaniards. It offered opportunities for increased status to indigenous people but not to Africans and mostly not to the African-descended.

This process was immortalized in what were called casta paintings, diagrams that were guides to the racial hierarchy and the status results of intermarriage, including the results of pairings involving the Spanish, indigenous, Africans, Jews, Moors, mulatos (black/ Spanish), lobos (black/indigenous), Asians (Gíbaro), and moriscos.

This casta painting illustrates various potential mixed procreative couples, unscientifically defining mixed-race variations that would result.

The second picture in the top row calls the child of a mestizo (Spanish/indigenous) and a Spaniard a *castizo*. Number three then shows how that castizo, in the next generation, can regain "Spaniard" status by simply procreating with a Spaniard. With one-quarter indigenous blood, this new Spaniard would still have access to all of the privileges of whiteness, something that would be untenable under US one-drop racial rules.

The crystallization of mestizaje ideology took place in the early part of the twentieth century as a reaction to Western race science (claiming a difference in propensity for intelligence and civil behavior among races) and eugenics that had been flowering in Europe and the United States. One of its principal theorists was Gilberto Freyre, who studied with Franz Boas at Columbia University and who was interested in a humanist, "melting pot" rejoinder to the grim message of race science. Freyre's ideas were crucial in imagining Brazil as a vast racial democracy that attempted to include its very large Afro-descended population in the national imaginary.

In his seminal book, *The Masters and the Slaves*—in which he thanks Boas for showing him "the difference between race and culture"—Freyre constructs a problematic (by today's standards) paradigm of Brazilian society centered around the "Big House" of a coffee or sugar plantation. Viewing the essence of Brazilian society as a re-creation of the master-slave dialectic incorporating aspects of European feudalism, and glossing over nonconsensual unions between masters and slaves as the engine of mestizaje, Freyre does little to paint the country in the positive light he desired.

In Mexico, José Vasconcelos, the minister of culture in the post-Revolution government, wrote *La Raza Cósmica*, which proclaimed that his country's diverse racial mixture, unified under a national ideology that celebrated it, constituted the fifth and final cosmic race, one that would finally transcend the race problems that countries like the United States, with its black-white binary, found so difficult to resolve. With his famous expression, "My spirit will speak for my race," Vasconcelos was attempting to move away from race science and eugenics and foresaw the emergence in Latin America of a "synthetical race, the integral race, made up of the genius and the blood of all peoples and for that reason, more capable of true brotherhood and of a truly universal vision."

Freyre's and Vasconcelos's ideologies—which found different, if more muted expressions in the Caribbean, Venezuela, Colombia, and Central America—were primarily a strategy to resolve the contradictions of a white-mestizo elite that held political and economic power in countries whose populations were majority people of color.

Intermarriage and rape were the mechanisms by which a middle ground, or buffer zone, was created between the Spanish conquerors and the majority indigenous and African populations in most Latin American countries north of the Rio de la Plata and the Southern Cone. Sex was the currency and mechanism of social fluidity that besmirched indigenous and African women with the irremovable stain of the conqueror and feminized indigenous and African men through subjugation. Translation of tradition and transculturation absorbed non-Christians into the Spanish mindset, and indigenous and African beliefs and religions were either erased or submerged in the magical/spiritual process of syncretism, inscribed in Christian symbols and saints.

Mestizaje was also a staging ground for the negotiations between the indigenous, the African, and the European, where difference is disappeared or, sometimes, where indigenousness or blackness can at times take the upper hand in the formation of culture. While this model mainly served to repress African and indigenous cultures in Latin America, mixed-race Latinx encountered a different dynamic after migrating to the United States. In their home countries they had been encouraged to mute their African and Native roots in favor of membership in an idealized mixed-race nationalism, where "Cuban," "Dominican," and "Mexican" rendered other identities irrelevant; in the United States they became brown, Aztec warriors, black Boricuas, Dominican-Yorks.

Blackness and indigenousness, particularly during the civil rights era, were revalued by Latinx migrants, forming the core of their new, hybrid Latinx-American identity. Claiming racial difference moved Latinx away from merely striving for off-whiteness—cultural or social-class-based "passing" being a kind of default state of Latinx identity—toward either claiming an ambiguous mixed-race identity or abandoning European identification altogether, identifying as Afro-Latino or Native American. Latina feminism has blossomed in the United States, particularly in reinterpreting the La Malinche tale from one of betrayal to one of survival, and the ability of women to create a different kind of non-Western intelligence and self-reflection. The theorizing and practical activity of Latinx feminists played a central role in the development of a perspective known as intersectionality, where race politics intersects with gender politics and queer theory and where fluid ideas about gender erase the male-female binary, as explicated in the classic anthology edited by Anzaldúa and Chicanx playwright Cherríe Moraga, *This Bridge Called My Back*.

Another critical contradiction of mestizaje is the need to distinguish the term from what has often been called *mulatez*, which specifically refers to African and European mixtures. *Mestizaje* can be a universal term referring to all race-mixing in Latin America, but it is more popularly construed as referring specifically to indigenous and European mixes. *Mestizo* has a generally positive connotation, conveying the sense of transcending a racialized indigenous identity, whereas *mulato*, which literally means *mule*, as in the offspring of a horse and a donkey, is less positive, and its English equivalent, *mulatto*, is generally pejorative. In its feminine usage, *mulata* is key to the construction of a sexualized feminine stereotype, attributing sexual desirability to women who possess traces or even strong hints of African phenotype.

Mestizo is used more often in countries with a larger indigenous population, such as Mexico, Central America, and Peru, whereas *mulatez* is associated with a sociocultural movement inspired by the Caribbean negritude movements of the early twentieth century. The term *mestiço*, widely used in Brazil, refers to a mix of Africans, indigenous, and Portuguese. Perhaps because of the general privileging of indigenous people over African people, *mestizo* seems to subjugate indios and privilege European-ness, while *mulatez* more aggressively asserts African-ness within a European context, though it views blackness positively only in the context of the mulato, and not the Afro-Latinx.

The result of mestizaje, mulatez, and their related ideologies is that blackness and indigenousness can be simultaneously venerated and denigrated, though white supremacy is not necessarily assured implicitly. The same kind of suspended judgment that allows an indigenous or Afro-descended Latino to imagine themselves as "white" can also lead an apparently light-skinned Latino to insist that their essence is somehow "black" or "Indian." Over time, biological utopianism has given way to the possibility of studying race within social and economic structures, the way the Cuban anthropologist Fernando Ortiz conceived of "transculturation," the creation of Cuban culture through the economic process of cultivating sugar and tobacco. These plantation spaces were the centers of not only exploitation but of negotiations that produced the porous hierarchies of Cuban mixed-race society. As Arcadio Díaz Quiñones describes in his examination of Ortiz's work, Ortiz imagines transculturation as a conversation between souls possessed by ancestral spirits, discarding the imperfect and forging a forward-looking "American" society.

Yet the arguments from promoters of mestizaje and transculturation usually fall into the trap of erasing difference, represented by African and indigenous people, and framing cultural negotiations with Western conceptions of dialogue like Ortiz's use of "counterpoint" to draw an analogy between Cuban music and culture, which in fact has an already mixed-race heritage of North African/ gypsy/French poetic folk song structure combined with the looping, repetitive matrix of West African drum ritual. Vasconcelos's cosmic race is imagined as an ending point, where in the future racial categories will no longer be necessary.

Latinx and the Category of Raza

In the years after the 1910 Revolution, Mexico did eliminate the use of racial categories in census-taking as a result of this kind of "forward thinking." But more and more this ploy is looking like the "post-racial" idea of American race discourse that has rapidly disintegrated ever since the moment George Zimmerman—a half-Peruvian—first imagined himself as an avenging neighborhood watch vigilante in his pursuit of Trayvon Martin. The cosmic race seems doomed to end up in a particularly undistinguished corner of the dustbin of history because of its misguided attempt to announce the End of (Race Discourse) History. Mestizaje idealism—under the harsh light of the NAFTA age Zapatista revolt, which demonstrated the utter failure of mestizo inclusivity in Mexico, and twenty-first-century Afro-Latinx movements that harshly reject liberal Colombian and Peruvian lip service toward coastal cultures—has become as obsolete as a dot matrix printer.

Yet what I'm describing here may be more of a failure of top-down construction of race categories clearly designed to contain the threat posed by the large non-white majority. There's something to be said for a more organic view of mestizaje, as proposed by anthropologist Peter Wade, who portrays it as a series of negotiations between people of color, whites, and off-whites, as well as among people of color themselves. The areíto circles organized by Taínos in the Caribbean, an indigenous group that reached the islands over a centuries-long process of raft travel from northern sections of Venezuela and Colombia, often merged with escaped African slaves, for instance, and were prototypes for hip-hop cyphers. The creation of cumbia in Colombia by merging African drumming with the oversized indigenous-constructed flute called the gaita has a way of obscuring whether its roots are primarily African or indigenous. Yet the clarion call sounded by Cuban nationalist José Martí by defining "Nuestra América," Our America, as one that is undeniably black and brown left it uncertain whether Latinx of color will ultimately be incorporated into the Western democratic project.

Often vague, yet somehow ambitious, are the building blocks of raza. Raza as tribe, as spiritual force, as unity of "others," that might even include a stray notion of off-whiteness. This is the raza one conceives of in the middle of a mosh pit at a show by Mexican ska-punk band Maldita Vecindad in the mid-90s, where youth from the northern sector of the Distrito Federal's Nezahualcóyotl reimagine the event as a Two Tone party from London's prelude to Thatcherism. It's a sense of raza that is cast in dark hues, the "mancha de plátano," or plantain stain that Caribbean mulatos and jíbaros are so proud of.

To illustrate raza's continuing ambiguity, I'll cite a recent experience of mine interviewing a hip-hop group from Colombia named Choc Quib Town. Hailing from the mostly Afro-descendent region of El Chocó, on the country's Pacific coast, the members of the group were not shy about addressing what they felt were continued micro-aggressions from their fellow Colombians, even after they had achieved a degree of fame and affluence. Colombia is typical of many Latin American countries in its public ideology of racial democracy deriving from the racial mix of its population. Choc Quib Town took the standard position of many groups and individuals that advocate for the rights of Afro-descendent Latin Americans, which is that the ideology of mestizaje, or mixed-raced democracy, does not eliminate, and in some ways obscures, the existence of racism. Despite this, they proudly spoke about a song on their latest album called "La Raza Llamada Sabor," loosely translated as "The Race That's Called Flavor," which advocated for solidarity around a "tribe" of music fans who agreed that the "flavor" of African-derived rhythms and melodies in their music constituted a "race." They seemed to imply that while mestizaje is a flawed narrative in practice, it symbolizes something about Latin America's unique view of race.

It's still not clear what the implications are of a tendency among Latinos—who find it difficult to identify themselves as belonging to one side or the other of the US racial binary—to view race as a choice. It also remains unclear whether this state of slipperiness in racial identity is best viewed as a transcendent opportunity or something along the lines of Rachel Dolezal's fall from grace—an ignominious, traitorous, and duplicitous masquerade, a grinding dance of misguided cultural appropriation. Just another Al Jolson minstrel show.

So we're left with the question of what kind of argument can be made for invoking "raza" as the way Latinos see themselves in the world. Raza's potential to be a cipher can push it in one direction or another depending on the political force that's driving it. One way of framing that idea is by looking back at late nineteenth-, early twentieth-century Spain. Joshua Goode's discussion of Spain's perilous journey into an era when its empire was rapidly deteriorating makes the case that, as race science was gaining force in neighboring Europe, Spain drew on the concept of raza to evoke its own exceptionalism, implying that there were qualities unknowable by science that Spaniards possessed: mystical qualities unrelated to people of color, yet another version of off-whiteness. This was religious-military fusion that had always been at the root of Spanish imperialism.

While Franco's Spain used *raza* to evoke a Christian purity, raza in the New World took hold as a catch-all category for mixed otherness that could slip into the zone of white privilege. In the United States, it took on more progressive meaning, whether in the indigenous pride surrounding Mexican American celebrations of Día de la Raza, or the formalized political advocacy group National Council of la Raza, now UnidosUS, an organization at once scarily separatist, invoking the threat of a twenty-first-century Reconquista that would take back California, Arizona, Texas, Nevada, Colorado, New Mexico, and Utah, and overly committed to working within the system, producing Latina leader Cecilia Muñoz, who oversaw the Obama administration's record-setting deportation binge in the 2010s.

In the New York of the 1930s there was yet another invocation of raza that coalesced around the activists from Spain and several Latin American countries who supported the Republican cause in the Civil War. These socialists, communists, and anarchists were aware of Vasconcelos's *Raza Cósmica* and Mexican poet Amado Nervo's "La Raza de Bronce," which invoked the bronze-skinned majesty of the same Cuauhtémoc conquered by Cortés, and they were interested in developing a class-based solidarity network that united Latinos of all stripes beyond destructive nationalisms.

Having been recruited to work in cigar manufacturing centers in New York, Puerto Rican migrants, who numbered around 50,000 in 1935, along with their Cuban counterparts, were very active in organizing the tobacco rollers into a union. Communist Party members like Jesús Colón, a pioneer of the bilingual bicultural Nuyorican identity, organized cultural activities and acted as "lectores," or readers of everything from the news to the great novels of the day from a high chair in front of a room of rollers. The anti-nationalist tendencies of socialist and communist organizing at the time helped generate a pan-Latino identity that sometimes used the idea of raza, which evoked Hispanization without regard to phenotypical appearance, in the service of progressive ideals.

Created by a Uruguayan military man named Angel Camblor, "La Bandera de la Raza," was for a brief period of time adopted by activists, cultural workers, and intellectuals alike in New York. The crosses were somewhat ironically symbolic of the three famous ships that Columbus set sail with, but were said to be imbued with a spiritual energy that could be reinterpreted in the service of whatever message Latin Americans, or fledgling US Latinx, wanted to use to represent their human liberation. Postage stamps were issued with representations of the flag in various Latin American countries, echoing José Martí's notion of Nuestra América. In New York, however, the bandera was used to amplify the idea of Latino identity while including those outside of the dominant group, Puerto Ricans. This universality and heterogeneity have remained a hallmark of the Latinx experience in New York, a solidarity based in part on common language, but also recognizing Latinx's occupation of the middle ground in America's racial binary.

These were the times of Marcus Garvey's pan-Africanism, as well as the more Eurocentric identities posited by Latin American expatriates and intellectuals who were still using Uruguayan essayist José Enrique Rodó's notion of Latin America as Ariel, the benign spirit of Shakespeare's *Tempest*, as a cultural symbol. According to this line of thought, Latin America's closer connection to the world of European letters and rejection of American anti-intellectualism cast the United States as Caliban, the uncivilized and brutish illiterate. La Bandera de la Raza and the solidarity with Spain, whose radical Republic rejected Christianity and at least in part embraced the multicultural ideals of Blas Infante's Moor-friendly Andalucían separatism, was a way of situating New York Latinx in a middle ground between Africanist and Europeanist poles.

While the idea of raza never quite took hold in New York as America lurched into the postwar era—its reinvention as a symbol of indigenous pride by Mexicans and Chicanx become more central in Latino nationalist and racialist ideologies—it did leave a legacy of Latino unity that has characterized community formations and cultural production to this day. Yet its firm rootedness in the problematic mestizo position did not do enough to clarify which path of racial identity would be best for Latino interests as a whole. The widespread identification of Puerto Ricans with African American identity that climaxed in the 1970s and 1980s, and that had roots in both proximity of social hierarchy reinforced by residential segregation as well as cultural affinities that reflected the repression of African identity in Puerto Rico itself, seemed to invalidate the dewy-eyed idealism of 1930s and 40s New York Hispanos.

Despite this and the embrace of negritude in both the Caribbean and New York, Caribbean blacks' ability to attain a cultural congruency with African Americans escaped many of New York's Afro-Latinos. If the mestizo middle was inadequate in its recognition of African-descended and indigenous Latinx, was language their only connection to the general framework of raza? Perilously close to the raza idea of exceptionalism first codified in late nineteenth-century Spain, the Latinx idea of race more clearly evokes "raza" as metaphor, particularly when contrasted with the rigid pseudo-science surrounding Anglo-American ideas of race and racialized borders.

So it was that over the course of several centuries, raza first invoked "blood purity," then "blood," and finally, in a strangely catholic way, "my people." Maybe it's necessary to hook up with raza on its own terms, viewing it more as a fluid space than a self-contained and concrete idea, a cacophony of voices rather than fingers balled together in a fist. Both Fanon and Spivak have hinted at the necessity of defining a movement for liberation around a strategic essentialism. As I've stated several times in this chapter, raza's essence is that it has no essence, yet at the same time contains all essences.

The mestizo middle, or muddle, can be rightly accused of carrying the disease of off-whiteness in order to enforce the hegemony of racial superiority over the rest of the darker tribes. But there is a fatal flaw to that model: the largely unexploited presence of the other, the seemingly controlled or uncontrolled inoculation of blackness and indigenousness, carried in bodies and language, which has the potential to destabilize such a racial order. Perhaps it's heady idealism or absurdly wide-eyed optimism, but "my people," as imagined by the idea of *raza*, carries that symbolic charge, and from where I sit, the voices that carry that otherness are growing louder and louder.

2

Mestizaje vs. the Hypo-American Dream

Very few Americans will directly proclaim that they are in favor of black people being left to the streets. But a very large number of Americans will do all they can to preserve the Dream. No one directly proclaimed that schools were designed to sanctify failure and destruction. But a great number of educators spoke of "personal responsibility" in a country authored and sustained by a criminal irresponsibility. The point of this language of "intention" and "personal responsibility" is broad exoneration. Mistakes were made. Bodies were broken. People were enslaved. We meant well. We tried our best. "Good intention" is a hall pass through history, a sleeping pill that ensures the Dream.

Ta-Nehisi Coates, Between the World and Me

When contemplating the enormous accomplishment of black identity in the United States, and its most recent triumph of letters in the form of the work of Ta-Nehisi Coates, it is crucial to value the connection between the Body of the other and the Dream that is used to erase unfortunate memories. The black body, as is true with other non-white, -male, and -heteronormative bodies, is the site of the scarring formed by the imposition of racial and sexual hierarchies, established in the project of colonizing the New World, that went hand in hand with (Western) science, democracy, capitalism, and modernity. Coates's narrative draws much of its strength through evoking the contrasting dynamics of violence and silence that characterize the social contract—covenant, if you will—of the United States, and how blackness is made visible by never betraying this painful history.

Yet while the tension between blackness and whiteness in the United States is clearly defined by a binary in which whiteness is privileged as an abstract set of moral ideas and social standards and blackness is excluded, immoral, and devalued, the narrative of race mixture—with some notable exceptions—is almost entirely absent. It is the binary notion of race itself, augmented by the logic of "hypo-descent," or the "one-drop rule" of racial definition, that upholds the fictitious notion of white purity and defines race discourse. Blackness insists on regarding the body as a site of a sustained violence with no apparent redeeming social value, and that embodiment of history disrupts the American Dream by revealing its complacent hypocrisy.

But as I've alluded to in Chapter 1, the race narrative of Latin America, which is transmitted through the social mores of Latinx that emigrate to the United States and remains influential until the point when immigrants completely assimilate into the American racial binary, is not a binary narrative. It is an ostensible embrace of mixed-race identity that privileges whiteness, and despite such flaws represents perhaps a more accurate framing of racial difference than is projected in the US racial binary model. One of its advantages is that it moves away from biological, "race science" fallacies toward the concept of race as a social construction.

The mixed-race narrative appears to be ingrained in many if not most Latinx, even the ones that acknowledge that there is racism directed towards them as a result of their perceived blackness or indigenousness, and is often central to their national identities. Like Coates's narrative, it refers to the body, but its notion of violence, while present, can be tempered by Latin America's history of consensual interracial sexual activity, cultural negotiation, and an illusory sense of racial democracy.

This mixed-race narrative is arguably the central factor in the long-argued truism that Latinx are slow to "assimilate" as Americans, and in fact resist it to the point of alarming conservative theorists like the late Samuel Huntington, whose *Who Are We? The Challenges to America's National Identity*, was one of the intellectual starting points of today's widespread Latinx-phobic anti-immigrant rhetoric. The idea that Latinx stubbornly resist learning and mastering English is one of the most fallacious—numerous studies show that by the second and third generation, Latinx become English-dominant and often do not retain Spanish in daily use. The notion that Latinx are inveterate Catholics—one of Huntington's bugaboos in the sense that it disrupts our ability to adopt the Protestant ethic of hard work and sacrifice—is also hard to sustain, since in successive generations Latinx are becoming less interested in religion in general at a similar rate to Anglo-Americans, or are adopting charismatic born-again Protestantism, religious sects whose origins are in Anglo-America and not in Spanish Catholic rule. With the exception of some "transnational" phenomena—best exemplified by Dominicans and more recent Mexican immigrants, who travel back and forth between their home country and the United States and remain involved in local and home-country politics, sometimes maintaining property in both countries—most Latinx firmly grasp the idea that the United States is their home. See, for instance, one of the dominant narratives of anti-deportation arguments by immigrant advocates: US-born children of immigrants most often exhibit horror and disorientation at the prospect of being forced to move to the country of their parents, where they have never lived, and with whose contemporary culture they are relatively unfamiliar.

So if Latinx are not assimilating quickly enough for some conservative pundits or observers, it is most likely due not to their inability to grasp English or embrace the United States' consumer-oriented

cultural framework, its "family values," its economic and legal
systems, or even the obligation of military service. It is more likely
a response to a binary racial apparatus that gives them little room to
assimilate as mainstream Americans unless they can be easily tagged
to the phenotypical poles of black and white.

Throughout their time in the United States, Latinx have been
racialized in a parallel way to blacks (and on the West Coast, Asian
Americans), at times assuming the role of binary "other." Yet
although a limited number of them are accepted as whites, they
have also sometimes been subject to the perception that they are a
"third race," or in other instances discriminated against as inferior
because of a perceived mixed-race status, as in Tampa, when Puerto
Ricans were separately racialized in residential segregation practices
as neither white nor black. Mexican Americans have also sought
through litigation by advocacy groups to be categorized as white
in order to avoid discrimination. Congressional testimony arguing
against the admittance of Puerto Rico as a state also referred to its
inhabitants as comprising a "mongrel race."

In the case of Mexicans in California and the Southwest, the
long-running social dislocation created by the absorption of seven
territories, and ultimately states, into the Union in the mid-nineteenth
century as a result of the US-Mexican War created what could be
interpreted as a "black" status in the absence of significant black populations, at least prior to the Great Migration of the Jim Crow era.
(This limited presence of blacks, which helped to create the idea that
states like California and Oregon were sublimated White Utopias,
was actively fostered by limiting migration and at times encouraging
expulsion, something that was more difficult to achieve with Mexicans, given their preexisting presence on the land itself and migratory
labor patterns.) Critical race theorists have recently focused on the
disadvantage in how legal cases interpret Latinx (in this case, largely
Mexican Americans) not as the victims of racial discrimination, but
instead as the subjects of discrimination as an "ethnic group."

Yet despite the pervasive reality of legal discrimination, social exclusion and segregation, and day-to-day racist practices, within both the United States and Latin America Latinx have always been "mestizo" and "mulatto" nations. Both the Anglo-American binary and Latin American mestizaje maintained a white supremacist ethos but in practice manifested differing social realities that while generally keeping intact racial prejudices, resulted in different dynamics. Nineteenth- and twentieth-century Latin American thinkers, reacting to notions of Anglo superiority, drew on these dynamics to imply that Latin America had more authenticity in its "American-ness" than Anglo-America. By willfully acknowledging, as Simón Bolívar, José Martí, and Gilberto Freyre did in various discourses and writings, that indigenous and African people were essential to Latin American self-perception and consciousness, the Spanish- (and Portuguese-) speaking Americas were more truly "American."

The racial mythologies about Anglo- and Latin America derive from the two opposing yet parallel tendencies involved in the conquest of the New World. Anglo-America was largely colonized by sectarian families escaping religious persecution in England, while Latin America was colonized by a triumphant band of re-branded "white" Spaniards who, while representing a "purified" Spain, were a racially diverse group of nominal Catholics who were mostly single men. In Anglo-America, the Christian settlers—dominated by Protestant sects—encouraged an attitude of intolerance, as well as a hidden, desirous fixation towards Native Americans, who were less thickly concentrated in "urban" areas than they were in Latin America, and an unforgiving, permanent enslavement of imported Africans in the South. In Latin America, the Spaniards left a legacy of genocide, rape, and slavery on indigenous and then African slaves. But they were also often encouraged to mate with both indigenous people and blacks, creating a mixed-race population that overlapped with social class. In addition, debates in the Spanish Catholic Church created a Spanish policy of legal tolerance, including relaxed laws about intermarriage and an easier path toward manumission through indentured servitude for blacks.

Another difference between the Spanish and Anglo conquest of the Americas was the Spanish system of promoting alliances between Spanish nobles and indigenous royalty—although this was also part of certain Anglo-American colonial behaviors. Some of the first intermarriages were between these two groups, with the mestizo offspring often shipped back to Spain to be instructed in the proper protocols of Spanish nobility. Yet there were many unions, consensual and forced, between Spaniards and indigenous women that produced a murky class of mestizo who were marginalized from power, as well as pairings between indigenous people, African-descended slaves, and free working-class men. There was much cross-identification that grew out of this—including those who at times identified "downward" as indigenous to avoid the military requirements of the Spanish. These processes, which were prefigured by a century of passing in Spain during the era of the limpieza de sangre statutes, made it clear that race identification was a fluid social construction, often determined by gradations in phenotypical appearance, class status, and even what modern sociologists would call "cultural capital."

These interactions imply that a space had been created for debate or controversy around raza. One example often noted in the writings of the decolonial school is the *Nueva corónica i buen gobierno*, a 900-page letter written in Spanish and Quechua by Felipe Guaman Poma de Ayala, against the colonial government in Perú. The letter represents the voice of the oppressed indigenous and mestizo population, subverting the Spanish presence by reflecting its contradictions. Poma de Ayala argues for indigenous purity in his retelling of the Inca empire, even as he acknowledges its hybrid nature. He rightly points out the absurdity of the Spanish model of purity even as their own identities potentially as hidden Jews and Moors escaping the Inquisition are in question. By using the problematic of the Spanish conquest through the caste system as a way to reject it, Poma de

Ayala makes an argument for indigenous purity that is equally untenable, but at the same time shows how the very act of communicating
via shared languages builds a forged worldview made up of ambivalent subjects engaged in a protracted negotiation.

An eerily parallel form of mirroring, or parody, was discovered
by María Elena Martínez, in her description of a 1612 incident in
Mexico City in which thirty-five blacks and mulattoes were hung
in retaliation for a planned rebellion against the Spanish colonists.
The rebellion would have established a black monarchy in which the
mixed-race reproductive hierarchy imposed by the Spaniards would
have been inverted. The black king would have a light-skinned mulata
as his queen; indigenous people would make up a surplus labor pool,
and Spanish women would be held for the purpose of procreation.
Spanish men would be castrated and the process of mestizaje would
be reversed through a gradual blackening of the population. The
significance of this scenario is instructive: the rebellion would not
concern itself with overthrowing the unjust nature of the colonial
system without reversing the triangle of power. It would use the
language learned from the system of conquest to effect "justice" by
subverting the hierarchy of domination and oppression.

Radical historians of the early Spanish conquest describe the hegemony that the conquerors imposed as a mixture of coercion and
instituting "practices and beliefs which eventually appear normal and
natural." This scenario of authoritarianism and negotiation is further
aided by the assumption that "by 1570 [the Spanish population] must
have had a 20 to 40 percent admixture of indigenous and African
blood." The creation of the so-called "creole" class meant that what
was considered "Spanish" allowed for a degree of mestizo-ness from
early on in the process of colonization. It meant that identifying as an
"American" (albeit "Latin" American) meant at least a tacit acknowl-
edgement that "white" purity was not essential. Abstracting this
further into the notion established earlier that Spanish-ness itself was
never quite "white," either in the eyes of Spain or in those of the rest of

Europe and Anglo-America, it's clear that we are dealing with a subject position that is not grounded in the typical white Western subject.

These examples imply that besides the mixing of bodies to create a mixed-race population, the ambiguous nature of power and the multiplicity of mixing spaces, from actual communities to structures of language and hierarchy, took hold in Spanish-conquered America early on, perpetuating a logic of mixing that reflected all of the ambivalence of conquest. It's no surprise, then, that by the time nation-state formation was sweeping across Europe and the Americas in the nineteenth century, Latin American concepts of "nation" were invariably imbued with the idea that the social contract was inseparable from mixed-race hierarchies.

The agendas of Anglo- and Spanish colonizers—the former described as "settlers," the latter as "conquerors"—were further distinguished by the sheer size of the African and indigenous populations in Latin America, which made "whites" or "Europeans" the minority population early on. Henry Louis Gates Jr. estimates that of the 10.7 million Africans that survived the Middle Passage to the Americas, only 450,000 arrived in the United States. This means that Latin America received almost twenty times as many African slaves as the United States did, and given that indigenous populations were larger, more concentrated in urban centers, and less subject to policies of extermination than they were in the United States, there were more indigenous people in Latin America as well. Yet the population balance in the South was closer to that of Latin America, as slave states depended on slavery for economic development rather than European industrial workers.

The small size of the lighter-skinned ruling class in Latin America also made mestizaje ideology more necessary as a form of state-driven social control. The implications of this are considerable for the present-day United States: As the white population sees its numbers shrink and its demographic majority disappear, a reaction is inevitable that might resemble strategies pursued centuries ago in Latin

America. The election of Donald Trump and his overt sympathies with white supremacy appear to reflect a reactionary racist sentiment among whites who see their majority status threatened, evidence perhaps of the long-term emergence of intolerance-based politics. This has happened despite the poll evidence suggesting that most Americans favor increasing tolerance toward minority races, ethnicities, sexual preferences, and gender identities. Whether Trump's ascension resulted from the vagaries of the electoral college system or Russian interference with social media, it seems to contradict the notion that American societal norms are extending honorary "whiteness" or more coded forms of social acceptance to people of color and members of sexual minorities, a process that will not necessarily end during his presidency.

In this sense, Anglo-America is in the process of transitioning from a fixed black and white racial binary to a model that includes more intermediary tones on the racial spectrum, while retaining an essential white privilege. The meaning of whiteness is changing: on the alt-right, it now merits its own "identity politics"; in the mainstream, it appears to have more porous boundaries. While various Latin American countries have self-consciously promoted themselves as mixed-race or mestizaje-defined societies, there has also been mestizaje and mixed-race discourse, albeit muted, forming in Anglo-America.

In his book *The United States of the United Races*, Greg Carter tells the stories of various figures in Anglo-American history—such as Thomas Jefferson's French-born ally St. John de Crèvecoeur and abolitionist firebrand Wendell Phillips—while touching on Louisiana's mixed-race creole class and its role as protagonists in *Plessy v. Ferguson* to make a case that an ideology of "mixture" in America has a considerable legacy. Yet the relative obscurity of these figures and the ideology's incompatibility with the logic of slavery-driven Southern capitalism have disconnected this tradition of advocacy from US history.

One of the crucial reasons why *raza*—or the Latin American idea that there can be a race defined by mixed-race people—matters, then, is that it represents a perspective that has been repressed in Anglo-American race discourse. It is a perspective that recognizes, inadequately or not, the inclusion of "other" races within a "national" subject and provides Latinx in the United States with a common bond: a shared difficulty in aligning with the white-black racial binary. *Raza* represents a fully formed "race" made up of several races while also representing a third dynamic in what is ostensibly a two-race system.

Yet Latinx do not necessarily transfer this "mixed-race" subject position intact from Latin America to the United States—during the process of our acculturation, we actually have several choices in how we fit into America's racial binary. The first option is assimilating as white, trading on the perception of lighter skin or Latin American "off-whiteness," through accumulation of wealth and cultural capital through educational and artistic achievement. A second possibility is becoming "black," either through perceived darker skin, acculturation in poor urban communities that are either contiguous with African American communities or neighboring them, subjecting ourselves to being marginalized in wealth accumulation, educational opportunity, and buying property through residential segregation/redlining practices, or, in more limited cases, becoming Native American by aligning ourselves closely with tribal practices or affiliation.

The third possibility, which can sometimes overlap with the previous two, is adopting either a pan-Latinx or Hispanic identity similar to the mestizo ideology from Latin America, which confers honorary whiteness onto a mixed-race core of people, or embracing an individual national identity such as "Mexican American," "Puerto Rican," "Dominican," and "Colombian." The compelling aspect of this last option is the possibility of addressing the exclusionary aspects of mestizaje as it was conceived in Latin America by reaffirming the prominence of indigenous and African culture within that mestizo matrix. This possibility allows for a mixed-race identification that prioritizes non-European cultural traditions, or at least emphasizes those aspects already folded into the Spanish/indigenous/African mixing that created discrete Latin American national identifications.

Anglo-America's Latent Mestizo Character

One of the essential storylines of this book involves the distinction and conflict between two ideologies about race. I have spent several pages now outlining the Latin American ideology about race, which evolved from the Spanish problem of limpieza de sangre to the Mexican and Latin American system of mestizaje and the caste system it created. The Anglo-American ideology of race centers on hypodescent. As opposed to the Latin American model of affording honorary whiteness to an elite of mestizos, the "one-drop rule" came to brand African-descended human beings in the United States as black—not mixed, not mulato, not mestizo, not honorary white.

Yet, in reality, America has always been to some degree a mestizo/mulato nation. Beside the fact that race is a social construction and it is almost impossible to conceive of anyone being of a "pure race" in the Americas, there have been several instances of mixed-race populations across the Americas, from the Dutch-Sephardic Jewish-Black-Asian people who lived in Manhattan when it was known as Nieuw Amsterdam in the seventeenth century, to the "mestizos" of the Carolinas, the Seminoles of Florida, and the Creoles of Louisiana. Anglo-America has been replete with racial mixing.

In Latin America, the idea of race mixture has been acknowledged overtly and explicitly, no matter how awkwardly and inadequately. Anglo-America's narrative about race-mixing has been covert, hidden, latent. It is this latent character that is still central to the race debate in the United States, the same one that is invoked in every tale of intense race conflict, from the O.J. Simpson murder trial to the Rachel Dolezal controversy, to every micro-aggression on every college campus in America.

The early United States in some senses tolerated mestizos and mixed-race people. Gary Nash begins his essay "The Hidden History of Mestizo America" by alluding to the marriage between Virginia colonist John Rolfe and "Rebecca," or Pocahontas, arranged as part of an effort to bring peace between settlers and indigenous inhabitants of Virginia. This strategy of intermarriage, echoing the "original sin" of procreation between Cortés and La Malinche, was used by the Spanish conquistadors in Mexico and two and a half centuries later in Texas and the Southwest territory by Anglo settlers following the absorption of a large chunk of Mexico as a result of the US-Mexican War.

There were also scattered incidents in mixed-race Anglo-America that never emerged from the shadows. Sociologist Brewton Berry writes of South Carolina's "mestizos," burdened with unfortunate appellations like "Red Legs" and "Brass Ankles," and descended from "Sir Walter Raleigh's Lost Colony and the Croatan Indians who befriended them, plus a subsequent admixture of Negro blood." When Berry wrote this tract, in 1945, he analyzed the South Carolinian mestizos in a way that recalled Latin American mixed-race people. There was "no infallible criteria" for identifying them, given their varied skin tones and hair textures, yet there was one certainty expressed by a mestizo Berry interviewed: "We know we ain't niggers, we know that." It has always been clear in both Anglo- and Latin America that mixed-race identification is often used to avoid being classified as black.

The relative tolerance toward intermarriage with indigenous people and disavowal of black-white unions, a common theme in colonial Latin America, was echoed in the words of founding father Benjamin Franklin:

> While we are, as I may call it, *Scouring* our Planet, by clearing America
> of Woods, and so making this Side of our Globe reflect a brighter Light
> to the Eyes of Inhabitants in Mars or Venus, why should we in the Sight

of Superior Beings, darken its People? Why increase the Sons of Africa, by Planting them in America, where we have so fair an Opportunity, by excluding all Blacks and Tawneys, of increasing the lovely White and Red?

Legal scholars point to an utterance, part of an opinion in a 1656 Virginia case called *Re Mulatto*, as the first judicial expression of the rule of hypodescent. The utterance was "Mulatto to be a slave and appeal taken," indicating that it made no difference that the plaintiff in question had an observable degree of European blood. Again, the parallel with Latin America is clear, though not exact. Blacks are marked clearly for exclusion as opposed to indigenous people, but the exclusion has more of a finality in the Anglo-American courts.

Early American figures like Patrick Henry and slave owner Thomas Jefferson actively encouraged intermarriage with Native Americans, with Henry advocating free public education for interracial children. In the early nineteenth century Sam Houston ran away from his home in Virginia and was adopted by Cherokees in Tennessee. He returned to Anglo society soon after but decided to return to the Cherokees in 1829. Seven years later he was president of the independent republic of Texas and enlisted Cherokees to fight against Mexico. As Nash explains it, subsequent skirmishes with Native Americans disrupted any policy toward an American "mestizo" nation in both Virginia and Texas, which then implemented policies that expelled Native Americans and prohibited intermarriage.

The painful process of establishing the colonies in North America also created affinity and intermarriage between escaped slaves and Native Americans. Crispus Attucks of Boston Massacre fame was half black and half Indian. Miscegenation prevailed among fur trappers, whose independent thrusts into the territories left them, like the Spanish conquistadors, with few options for procreation. Sadly, Cherokee Indians decided to adopt the Anglo-American strategy of enslaving blacks and by 1824 prohibited intermarriage with them. Many writings about the early colonial era mention the phenomenon of "white Indians," in which European settlers are either kidnapped or run away to join Native Americans, never to return, while Indians almost never chose to stay among European settlers.

Rhetorically, the United States' ideas about race-mixing grew out of the early debates around abolitionism and whether freed blacks could become "amalgamated" with white Americans or simply shipped back to new colonies in Africa. Fear of slave revolts morphed into fear that freed slaves might take revenge on their ex-masters; this happened in the context of several nonconsensual relationships between slaves and their masters, most famously the one that produced Sally Hemings, the daughter of Thomas Jefferson. One of the early climaxes of this debate was when Kentucky representative Henry Clay, who would one day author the Missouri Compromise, addressed a meeting of the pro-repatriation American Colonization Society in 1816.

> The class of the mixt population of our country was particularly situated; they neither enjoyed the immunities of freemen, nor where they subjected to the incapacities of slaves, but partook in some degree of the qualities of both. From their condition and the unconquerable prejudices resulting from their colour, they never could amalgamate with the free whites of this country. It was desirable … to drain them off.

Lawyer and abolition activist Wendell Phillips was among the most pronounced advocates for "amalgamation" in the mid-nineteenth century. Carter, who titled his book after one of Phillips's speeches, credits Phillips with anticipating Martin Luther King Jr.'s urging to judge humans "by the content of their character," and not their skin color, as well as an early conception of "color-blind citizenship." But as abolition became a reality after the Civil War, many of Phillips's ideas were tainted by a hoax, the creation of a pamphlet called *Miscegenation*, which used some of his ideas to stir fears of race-mixing and interracial sex.

The post–Civil War era also saw the birth of race science. Arthur de Gobineau's 1855 *Essay on the Inequality of Human Races* conceived of at least three different races (European, African, and Asiatic), comprising several different sub-races. The haggling of de Gobineau's intellectual descendants over, for instance, the distinction between Nordic and Alpine whites, or Semitic and Mediterranean whites, was replicated in the United States in the early part of the twentieth century (hence the melting pot narrative); by the end of the Civil War, however, his taxonomy had become part of a new ideology of whiteness. The reduction of racial categories to black and white, which took hold in the United States in the mid-nineteenth century, was motivated, according to many historians, by the need to maintain the highest profit margins for slaveholders.

Ned and Constance Sublette's *The American Slave Coast: A History of the Slave-Breeding Industry* asserts that after the importation of slaves from foreign traders was banned in 1808, part of a provision argued at the original Constitutional Convention, US slave traders were intent on consolidating their profit-making structure through internal "production" of slaves by procreation and breeding. This produced a monopoly that permanently undercut whatever vagaries the international slave trade might endure. As David A. Hollinger puts it:

> Children begotten upon slave women by their owners or by other white men would grow up as slaves, adding to the property of the owners of the women and preserving the amazingly durable fiction that male slave-holders and the other white males in the vicinity were faithful to their wives.

So, in a kind of parallel mechanism to, as described by María Elena Martínez, the casta system controlling the sexuality of Mexican women, the hypodescent strategy was not only concerned with preserving sexual "morality" but also intent on the profit-making possibilities of controlling the offspring. Rather than allowing for the possibility of mixed-raced offspring whitening their way over generations into privileged society, Anglo-American slave owners viewed these children as "interest" to be added to the exchange value of their stock of slaves in the creation of new capital accumulation. The rule of hypodescent formed over 200-plus years, making the US racial binary unique among nations.

As Hollinger writes, the rule of hypodescent "gained currency as the customary social, informal, and 'commonsense' definition of blackness" in the eighteenth century. While anti-miscegenation laws were much less common or nonexistent in Latin America, and the legal possibility of African-descended people to ultimately work or buy their way out of slavery more pronounced, in the United States laws of stark separation between whites and blacks became more strongly codified over time. Yet despite being initially motivated by slaveholders' need for more slaves, its ultimate inscription into American social and legal mores was made even more urgent during the Jim Crow period, after slavery had officially ended.

Once a Spanish, then a French territory, Louisiana featured a festival of mixture where sexual unions between French settlers and Native Americans were common and an entire segment of society in New Orleans took on the Creole identity, parallel to the "criollo" identity of Latin America. The dynamic in Louisiana was closer to that of Latin America because Native Americans were taken as slaves at first, and much of the race-mixing occurred before the importation of African slaves. The Spanish *cabildo* system of local governance also had a lasting effect on racial hierarchy in New Orleans. Unlike much of the rest of the United States and its territories, mulattoes were recognized and not erased by the rule of hypodescent until the Jim Crow era began.

Like the criollos of Latin America, New Orleans Creoles used their lighter-than-black free status to create a cultured, superior myth about themselves that was shattered by the end of the Civil War and the imposition of Jim Crow segregation. When the tyranny of hypo-descent struck New Orleans, Creole musicians, who were as studied as the black violinists and flautists of Havana, were forced to play with black blues musicians in the French Quarter. While there were many antecedents to the creation of jazz, this sudden shift in cultural and class milieu was perhaps the most significant.

Yet one of the most obscured interventions of Louisiana Creoles in the story of the American racial binary is their involvement in the *Plessy v. Ferguson* case, which ultimately enshrined the principle of "separate, but equal" that held sway until the Civil Rights Act of 1964. The team of lawyers that argued the case constructed it as a kind of legal theater—the passenger who was removed from the whites-only railroad car was a Creole light-skinned enough to pass for white, and removed at the behest of the legal team. The elaborate performance was staged so they could argue in favor of mixed-race Creole rights and defend their refusal to deny their non-white identity. The decision, of course, set the stage for decades of legalized segregation and civil rights violations.

W. E. B. Du Bois played a significant role in trying to reconcile mixedness with the reality of the racial binary by devising a black identity that, while embracing varied shades of skin color, asserted a clear identification with blackness. In Du Bois's somewhat obscure tract "Miscegenation," he concedes that "white women of the indentured servant class married slaves or free Negroes." The impetus here was the prospect of freedom for the indentured servant, which was granted through marriage. "As a free Negro and a mulatto class began to multiply," Du Bois continued, white men began to raise families of mulatto children. Du Bois's participation in the Paris World Exhibition of 1900 with a series of photographs of differently pigmented African Americans could be seen as an echo of the Mexican caste paintings, but had the opposite purpose—moving away from the vagaries of mixedness and toward a strong black identity.

Although the US census counted mulattos from 1850 to 1920 (and mulattos were found to account for anywhere between 11 and 20 percent of the Negro population), the category was eventually eliminated in 1930. The key moment for cementing the black-white binary was the Virginia Racial Integrity Act of 1924, which was passed in the context of the increasing popularity of race science and eugenics, to "defend" the integrity of those who might be categorized incorrectly due to the vagueness brought on by racial mixing. The Virginia Racial Integrity Act helped end the public discourse about race-mixing that began around the time of emancipation, and was used to sterilize black women.

Over the last half of the nineteenth century, nativism, through organs like the anti-immigrant Know-Nothing Party—a predecessor to Trumpism—had given way to a debate over the "melting pot," which was used to describe proscriptive ends for new non-Protestant Northwestern European immigrants. Derived from the famous play by Israel Zangwill, which featured a Russian-Jewish family with a Spanish Sephardic–sounding name, the Quixanos, the melting pot idea was similar to the mestizaje ideal of Latin America, except that it was Southern and Eastern European immigrants that were given approval to "melt" with white America as long as they absorbed the unwritten and written rules. The privilege of whiteness, as Roediger writes in *The Wages of Whiteness*, was extended to the working class to manufacture loyal consent to white supremacist capitalism and protect them from some of that system's worst excesses. Yet the acceptance of the new immigrants, as full of strife as it was—with some of the problems coming from nativist Progressives—coincided with a retrenchment in anti-black racism that sounded the death knell for miscegenation and amalgamation.

It was a moment of American exceptionalism par excellence. When describing Hannah Arendt's disgust while observing the 1958 *Loving v. Virginia* trial, which finally struck down the Virginia Racial Integrity Act, Hollinger points out that "even the union of South

Africa did not have a miscegenation statute until 1949," and that according to Werner Sollors, the Nuremberg Laws of Nazi Germany were inspired partly by the miscegenation laws of the United States. Yet out of all of this obvious evil, there arises a clear case of good, at least in terms of identity construction and political power for blacks in the United States. Christine B. Hickman in her classic *Michigan Law Review* article, "The Devil and the One-Drop Rule," invokes the Faustian bargain carried out by the advent of hypodescent as the ruling principle of the US view of race:

> As we examine the one drop rule and its importance in the current discourse, we should recall the famous exchange between Faust and Goethe's Devil:
>
>> Faust: Say at least, who you are?
>> Mephistopheles: I am part of that power which ever wills evil yet ever accomplishes good.
>
> So it was with the one drop rule. The Devil fashioned it out of racism, malice, greed, lust, and ignorance, but in so doing he also accomplished good: His rule created the African-American race as we know it today, and while this race has its origins in the peoples of three continents and its members can look very different from one another, over the centuries the Devil's one drop rule united this race as a people in the fight against slavery, segregation, and racial injustice.

Hickman's argument applies to the construction of black identity in the eighteenth-century plantation South, with enslaved people appropriating symbolic power from below to create a unified oppositional culture. But she also captures the essence of the contradiction between acknowledging and embracing a mixed-race identity, which is the essence of both mestizaje ideology and voices like that of philosopher and cultural critic Kwame Anthony Appiah, and throwing down with what is strong, unified, and black. She sees the unified black identity as a much more effective force in combating racism and even argues that the three-tiered White/Coloured/Black system of racial classification in South Africa was "more effective than the one-drop rule in ensuring the subordination of Black South Africans."

Hickman's message, first published in 1997, is still significant today for the African American community in the United States, and for Latinx, who also grapple with how they fit into the hypodescent-determined racial politics of the United States today. It locates more power for African Americans within the context of the binary and implies that a more complex racial hierarchy only serves to delay racial justice.

Clash of Ideologies: Zero Sum Game or New Latinx Utopia?

> After the Egyptian and Indian, the Greek and Roman, the Teuton and Mongolian, the Negro is a sort of seventh son, born with a veil, and gifted with second-sight in this American world,—a world which yields him no true self-consciousness, but only lets him see himself through the revelation of the other world. It is a peculiar sensation, this double-consciousness, this sense of always looking at one's self through the eyes of others, of measuring one's soul by the tape of a world that looks on in amused contempt and pity. One ever feels his two-ness,—an American, a Negro; two souls, two thoughts, two unreconciled strivings; two warring ideals in one dark body, whose dogged strength alone keeps it from being torn asunder.
>
> W. E. B. Du Bois, *The Souls of Black Folk*

> We are descended from Valencian fathers and Canary Island mothers and feel the inflamed blood of Tamanaco and Paramaconi coursing through our veins.
>
> José Martí, *Nuestra América*

In the early twentieth century, Hungarian philosopher Karl Mann-heim's book *Ideology and Utopia* tried to identify how sociological and historical inputs shaped thinking among groups, setting up an opposition between what he called ideologies and utopias. The former concept refers to systems of thinking based on conscious deceptions, perhaps intended to bypass myriad ethical and political contradictions, that impose an order on societal thinking. The latter, Mannheim feels, are based on leaps of faith that are incongruous with reality yet seek to create radical change.

This binary proposition falls into the same trap as current commentators of the moderate center who assign a false equivalence to the candidacies of Donald Trump, on the far right, and Bernie Sanders, on the far left. In some senses the analogy holds true, as the possibility of Sanders—despite his explicit references to "socialism"—effecting real change in the American bankster-industrial complex might be as far-fetched a utopian idea as the hope promised by Barack Obama. But while it is obvious that the Trump candidacy is a pack of lies, pack-ier and lie-ier perhaps than anything American politics has produced, it is a profound disservice to the truth to claim that the essence of what Sanders strives for is equivalent to the cynical kleptocracy and naked corporate takeover of politics that Trump represents.

It is in this context that the confrontation between the hypodescent ideology of race and Latin America's mestizaje/mulatez utopia is in the process of playing out in the United States, accelerating since the immigration explosion of the late twentieth century made Latinx the "largest" minority group in the country. Yet the relationship between the two ideologies is more complex than a simple binary opposition. The hypodescent ideology has been a tool for capital accumulation central to the United States becoming the world's most dominant economy, at least until the recent rise of China. Yet in terms of politics and identity, it has also been embraced by African Americans as an organizing tool that exposes how white supremacy reigns in a self-consciously liberal society. The unfortunate conflict, politically and socially, between African Americans and Latinx is grounded in the fallacy of the mestizaje ideology that many Latin Americans and

Latinx have used to claim a political or moral superiority over American imperialism.

As Marilyn Miller suggests in her book *Rise and Fall of the Cosmic Race*, the Latin American utopic vision of mestizaje is a cauldron of contradiction, at once serving the purposes of racists and anti-racists and arguing that mixed-race societies were the superior wave of the future—a future imagined by Simón Bolívar to anoint Latin America with an identity that distinguished it from the North, out of frustration with the lack of support from the United States for his efforts to break away from Spain. Bolívar's cult of personality also had its problems, including his beliefs in European intellectual superiority and the inherent passivity of indigenous people and his fear of black slave revolts. Yet Bolívar was a major influence on Cuban independence fighter José Martí, who insisted that an alliance between races was necessary to fight not only for independence from Spain, which kept Cuba as a colony until the war with the United States in 1898, but the devil to the North as well. "The rise of the mestizo," said Martí, who included indigenous and African roots in his definition of the term, is a "guarantee of Latin American autonomy in the face of the United States' expansionist designs on Cuba, Puerto Rico, and large chunks of Central America."

Martí's *Nuestra América* helped define that American-ness and explain that both North and South land masses were part of a New World that had experimented in different ways with assimilating, amalgamating, and miscegenating Europeans, Native Americans, and African people. The text also created a subversive identity for Latin America that transcended the black-white binary. Martí's ecstatic appropriations of the blood of Tampuco Indians as part of his and Nuestra América's essence contains considerably more weight than Emma Lazarus's famous poem about the American melting pot.

Martí had already rejected the utopian argument previously framed by Enrique Rodó, who called the United States the seat of barbarism and Latin America the seat of civilization, by asserting that "the struggle is not between civilization and barbarity but between false erudition and Nature." This claim, falling into the static binary of ideology versus utopia, is overly romantic about "natural" Latin America, but it correctly points out the deluded, false erudition obscuring the US origin story: the taking of a continent through genocide and forced displacement, with a slave economy as the hidden source of reserve capital for a budding industrial empire. It is also consistent with Ta-Nehisi Coates and with radical feminists' privileging of the body as the site of history and radical social change, a permanent reminder of the genocide of colonialism.

The flow northward of the imperfections and utopian notions of mestizaje and mulatez has already had a considerable effect on the evolution of social, political, and cultural life in the United States. Will these ideas take control of the more open-source tendencies of the US democratic polity and narrative? Or will they merge with binary notions of white supremacy to create a new, more sophisticated self-deceiving racial ideology?

This merging between Anglo- and Latin America is marked by the historical fact that for Latin Americans, the United States represents (as suggested by the Ariel-Caliban writings of the nineteenth century) a "second" conquest. While American ideology keeps trying to solidify and in some ways rehabilitate its identity as the Great Democratic Hope for the World, Latinx immigrants are reassessing the way race ideology has categorized them and figuring out how to navigate a new system founded on white supremacy. In the process, they are also confronting the nakedness of the horror and violence perpetrated on their indigenous and African ancestry.

To paraphrase Du Bois, there are double consciousnesses, and there are double consciousnesses. Will the two meet and enter into a dialogue with the Native American and Asian American legacies in the United States? Perhaps Latinx, simply by meditating on their African and indigenous roots, will expose the worst excesses of hundreds of years of racism and colonialism in the New World.

3

The Second Conquista

Mestizaje on the Down-Low

As the cavalry came round by the rear of the Indians, who were entirely occupied in their attacks upon us, the latter did not perceive them until they made their charge. The ground being very level, most of the horses active, and the men expert, they now rode through the bodies of the enemy as they chose, and we, encouraged by this support, reiterated our efforts on our side. The Indians struck with surprise thought that the horse and his rider were one; they were terrified at the fight, and in an instant fled to the adjacent woods and marshes, leaving the field and victory to us.

Bernal Díaz del Castillo, *The True History of the Conquest of Mexico*

The nonlinear, polytheistic worldview of the Aztec tribe that first confronted Hernán Cortés, a member of the hidalgo class of Spain who found himself in the unique position of conqueror in the early sixteenth-century city of Tenochtitlán, allowed them to see him as a chimera, a centaur, half-man, half-horse. Imagine their shock when he alighted from the horse, and they saw what they had assumed was one hybrid split in two. The encounter was a bridging moment, not only encapsulating the clash between Iberia and the New World but foreshadowing a future encounter between Mexico and the United States.

While the union between Cortés and his translator, La Malinche, symbolized the beginning of the process of miscegenation between Spaniards and indigenous people, locating mestizaje in a sexual act between bodies, the story of Cortés's appearance as a chimera is an even more symbolic manifestation of mixture. A hu/man on a horse is a vision of the movement of cultural hybridity from Spain to the New World and northward, revealing that the symbol of the American West, the cowboy/girl, is the quintessential representation of the new mixture that occurred as Latinx intersected with Anglo-America.

We've already seen how the Latinx notion of raza began with the early modern racist thinking of the Iberian peninsula and then was reconfigured by the conquest of the New World in Latin America, the Spanish Triangle dissolving into the murky mess of mestizaje and mulatez. Through this series of conquests, the ambivalent coexistence of self and other reimagined as a series of selves and others created a mixed-race consciousness with the potential to either permanently erase the indigenous and the African or allow those legacies to emerge forcefully at some opportune historical juncture. But a third conquest is involved when Latinx engage with Anglo-America, one that has been obscured for the most part in official US history even as its legacy becomes a living, breathing part of that history. Contemporary cultural institutions have attempted to unearth that history: A 2017 exhibition at the Studio Museum in Harlem called "Black Cowboy," for example, featured images of cowboys of color on urban panoramas, as the Federation of Black Cowboys, who were featured in the exhibit, struggled to hold on to its space in Southern Queens that it had held since incorporated in 1994 to celebrate the history of black cowboys. The thriving subculture of bicultural Mexican "charros" in Los Angeles spurred the production of a Hulu reality show series called *Los Cowboys* that was eventually picked up by Univision. A quick scan of the top-selling norteño or banda albums—Mexican regional music made by northern Mexicans that accounts for massive record sales among West Coast and Texan Latinx—reveals that acts like Intocable, Banda Sinaloense, and Julión Álvarez always dress in cowboy hats and boots. These manifestations of the cowboy figure may seem unconnected to each other, but they point to the threads that created this image. The cowboy was black, indigenous, Mexican, and African American and came to be in the region where North met South, a contact zone of movement and cultural innovation.

One can trace a direct lineage to the American cowboy from the roaming Arab horsemen active during the pre-Iberian conquest of Northern Africa. During the seventh century, the epoch of Mohammed, Arabs set out from Egypt to the west and encountered the nomadic desert- and mountain-dwelling Berbers. Decades of cultural intermingling and the creation of a hybrid Arab-Berber language created a mestizo culture, the prototype for the Moorish culture that in 710 C.E. crossed the Straits of Gibraltar to begin the long Islamic occupation of Iberia.

The Moorish style of horseback riding, *jinete*, became so entrenched in the culture of southern Andalucía, and ultimately the rest of Spain, that it continued to be practiced, with acknowledged Moorish influences, long after the expulsion of the Moors and Jews in the fifteenth and sixteenth centuries. The related word *jinetero/a* is still used in Cuba to describe all forms of street hustling. The *jinete* style, according to Barbara Fuchs in her book *Exotic Nation: Maurophilia and the Construction of Early Modern Spain*, was associated with the frontier and "emulated the Moors' consummate horsemanship" with "shortened stirrups and much higher set in the saddle," allowing "the rider [to] use knees and heels to guide the horse through tighter maneuvers."

This tradition was brought to Mexico by Cortés and his

accomplices and evolved over time to become standard practice in New Spain, the territory that encompassed Mexico and Central America. In *Vaqueros, Cowboys, and Buckaroos*, Jerald Underwood asserts that the vaquero tradition of Mexico used a lower-class labor force, with African and Indian slaves, mixed-race moriscos, and mestizos contributing to its development. He even speculates that the very first vaquero was a half-Moorish, half-black slave belonging to Cortés himself. Underwood also claims that "the cattle that became the Longhorn breed in the United States was actually crossbred from three original breeds" from Spain.

The horsemanship that developed over decades in what is now Mexico fostered the seventeenth- and eighteenth-century incursions north by Spaniards into Texas, New Mexico, Arizona, and California. Underwood locates the origin of the US cowboy in the 1850s when a group led by José de Escandón crossed the Rio Grande to collaborate with Richard King, who founded the King Ranch. The Kinéños, as they were called, pioneered a new, open-ended mixture of people and styles that would eventually become the American cowboy. While there are numerous stories claiming contact between Anglos and vaqueros dating back to the 1830s, the Spanglish effect was the most important consequence of this contact: Spanish words like *lariat*, *rodeo*, *riata*, *lazo*, *bota*, and *sombrero* became part of the English vocabulary.

The cowboy, like the Mexican vaquero, reflected a mixture of razas that began in the early years of Cortes's conquest and continued through the increased presence of freed blacks in Texas and crossover by neighboring Apache and Yaqui tribes. The American cowboy would not have been possible without the US-Mexican War of 1846–8, ostensibly provoked by incursions by Native Americans, the controversial settlement of Texas (leaving both Anglos and northern Mexicans unhappy with the ruling center of power south in Mexico City), and a utopian idea called Manifest Destiny. It was also strongly associated with efforts by Southern Democrats, led by their president, James Polk, to expand the amount of territory used for slavery. So although the conquest of the Southwest and California presaged the first Anglo-Latinx mestizaje, it was rooted in an act that symbolized one of the last gasps of the still-burgeoning Southern slave economy.

Mexico has a long history of blackness that until now, with the emergence of various Afro-Mexican advocacy groups, has been largely elided. The second president of Mexico was Vicente Guerrero, who was of black and indigenous descent. He ascended to the presidency in 1829 in a coup d'etat, abolished slavery five months later, and was abruptly removed from office by year's end. He was ultimately executed a year or so later, but the effect that Guerrero left on Mexico was the fatal flaw of mestizaje ideology. He had defied his predecessor and erstwhile collaborator Agustín de Iturbide by insisting that Afro-Mexicans be granted the same rights as indigenous people as part of the Mexican War of Independence. His execution stifled what was left of Afro-Mexican advocacy in a society that was increasingly moving toward pro-whitening ideology by granting social mobility to educated and moneyed mestizos. The eventual elimination of the social caste system with its mixed-race categories and hierarchies was intended to promote a nationalist idea of Mexico but resulted in a breakdown of political power articulated by indigenous and African identity.

Yet the mythological Anglo-American cowboy—a parallel construction to that of the noble white Spaniard peasants of the Caribbean (the Cuban guajiro and the Puerto Rican jíbaro)—remains an enduring symbol of whiteness, re-configured in the person of actor John Wayne, despite his three Mexican wives and purported fluency in Spanish. The emergence of white archetypes from the border narratives in which Wayne flourished was central to the erasure of Mexican blackness and indigenousness from the American character in the century following the war with Mexico. But the erasure was never complete.

The Jíbaro Masquerade and Playing Indian

In June 1820, the Puerto Rican newspaper *El investigador* published a lengthy anonymous poem called "Coplas del jíbaro" (The Jíbaro's Verses), which used gruff peasant language to critique the imposition of a constitution by the Spanish monarchy that irked local liberals. After an outcry over the poem, the writer revealed himself to be Miguel Cabrera, a liberal of the educated class, a Creole seeking liberation from Spanish absolutist monarchists. In what historian Francisco Scarano calls "The Jíbaro Masquerade," political dissidents like Cabrera "disguised their opposition politics behind a discursive mask, passing themselves off as native peasants."

While this tendency may have been informed by Spain's century of passing, it appears to be a strategy through which "American" identity was formed in both Anglo- and Latin America. Scarano compares the jíbaro masquerade to the white Indians of early eighteenth-century, post-revolutionary Maine. Much like the Boston Tea Party participants who dressed as "Indians" to protest the English colonial government's imposition of a tea tax, the white Indians went through an elaborate performance to voice their grievances. Elizabeth Maddock Dillon and historian Alan Taylor describe these performers' "uniform of moccasins, an Indian blanket, and a masked and elaborately decorated hood that usually ended in a conical peak." Beyond strategically disguising their renegade interests, the costumes contributed to, as Dillon describes, "a detailed new identity complete with songs, flags, effigies, speeches, and rituals designed to proclaim rebel 'laws' and to degrade local men regarded as turncoats." Mere concern with disguise cannot explain the pains they took to elaborate rebel appearance. Dillon suggests the creation of a white nationalist American identity in the early nineteenth-century Jacksonian era, where dressing as Africans and Native Americans in New York's Astor Place theater circuit allowed post-Revolution "Creoles" (that is, English-Americans born in the United States) to create a moral claim to their new land by mythologizing Indians' claim to a "moral economy."

The idea of "playing Indian" in the Americas lays crucial groundwork in the formation of American "Creole" identity. (*Creole* is more often used in the United States to describe mixed-race people of Louisiana; its counterpart, *criollo*, is used by Latin Americans of Spanish descent who were born in the Americas to describe themselves.) In his book titled *Playing Indian*, Philip Joseph Deloria quotes D. H. Lawrence's analysis of this seemingly bizarre convention in the construction of Anglo-American identity: "Americans … had been continually haunted by the fatal dilemma of 'wanting to have their cake and eat it too,' of wanting to savor both civilized order and savage freedom at the same time."

For Dillon, the "colonized subject is expected to disappear" in "a logic of elimination," which "requires the presence of the native whose vanishing becomes the work of the present in creating a fictive past—one that includes the death of the Indian." In a sense, then, one can almost understand the cognitive dissonance that seems to afflict American sports fans who feel threatened by calls from Native American groups to change the names of professional teams like the Washington Redskins and the Cleveland Indians. In 2016 white men dressed in garishly repulsive "Indian" costumes confronted Native American activists protesting outside the Cleveland stadium, reminiscent of a 1768 *Boston Evening-Post* dispatch describing the white Indians of Maine's efforts in this way:

> Their caps and masks were decorated with the most uncouth images imaginable. The masks were some of bearskin, some sheepskin, some stuck over with hog's bristles. To give a true description of them is impossible. The frantic imagination of a lunatic in the depth of desperation could not conceive of more horrid or ghastly spectres.

This tradition continued well into the twentieth century, as Iris Marion Young describes the "secret brotherhood of revolutionary patriots" in the Tammany societies that held meetings featuring "Euro-Americans dressing as Indians, singing songs and dancing in their own fashions 'as' Indians, and pledging their loyalty to the American Republic." In fact, it was a group of owners associated with New York's Tammany Hall that bought the National League's Boston franchise in 1911 and renamed it the Braves.

The less offensive Native American costumes worn by both whites and blacks in New Orleans's Mardi Gras Carnaval can arguably be attributed to that city's history of previous occupation by Spanish and French colonial regimes. At the same time, mocking performances at the turn of the twentieth century by young upper-class white Argentinean men attempting to imitate Buenos Aires's black culture and dance are at the root of the emergence of tango as a "white" cultural form.

Is it possible to draw a provisional line between the Anglo-American settler colonialist "replacement" of the native, leading to its extinction, and the more fluid Latin American cultural mix? How can one explain the contemporary rash of university campus parties that encourage white students to dress up as urban blacks or sombrero-wearing Mexican *campesinos*, when these tendencies are largely absent in the Mexican upper and middle classes, who prefer to disguise themselves as denizens of Southern California's San Fernando Valley?

Some writers, including legal scholar Tanya Katerí Hernández, argue that post-slavery legislation in Latin American countries has acted as a pernicious form of social control to enforce racial hierarchies, even as the absence of overt Jim Crow laws allows such societies to claim "racial innocence." I have observed in Puerto Rico, Mexico, Colombia, and elsewhere a persistence in racist attitudes in everyday life, but those attitudes, aside from some noted incidences on Peruvian and Colombian television, where comedy skits and

Ramón Frade's painting *El Pan Nuestro* (1905) codified the Puerto Rican jíbaro as a noble, light-skinned mountain-dwelling subsistence farmer (Instituto de Cultura Puertorriqueña).

sometimes whole programs feature blackface, mostly stop short of the open mockery and cruelty that have bubbled up in twenty-first-century America.

If the Latin American race dynamic is indeed different, its distinction might lie in the way racial "cross-dressing" happens in a more seamless and less shocking way there, and how the charged, symbolic identity of the "jíbaro" has transformed through our migration to the United States. Unsurprisingly, Puerto Rican writers and intellectuals went on a wild spree of lionizing the jíbaro after the US takeover in 1898 as a result of the War with Spain. Writers like Antonio S. Pedreira, who wrote the classic set of essays *Insularimso* describing the peculiarly insular character of the Puerto Rican experience, meditated on "jíbaro authenticity," while Ramón Frade's painting *El Pan Nuestro* (Our Daily Bread) created an iconic image of a "white" or "light-mixed" agricultural peasant hero that, as Scarano specified, was "ambiguously inclusive of the racially mixed peasant majority."

The negritude poetry of Luis Palés Matos used a minstrel-like imitation of the African dialects of Puerto Rico to merge the island's world of letters, and, by extension, its political corpus with Afrocentrism. Yet the resonance of jíbaro, when transferred to New York—the central destination for the Puerto Rican diaspora in the twentieth century—allowed for affirmation and awareness of racial difference for an ethno-racial group that, in the gaze of Anglo-America, was racially uncategorizable. In other words: you ain't black; you ain't white; what are you, son?

I saw the jíbaro strategy on display in my own father while I was growing up in New York. "Jíbaro!" my father would shout at his friends as they loped up the street from the subway, through the relentless slog of life in postwar New York's reserve industrial labor force. No matter where they fit on the colorist spectrum of racial identity, they nodded at my father's attempt to engage in class and (mixed-race) national solidarity. They may have thought he was being sincere or condescending, or they may have found themselves sharing a beer one night at an impromptu rooftop party in the middle of a citywide blackout, left suddenly to their new identity as New Yorkers.

As a working-class man who felt not only racialized in the job market, but scrutinized by both Anglo-Americans and Latinx for having a relatively dark-skinned wife, my father was constantly seeking to make alliances and racial identifications outside of his self. In contradictory fashion, he traded on Anglo-Americans' perceptions of his whiteness if it helped him in financial or social transactions, yet sought to avoid complete identification with whiteness when it came to his "real" identity.

The rooftop party scenario comes from a short story by the half-Dominican Afro–Puerto Rican writer and activist José Luis González titled "La noche que volvimos a ser gente" (The night we became people again). It describes such a worker who finds that all his neighbors are gathered around a quartet, or *conjunto*, of guitar, *güiro*,

maracas, and drums playing the Pedro Flores classic "Preciosa."
When he asks what the party is for, a neighbor replies, "Haven't
you noticed, you can see the moon and the stars." In that moment of
tropicalization, one of the four moments of the awakening of what
Juan Flores has called the New York Puerto Rican consciousness, the
narrator realizes that in the bright lights of the city that never sleeps,
he has forgotten that the stars had ever existed. With the replication
or transference of the music, smell, sights, and sounds of laughter
that he associates with his Puerto Rican identity, he realizes that he
has found a new home.

Yet this new nation-territory of the jíbaro was built on a fiction
about race—a utopian ideology that lied about its implicit white
supremacy. Benedict Anderson might have called it an Imaginary
Nation, codified by the city's vibrant Spanish-language media and
emerging bilingual codes and dialects. González knew this, and
would eventually renounce his American citizenship to live in exile
in Mexico because of his Marxist and pro-independence views. In his
classic essay "El país de cuatro pisos" (The country with four floors),
González claims that Puerto Rico has been incorrectly viewed as a
majority white "country" because of nineteenth-century European
immigration and the erasure of black Puerto Ricans. In the country's
early years, the latter were almost a majority of the population. He
continues:

> As for the white campesinos … in other words the first jíbaros, the truth
> is that this was a poor peasantry that found itself obliged to adopt many
> of the life-habits of those other poor people already living in the country,
> namely slaves … When people today speak … of *jíbaro* food what they
> really mean is "black food."

The battle over the racial content of the jíbaro/a ultimately became
a vehicle for New York Puerto Ricans' struggles with racialization, a
dynamic that felt a push and pull from above and below. Flores argues

that this dynamic put Puerto Ricans at odds with non-Caribbean Latinx, who viewed them as "less than" or "blacker" than other Latin Americans, and non-Latinx Caribbeans (from islands colonized by the English, French, and Dutch), who viewed them as "whitened." In New York, which was already following a model of pan-Latinx solidarity because of its diverse Latinx national groups, the conditions were ripe for Puerto Ricans to move towards a "mixed" identity, which also included the "black" and "white" binary categories.

The contrast between the Puerto Rican jíbaro and the cowboy of the Southwest is seemingly one of opposites: the jíbaro remained outside of any discussion of American-ness, and served as a site for the creation of a new hybrid identity that emphasized "outsider-ness," while the cowboy was completely incorporated by white America as a symbol of rugged individualism. But while the cowboy's story was one of migration, mixing, and ultimately erasing of "others" to create a white supremacist myth, the jíbaro underwent a kind of under-the-radar transformation reflecting the experience of Latin American migration.

The intersection of the United States and Latin America arose from American expansion and imperialism affecting almost every Latin American country and completely disrupting today's often-invoked neoliberal immigration narrative: that Latin American immigrants are simply compelled by the inability of their nation states to sustain an economy vibrant enough to employ them and have no choice but to flee northward, searching for a better life for their families. As Juan González innovatively claimed in his book and subsequent documentary *Harvest of Empire*, Latin American immigration substantially differed from European immigration because it was caused by direct American military and economic intervention. The expansion and emergence of US imperialism was the main driving force behind Mestizaje on the Down-Low. The US war with Mexico and the Spanish-American War, occurring in the mid- and late nineteenth century, respectively, coerced contact between the

United States, Mexico, and Cuba and Puerto Rico: the first three Latinx cultures to become intertwined with US culture, and fodder for all of the original racial stereotypes placed on Latinx.

This racialization also included sexual stereotypes, as racial and sexual oppression combined with the colonial dynamic as employed by both Anglo- and Latin American colonists. While men were seen as lazy, mentally inferior, and defined by their physicality, women were portrayed as sexually promiscuous, their "mixed" appearance already implying a deviant interracial sexual creation story. Although Cuba is often perceived as having an "off-white" racial identity, it has the largest black population of any of the Spanish-speaking Caribbean islands, and during its heyday as a Las Vegas–like holiday destination for Americans, was known as paradise of sexual fantasies, mainly driven by its mulata sex workers. In *Our Man in Havana*, for example, Graham Greene luridly describes Cuban women with "brown, eyes, dark hair, Spanish and high yellow, beautiful buttocks lean against the bars, waiting for any life to come along."

The ways in which Latinx are racialized in the United States are as complex and ambiguous as the Latin American system of racial categorization itself. Mexicans were racialized as "brown" if their phenotypical appearance had any hint of indigenous stock, and in California and the Southwest, became "black" through policies like residential segregation, separate water fountains and bathroom facilities, seating in movie theaters, and access to swimming pools that paralleled those applied to African Americans in the Jim Crow South. Yet their history in the US court system, on both the state and federal level, includes attempts to classify them as "white" to avoid legal racial discrimination. Another complicating factor is that the history and continuing presence of African-descended people in Mexico is repressed both in Mexico and wittingly or unwittingly by Mexican Americans themselves. This explains how, in popular culture, both Mexicans in Mexico and Mexican Americans see them-selves as members of a "brown" raza.

Puerto Ricans and Cubans, on the other hand, are seen in the United States as having widely varying racialized identities. Despite having been characterized by Puerto Rican poet Lola Rodríguez de Tío as "two wings of the same bird"—their flags, designed in Manhattan during the period leading up to the Spanish-American War, are of the same design, with inverse color schemes—the two islands' twentieth-century history has been one of a reversal of roles, racially and economically. After seizing them as war booty from the Spanish, the United States gave Cuba its nominal independence, seeking to control its economic development through other means, while retaining Puerto Rico as a colony.

The end result of US involvement was the Castro Revolution, whose ideological fierceness led to the migration of Cuba's mostly white, professional, landowning upper and middle classes to South Florida, while the United States' reboot of Puerto Rican governmental autonomy was accompanied by a rapid industrialization program that led to thousands of Puerto Rico's mostly creole, mulatto, and black landless peasants relocating to New York. The latter migration reinforced the increasingly circulated myth that Puerto Rico was a "white" island because of the whiter population left behind. The Cuban migration to Miami, on the other hand, created the whitest Latinx population of any US city, determining the relatively favorable way that Cubans are regarded in the United States, and Cuba's remaining population became symbolically black—although, due to racism in Cuba, not significant members of the ruling party. (The increase in Afro-Cuban lawmakers in Cuba's 2018 national elections was an attempt to address this.)

The growing presence of Mexicans, Puerto Ricans, and Cubans that characterized the Anglo-American twentieth century had little impact on the firmly entrenched US racial binary. These three groups introduced new cultural mechanisms that played with race and, through interactions with blacks, Native Americans, and whites, redefined those identities in ways that, while not yet disrupting the binary, laid the groundwork for what might happen in the twenty-first century.

Latino Late Modernisms: Unstuck in Time

The murals of Aztec warriors and goddesses that line the streets of East Los Angeles and the hybrid tribalism of Caribbean Afrophilia that informed the creation of hip-hop in the South Bronx can be viewed as merely re-imprinting ancestral memories on new terrain. But more than just planting a flag, they represent the shock Latinx feel when they migrate to the United States and realize that they have been subjected to yet another conquest. As anthropologist Serge Gruzinski suggests in his book *The Mestizo Mind*, the cultural mixture of Latin America represented an adaptation in the context of disorientation, destruction, and ultimately, acculturation. Aspects of African and indigenous identity are sometimes subliminally, sometimes overtly embedded religiously, culturally, and politically in experience and historical memory. These processes, sometimes latent, sometimes sharply manifested, have been unifying, at least for those who hold on to that notion of themselves. Clearly migration or immigration can allow some Latinx to blend into whiteness

The mural *La Pared Que Habla, Canta, y Grita* (The Wall That Speaks, Sings, and Shouts, 2001) represents Chicanx mysticism on Whittier Boulevard in Southern California.

entirely, extending a preexisting goal from the whitening dynamic of mestizaje. But many choose to embrace blackness, indigenousness, or some racialized notion of mixed-ness in defiance. Just as Black Lives Matter activists assert that the work of black liberation is far from done and that not enough has changed since the civil-rights-era victories, Latinx may be motivated, in a less coherent or explicit way, to assert that they have not yet resolved the shock from the destruction imposed on them by the Spanish conquista.

There is a staggering preponderance of what faded and graying Marxists might call *dialectics* involved here. In Latin America the shock of conquest involved Antonio Cornejo Polar's idea of heterogeneity, which describes a "double relationship of antagonism and supplementarity as part of the process of transculturation." Both the conquest process, which was unique in its institutionalization of racial mixing through coercion and persuasion, and the migration northward imply a degree of deterritorialization—losing one's sense of homeland, culture, and self—before you can even think of using that stubborn favorite of globalization-speak: hybridity.

One can go a long way in demystifying globalization—the neoliberal consensus of Soros think tanks and world banking conspiracy theorists alike—by invoking a prominent doubter of Marx, Immanuel Wallerstein, who argued that globalization began with the era of mercantilism in the sixteenth century. This point of view makes it easier to understand that the "mestizo mind" of Latin America was the product of a globalization that is now transposed, transfigured, and translated in the context of another conquest shock.

What does the organic mestizaje formed by centuries of evolution of Latin American societies look like in the age of globalization, practiced in the center, rather than the periphery? It might be useful to use a definition of hybridity coined by Néstor García Canclini, an Argentinean anthropologist based in Mexico City. According to Canclini, hybridity can be defined as "sociocultural processes in which discrete structures or practices, previously existing in separate

form, are combined to generate new structures, objects, and practices." Latin America seems filled with examples of this, but in the
United States, it's a phenomenon that seems to have barely begun.

Take Afro-Cuban music, for example, which in the United States
has come to be known in genres like "mambo" or "salsa." Afro-
Cuban music consists of previously existing practices like Yoruban
religious ritual, Italian opera buffo, Arabic-Andalucían folk music,
New Orleans jazz, and the Franco-Iberian poetry form known as
décima. Mambo and salsa exist as discrete genres but are actually
vibrant crucibles of cultural activity deriving from cultures stretch-
ing from Syria to Northern Africa and Southern France, revealing
how traditional skills or heritages can be reintegrated into new
conditions of production and distribution. Defying accusations of
cultural or ethnic essentialization, the process is defined by continual re-contextualization of cultures that already overlap in mestizo
societies.

Afro-Cuban trumpeter Mario Bauzá (center), pictured here with Chick
Webb and Ella Fitzgerald, found Afro-Latinx heaven in 1930s Harlem.

Latinx art forms, or identities, or cultural trends, or political phenomena are predisposed to become coherent categories that defy
categorization. What this makes possible is hybrid categories like
"Latin Music," or "Afro–Puerto Rican culture in New York," or
"Chicano culture in California." These are all cultures or identities
defined by an adaptation or acculturation to suit the particular needs
of each successive generation. What follows are some examples of
Latinx cultural adaptations to the United States that exemplify the
way this plays out in the new Anglo context, simultaneously adapting
to and disrupting the black/white racial binary.

The Afro-Cuban Tinge in American Jazz

Race narratives are central to Cuban jazz trumpeter and bandleader
Mario Bauzá's early twentieth-century transnational intervention in
Harlem's jazz scene. His story is a reminder of how the hypodescent theory of race in the United States can be juxtaposed with the
obscured racism of Latin America. Despite the utopian narrative of
mulatez that had been forming in Cuba, driven by poet, journalist,
and Communist sympathizer Nicolás Guillén, Bauzá found that the
liberation he never could find as a frequent performer in the whitened
Hotel Tropicana in Havana would come through the Harlem Renaissance. Bauzá made a break from the sphere of mulatez to the identity
of (N/n)egro in America, the embrace of the Harlem Renaissance,
and the freedom that segregation gave to black people unburdened
by the imperfect conciliatory gesture of mulatez.

Early in the course of his career of more than sixty years, Bauzá
was the musical director for the Chick Webb band, one of the most
popular in Harlem in the 1930s and 40s, and played with Fletcher
Henderson and Cab Calloway. His stint with Calloway allowed him
to join forces with trumpeter Dizzy Gillespie, whom he eventually
united with Machito (Mario Grillo), a Cuban bandleader who formed
a group called Machito and His Afro-Cubans. During this period,
Gillespie, Bauzá, Machito, and Charlie Parker experimented with a

music called "cubop," an offshoot of "bebop," with which it shared elements such as syncopated rhythmical structure and bass-playing techniques derived from Cuban mambo.

In New Orleans in the early 1900s, jazz had already come under the influence of what pianist Jelly Roll Morton called the "Spanish tinge," essentially an incorporation of the Cuban style of playing piano by using the left hand to unleash rhythmic attacks and the right to improvise melody and harmony. Yet when Bauzá tried to teach certain aspects of improvisation and rhythmic underpinnings to African American musicians in New York, they balked at what they considered "primitive" associations with African music.

New York music promoters agreed. The attachment of watered-down jazz elements to highly stylized Cuban fusions created a product exemplified by popular songs like "El Manisero," which became the first ever "Latin music" hit, and a slew of shallow imitations like white Cuban bandleader Xavier Cugat's orchestra and Desi Arnaz's infamous "Babalú," piggybacking on a version of the song by Miguelito Valdés. Valdés was, ironically, the product of a Spanish-Mexican marriage in Havana; yet despite his chameleon-like appearance, was reputed to have the blackest-sounding voice that mulatez could produce.

Cuban music became part of the American scene at the price of being presented as a novelty, with cutesy ethnic stereotyping. This, along with the language barrier, obscured how influential Cuban music had already become on American musicians. By 1931, "Latin music," or whitened Afro-Cuban music, began to cross over. In the 1931 film *The Cuban Love Song*, Mexican film star Lupe Vélez taught "The Peanut Vendor" to American actor Lawrence Tibbett. George Gershwin went to Havana and was so inspired that he wrote an orchestral piece called "Rumba," incorporating Afro-Cuban instruments. He even quoted "Échale Salsita" by Ignacio Piñeiro, a song that suggests the eventual naming of salsa through the oft-used sauce or stew paradigm.

The rejoinder to the pop fad of "El Manisero" was Puerto Rican singer Rafael Hernández's "Lamento Borincano"—a song that, rather than commodifying the Cuban genre son from above, served as a subaltern message from below. "Lamento" narrated the plight of the subsistence farmer during the height of the Great Depression, who sets out down the mountain to sell his wares to "buy my old lady a dress." But when he arrives at the market, "everything is deserted, the town is filled with need." Hernández is describing an experience similar to that of my grandfather, a subsistence farmer who lived in the mountains and found the Depression years as challenging as they were in the United States, to whose economy Puerto Rico's was directly linked. Yet this song was written years later by Hernández in Manhattan, and became immensely popular among migrants to New York whose nostalgia for their Caribbean home was made more poignant by such memories of deprivation.

The jíbaro image, already contested as a symbol of "authentic" Puerto Ricans in opposition to increasing US influence, was slowly transforming into blackness in New York. Hernández, who got much of his musical and traveling experience as a member of the US military, is widely recognized as an Afro–Puerto Rican, and was part of a migration that tended to be on the darker range of the Puerto Rican racial spectrum. Hernández was also part of a group of musicians in New York that were beginning to use bilingualism as a marker of a racially charged identity. The stammering mispronunciations of newly formed "plena" groups singing songs like Conjunto Típico Ladí's "Un Jíbaro en Nueva York" were at once an admission of being less than American but also a defiant way of establishing a new, acculturated status, attitude, and identity.

The song features an early recorded use of Spanglish as a way to express, as Urayoán Noel observes, a simultaneous defiance and disarticulation. Describing a confrontation to a jíbaro who has been in New York for a while, the narrator complains that his new friend has lost his Spanish, only to hear him respond, "Oye esto, brother/I love my father and mother/igual que un Americano," refusing to concede his assimilation since he has continued to speak "Spanish and inglés."

Yet although "Un Jíbaro en Nueva York" belonged to the seis con décima genre, itself derived from the poetic style of Moorish-dominated Andalucía, the African-derived plena style became increasingly emblematic of an emerging New York Puerto Rican jíbaro expression. Devalued in Puerto Rico because of its African origins, plena music ironically expanded into a more elaborate big band format using singers like the lighter-skinned Canario, who abandoned his previous attempts at popular bolero music to become a star in a style that was marked as black from its origins.

In the mid-1940s, zoot suiters wore flamboyant clothing to make an identity politics point.

In almost the inverse of the development of Cuban music, record companies designed Puerto Rican music as an ethnic music industry, marginalized by the mainstream the way regional Mexican music is today. But the roots appeal of "Lamento Borincano," which transposed a national identity derived from a performance about a rural figure of ambiguous racial origins, fit in well with the general atmosphere in New York, where Latinx were brought together through appeals to working-class solidarity among national identities, as well as by the pro-Republic Spaniards and sympathizers in the lead up to and aftermath of the Spanish Civil War.

Pachuquismo

In the 1940s a new Mexican identity was evolving through *pachucos*: wearers of the bold, bright exaggerated uniforms known as zoot suits, which originated in Harlem. Pachucos and pachucas were young working-class Mexican Americans who traded on the flamboyance of the suit, which was most famously worn by jazz artist Cab Calloway, to defy the white supremacist code of desired Mexican American behavior: submissive, unwilling to speak Spanish in public or call attention to oneself on the street. They also sported wide-brimmed hats, teased hair, and a tattoo between the thumb and the index finger.

Pachuquismo spread far beyond its origins in cities such as El Paso and Tucson and throughout the entire Southwest and California. It was even picked up by Mexico City comedian Tin Tan, which prompted Octavio Paz to denounce the subculture in *The Labyrinth of Solitude*. Pachuquismo's transnational characteristics also included caló, an informal street slang used as a form of protection from outsiders, similar to a secret jargon of the same name used by Gypsies in Spain. Some speculate that caló spread northward from Gypsy bullfighters passing through Mexico City or drug smugglers and youth traveling northward and out of El Paso in railcars. Still, its development in the Southwestern border areas is considered to be fairly autonomous, and caló words like *vato*, *cholo*, and *ese* have been immortalized in the poetry of José Antonio Burciaga, Mexican American gang movies, and even Cheech and Chong routines.

> *Sabes qué, ese?*
> I'm a loco from the word go,
> In the purest sense
> Of the word loco
> From the Latin
> Loco citato
> The place cited
> I know my place, *ese*
> I know my location
> My station
> *Es aquí*
>
>   José Antonio Burciaga, "El Juan from Sanjo"

This new subculture, a deviation from both Mexican American and traditional Mexican identity, threatened the homogeneity of Anglo-American identity. It paralleled African American "juvenile delinquency" and was a forerunner of the Anglo-American juvenile delinquency that was subsequently romanticized and pathologized in post–World War II American cinema.

Two race-related incidents during the World War II years helped to define the zoot suit and its importance as a symbolic performance of a hybrid Mexican American identity. The Sleepy Lagoon incident in 1942 involved the railroading of several pachucos and pachucas, after a murder following a party in a swimming hole near Los Angeles. Many of those arrested were not at the party and little evidence existed that connected the accused with the crime, yet the jury found the defendants guilty, although they were released two years later. The next year, negative newspaper coverage of Mexican American youth helped provoke the so-called Zoot Suit Riots. The Los Angeles mainstream media claimed that zoot suit wearers were not patriotic because the suits required excessive amounts of material that was being rationed at the time. During these "riots," American servicemen on shore leave roamed the streets of Los Angeles, beating and stripping naked not only Mexican, but African and Asian American youth as well.

During the postwar years, increased awareness of Mexican Americans in the West and Puerto Ricans in New York spurred criminologists and psychologists alike to characterize them as social problems. Puerto Ricans began to be featured in movies about juvenile delinquency such as *Blackboard Jungle*, appearing ultimately in the Broadway play *West Side Story* as largely racialized hoodlums (with the exception of the light-skinned Maria, who acts as the Malinche figure of translation/miscegenation in a last-ditch attempt to allow her group to be absorbed into the ethnic melting pot).

The 1950s were a crucible for what would become the 1960s counterculture. Although that social phenomenon is largely attributed to the alienation and downward mobility of middle-class white American youth, these elements also intersected with the mestizo, mulatto, and African American subcultures that had arisen in response to the exclusion of Latinx and blacks from the benefits of FDR's welfare state and the postwar explosion of the US economy. The "white" counterculture was steeped in a romanticism that mirrored previous tendencies toward isolationism, resisting notions of collectivity.

In 1957 Norman Mailer published an essay in dissent called "The White Negro," which echoed the concerns of Beat writers such as Allen Ginsberg and Jack Kerouac about the profound alienation of many young white Americans in the aftermath of extreme wartime violence, exemplified by the firebombing of Dresden and the nuclear bombing of Tokyo and Nagasaki. "It is on this bleak scene," writes Mailer, "that a phenomenon has appeared: the American existentialist —the hipster, the man who knows that if our collective condition is to live with instant death by atomic war ... why then the only life-giving answer is to accept the terms of death."

For Mailer, American society is divided in typical binary fashion between the hipster and the square: "One is a rebel or one conforms, one is a frontiersman in the Wild West of American night life"— an unconscious allusion, perhaps, to Deloria's suggestion about "Playing Indian" in the jungle-y precincts of singles bars in Manhattan. For Mailer, the true source of hipness was of course "the Negro, for he has been living on the margin between totalitarianism and democracy for two centuries."

Yet for Jack Kerouac and his *On the Road* alter ego, Sal Paradise, hipness embraced African Americans, mulattoes, mestizos, Mexican Americans, and migrant Mexican workers, a realization he made after leaving the safe precincts of Morningside Heights to hitchhike across the country and examine the vastness of hybrid/mestizo America. He explains in this excerpt from *On the Road*:

> The only people for me are the mad ones, the ones who are mad to live, mad to talk, mad to be saved, desirous of everything at the same time, the ones who never yawn, or say a commonplace thing, but burn, burn, burn like fabulous yellow roman candles exploding across the stars.

Those mad ones were the nascent Beat generation, precursors of the counterculture, alternative rockers, even in some ways the hip-hop generation, dance club kids, and the entitled hipsters of the yearly Burning Man festival and the far-flung industrial lofts of Bushwick. Yet what is only hinted at in Kerouac's prose is that these "mad ones" were sometimes African American, or mixed-race, or Latino, or that they were African Americans, Latinx, mixed-race people, and queers building their own subcultures when they weren't crossing over.

Despite spending multiple pages on his sublimated bromance with Dean Moriarty, Kerouac's Paradise finds his first love after a failed marriage in Terry, a "sweet Mexican girl" whom he meets on a bus in California. They take jobs picking cotton, a nightmarish task most often associated with African Americans, but practiced out West by huge numbers of Mexican migrant workers. (Even Puerto Ricans were enlisted in the mid-1920s to pick cotton by Arizona growers frustrated with Mexican workers.) Kerouac writes:

> One night the Okies went mad in the roadhouse and tied a man to a tree and beat him to a pulp with sticks. From then on I carried a big stick with me in the tent in case they got the idea we Mexicans were fouling up their trailer camp. They thought I was a Mexican, of course; and in a way I am.

Kerouac also liked to think of himself as a "Negro," waxing poetic, like Mailer, about the transformative power of jazz:

> At lilac evening I walked with every muscle aching among the lights … in the Denver colored section, wishing I were a Negro, feeling that the best the white world had offered was not enough ecstasy for me, not enough life, joy, kicks, darkness, music, not enough night.

The world of Beat was firmly entrenched in the world of bebop, a jazz style made famous by Charlie Parker, Dizzy Gillespie, Mario Bauzá, and Chano Pozo, who had escaped the commercialization of Cuban rumba through continually subversive mambo improvisations in both the mainstream mambo dance genre and African American jazz. When Paradise and Moriarty go out in San Francisco to see jazz, they go to see Slim Gaillard, a singer and pianist who embodies the hybrid multicultural roots of bebop. While some accounts claim he was born in Detroit, Gaillard was also rumored to have been born and cut sugar cane in Cuba, in addition to inventing a nonsense "jive" language similar to caló and representative of the confusion of Anglophones when encountering Spanish.

In the end, after disappointing all of the women in their lives, Sal and Dean head for Mexico for what would become a rite of passage for the nascent hipster counterculture. A 1957 article in *Life* magazine describing the hallucinogenic powers of psilocybin mushrooms would eventually bring flocks of hippies to Oaxaca, Mexico, to visit a *curandera* named María Sabina. Years before, William Burroughs had visited the Amazon rainforest to sample the hallucinogenic plant yagé and wrote Allen Ginsberg several letters about it, which were published as *The Yage Letters*.

Yet as Manuel Martínez writes in *Countering the Counterculture*, the Beat writers were perhaps closer to upholding the racist, sexist, and imperialist nature of America than diverging from it. Writers like Kerouac and Burroughs sought to "find freedom through liminal others," and through a decadent and romantic individualism created new spaces for exploitation and marginalization, erasing the genocidal history of the United States in the process. In Kerouac, Mexican others symbolized sexual freedom or freedom of movement, and in Burroughs they represented cultural practices around new exotic drugs as objects of consumption.

Many of these countercultural roots, derived from the urban cultures of Latinx and African Americans, are clearly forgotten in the contemporary notion of the hipster, due perhaps to the imperative of the racial binary or simply an example of cultural appropriation designed to claim it all for white ownership. Yet Kerouac, in the published novel at least, seemed to acknowledge in a way that some found condescending and others compassionate that Mexicans were free in a way he wanted to be, but Americans weren't.

Describing his feelings as he makes his way out of Mexico after his ill-fated adventure with Moriarty, he imagines what the Mexicans might have thought of him and his companion: "They knew this when we passed, ostensibly self-important moneybag Americans on a lark in their land. They knew who was the father and who was the son of antique life on earth ... All Mexico was one vast Bohemian camp."

Chicanx and Nuyorican Resistance Emerge
as Mestizo on the Down-Low

In California, Mexican Americans became the demographic in the late 1950s that sustained rock music, turning up in huge crowds for R&B and doo-wop shows in El Monte Legion Stadium in the San Gabriel Valley. Playing to a subculture of lowriders and Pendleton plaid shirts, the shows gathered an audience of mixed races and ethnicities just as the Palladium Ballroom did in Manhattan for crowds to dance the mambo. Garage bands popped up all over Southern California, featuring heavy use of the same Farfisa organs used in the norteño music of reconfigured Texas rancheras.

Mario Suárez's short stories set in an inner-city barbershop in El Hoyo, a neighborhood in Tucson, Arizona, echo the importance of that location in African American communities. *Pochismo*, a catch-all term for Mexican American subcultures that abandoned the use of Spanish—sometimes as a symbol of rebellion, other of conformity—paralleled the outlaw phrasings of caló. The Mexican roots of rock and roll were clear in the figure of Ritchie Valens, née Valenzuela, who worked to actively transform himself from a pocho, non-Spanish-speaking California Mexican American into someone connected to his roots. His rock adaptation of "La Bamba," a song he had heard in Tijuana, which was rapidly developing into one of the hemisphere's most dynamic border cultures, revived a song in the *son jarrocho* genre with African origins. "Louie, Louie," a song that became a staple of white frat rock, was actually written by Richard Berry, an African American devotee of the El Monte Legion Stadium rock shows, who adapted the rhythm pattern for that song from a Cuban cha cha cha written by René Touzet.

Yet the emergence of rock music and the US counterculture spelled doom for both the multiracial El Monte Legion Stadium phenomenon and the Palladium Ballroom mambo battles, which featured Mario Bauzá's Machito band and hybrid New York Puerto Rican bandleaders like Tito Puente and Tito Rodríguez. The Friday-night

dance culture that had flourished in the United States in the 1920s
and embraced Afro-Cuban genres and dance styles as mainstream
in the 1950s crashed and burned with the advent of British invasion
rock and, ultimately, the Playing Indian excesses of San Francisco
psychedelia. Manhattan's Palladium shut down in 1966, in part due
to a drug bust, just as the Fillmore Auditorium in San Francisco,
the brainchild of promoter Bill Graham, was about to welcome the
Summer of Love. It was no coincidence that Graham grew up in
New York going to dance mambo in the Palladium; Graham brought
a glittering, spinning ball just like the Palladium's to the Fillmore's
dance floor and encouraged his protégé Carlos Santana to record a
rock version of Tito Puente's "Oye Como Va." But the Fillmore's
dancing was free form—closer to the roots of African dance, albeit
with considerably less discipline—and the counterculture hippies
who emerged had no memory of Mexican American garage bands
or the Afro-Cuban rhythms that informed the R&B cum Beatles rock
classic "Twist and Shout."

There was no longer room in the American Dream for the multicultural bohemia that briefly provided an intersection between
beatniks, bebop, mambo, R&B, and roots rock and roll. While
Mexican Americans regrouped around a new idea of indigenous
roots, in New York a new generation of US-born Puerto Ricans
raised on soul, rock, and R&B began to vacillate between updates
on Cuban genres such as charanga and pachanga. They eventually
settled on a genre called bugalú, which acknowledged the Southern migration of African Americans to New York as parallel to their
own. But as Angel Quintero-Rivera writes in his essay "Migration
and World View in Salsa Music," this nascent identity of Nuyoricans
and New York Latinos in the 1960s and 70s did not share a common
ground with the emerging middle-class counterculture:

> For the youth of the (im)migrant world of the Caribbean populace, for
> whom the image of the consumerist "paradise" came crashing down in

the ghettos, the future did not appear as a telos toward which the ascendant line of modernity led, but as an aspiration, as an identity project that, as a result, needed to be gradually constructed from the valued remnants of their present and their past ... Generational identity thus remained thoroughly suffused with other identities: national, ethnic, and class.

Without generational identity as the central undertaking of salsa musicians, Nuyorican and other New York Latino musicians made a cultural turn to the nutritive nostalgia pioneered by Rafael Hernández, abandoning the English-language bugalú project. The nationalist art and cultural forms that emerged in the 1970s for Puerto Ricans and Mexican Americans did not abandon themes of race and social class. Instead they formed a modernism that lagged slightly behind the rest of the developed world, reflecting the need to work out its last expressions, ultimately coinciding with the beginning of postmodern scratching, cutting, and pasting of rapping, DJing, graffiti, and break dancing. These were the essential components of *Mestizo on the Down-Low*.

4

Raza Interrupted

New Hybrid Nationalisms

I am the sword and flame of Cortés the despot
And I am the serpent of Aztec civilization
                                Corky Gonzales, "Yo Soy Joaquín"

Coño Papo. Te parece como un moreno, brother
Word up, bro. You look like a stone black kid
                                Willie Perdomo, "Nigger-Reecan Blues"

Two languages coexisting in your head as modes of expression can either
strengthen alertness or cause confusion.
                                Miguel Algarín, "Nuyorican Language," 1975

In Juan Flores's essay "Qué Assimilated, Brother, Yo Soy Asimila'o" (What Do You Mean Assimilated, Brother, I Be Assimilated), he lays out four paradigmatic moments in the awakening of Puerto Ricans who came of age in New York, colloquially known as Nuyoricans. The first is what he calls the state of abandon, or what I might call the shock of urban wage slavery, a new version of the shock of Spanish conquest. The second is a moment of intense nostalgia, where the home country and its paradisaical landscape of palm trees, warm waters, and agricultural bounty are fetishized beyond what the emigrant ever imagined. The third involves something akin to "tropicalization," when the symbols and codes of the home country are mythically attached to the mean streets of New York to create a new home, and the fourth is integrating this new, wholly formed identity into the new surroundings and interacting with concrete historical conditions that are playing out in the present.

While Flores's essay focuses on Nuyoricans, the essence of his model is applicable to Latinx groups in general, even those with varying political and social class positions. Most of this chapter will concern itself with the third and fourth moments, which, for Puerto Ricans, Mexicans, and Cubans, coincide with the civil rights era and the national liberation movements, radical direct action against government authority, and their social and political expressions in the 1960s and 70s. In this era Latinx confront America's increasingly violent negotiation of racial difference, redefining identity and generating a different model from the ideal of melting pot assimilation. While Latinx hybrid identities typically have been considered the result of cultural and linguistic mixing, their staying power has always been grounded in the peculiarly American racial experience.

In the 1960s and '70s, Puerto Rican and Mexican migrants to the United States found themselves racialized through explicit segregation, as Mexicans faced in the West and Southwest, or stereotyped as criminals and discriminated against through segregation and exclusion as Puerto Ricans were in New York. The postwar years leading up to the civil rights era had included some victories for both groups, but the promise of postwar suburban affluence that was being enjoyed by the United States' white majority had eluded Latinx (as well as, of course, African Americans). As had happened with African Americans, Mexican and Puerto Rican soldiers came home from World War II and the Korean War and were chagrined at having remained second-class citizens. After decades spent establishing core communities in large cities in the East and West, they began to embrace the militant questioning of authority of the African American black nationalist movement.

As national liberation movements began to gather steam, they shared utopian elements with the emerging, "white" counterculture. Yet while the latter engaged in an angry self-negation of the American character, Puerto Ricans and Chicanos were assembling a new "nationalist" identity, abandoning the goal of passing for white and creating a new deterritorialized nation that, in anticipation of full-blown globalization, was not fixed to a specific space, and was based on themes derived from the marginalized razas of mestizaje, *lo africano y lo indio*.

The emergent identity for New York Puerto Ricans was encapsulated in *Nuyorican*: newness, Nu Yor', as it would be pronounced by a Spanglish-speaker, grafted to Rican, an allusion to a charged metal currency, the Rich Port transferred from one harbor (San Juan) to another (Upper New York Bay), reminiscent of the triangular slave trade. It flows easily from bilingual lips, describing a repositioning and recontextualization of one colonial port to another.

The synergy between the Caribbean and New York's five-borough archipelagoes has historical roots. The spirits of the old Dutch East India Company remain in power on Manhattan Island, and the dead and living generations of seagoing commerce are always murmuring: New York, in its past life as Nieuw Amsterdam, had been in a constant trading circuit with Jakarta, Cádiz, Cape Town, Barcelona, New Orleans, San Juan. The famous last mayor of the Dutch colony of Manhattan, Peter Stuyvesant, had come to the job after serving as the commander of Dutch political and military operations in the Caribbean, based in the island colony of Curacao. Neoliberal progressive hero Alexander Hamilton was born in the Caribbean island of Nevis. His ambivalent relationship with slavery and murky racial status made his life's distorted miscasting as a typical immigrant story in an extremely successful Broadway play possible.

The islands in the Caribbean, linked to the island archipelago of Manhattan, were the headquarters for the Captains of Commerce and the revolution they would bring to the New World. They began, in the Cape Verde Islands almost midway between Africa and the Caribbean archipelago, to throw together a social system of Iberian military and noblemen, Moors, Jews, mixed-race entrepreneurs, free blacks, and slaves. New York became the slave-trading capital of the colonies for a period in the eighteenth century, and spirits echo from Wall Street caverns as they did from the walls of San Juan's fortress, El Morro.

When considering the process of relocation of Puerto Rico's spirit to New York, I like to draw on the words of the Cuban writer Antonio Benítez-Rojo about the general nature of the Caribbean archipelago: "its fragmentation, its instability, its reciprocal isolation, its uprootedness, its cultural heterogeneity, its lack of historical continuity, its contingency and impermanence, its syncretism." The Caribbean island plantation machines, as Benítez-Rojo calls them, were antecedents to patterns that were replicated in the Anglo-American colonies. The model of Barbados was almost literally translated to Virginia and South Carolina, and the slave market of Seville became the slave market of New York. When I think of archipelago I think of New York, and how Puerto Rican migrants read between the lines and found a way to make a home among a series of chaotic and unstable islands where African drums marked time like rumbling subway trains.

Anticipated by Mario Bauzá's immersion in Harlem and the Jazz Age, Puerto Rican New York was pioneered by black and mulatto fusionists, from Jesús Colón's socialist activism and writing to poet Julia de Burgos's championing of José Martí, the autonomy of women, and her own identification with negritude. It grew out of

Piri Thomas's mean streets, where he discovered the "Porty-Rican" in-between of blackness, Tato Laviera's Afro-skewering of proper Spanish, and Tito Puente's reinvention of Gene Krupa and Glenn Miller. It was a three-pronged explosion of words, rhythms, and political action that birthed Nuyorican and its homeland, the Spirit Republic of Puerto Rico in New York.

Nuyorican identity developed out of three spheres, which each represented a temporal orientation and a different acculturation strategy: salsa, which reached back to Caribbean musical forms and insisted on Spanish as a lingua franca to preserve a sense of origin; the radical cultural nationalism of groups like the Black Panther–like Young Lords that responded to the present political ferment of the anti-war movement and black nationalism; and Nuyorican literature, whose bilingual aesthetic and postmodernizing of the oral tradition pointed to the future. As Flores insisted in his essays on the subject, Nuyorican was a form of assimilation that refuted the melting pot framework. The gradual increase in the use of English—more often than not "black" English—as well as the participation in evolving Anglo/African American culture and tradition made Nuyorican identity and culture a mechanism that established a homeland away from home.

Salsa was a modernist re-contextualization of the mulatez aesthetic of Afro-Cuban music, redrawn to fit the 70s crisis of capitalism and the collapse of industrialization in cities like New York. It drew from nationalist populism to turn both time and consciousness back to the home country while creating a hybrid Spanglish identity for English-dominant Nuyoricans, most of whom had never seen the island. Movements like the Young Lords and the Real Great Society focused on housing reform and advocacy, and the Independence movement repped by local chapters of the Puerto Rican Socialist Party made clear not only the colonial problem that had gripped the island since 1898 but also theories of internal colonization to which black nationalism and the Chicano movement also subscribed. Nuyorican poetry, on the other hand, pre-figured the postmodern genres of rap and spoken word, acknowledging discourses of intersectionality, the shift to digital information, and the primacy of looping, repetitive rhythmic structures while—for the most part—abandoning traditional, Western, lyrical poetic forms.

With the overlapping of modern/postmodern, nation-state/ global eras came inevitable contradictions in Nuyorican and New York Latino identity formation as a postcolonial activity. Puerto Rico lives in a postcolonial limbo while awaiting its effective decolonization as a national territory. The Nuyorican moment was the leading edge of a postcolonialist liberation movement that has trickled down to the island in the form of cultural remittances such as those described in Juan Flores's *The Diaspora Strikes Back*. The re-encounter with blackness achieved in New York allowed reverse migrants to return to the island and affect local politics, influence the creation of hip-hop–inflected genres such as reggaetón, and even bring a streetball aesthetic to the Puerto Rican national basketball team.

The ranks of early salsa were dominated by English-heavy Spanglish speakers including Willie Colón, who mixed a *Superfly*-influenced street gangsta aesthetic with the mulato-jíbaro nasal inflections of his lead vocalist Héctor Lavoe, embracing cultural nationalism and defying the hegemonic attempt at rock and roll by the Anglo counterculture. There were also echoes of modernism: most notably the Debussy-ish jazzy dissonance of pianist Eddie Palmieri, who had cut his teeth in the Palladium mambo scene and in collaborations with R&B group Harlem River Drive.

Salsa music for the most part was not regarded as part of mainstream American entertainment, unlike its Afro-Cuban predecessors son, rumba, and mambo. This was partly due to the collapse of the mainstream Saturday night dance culture that made Afro-Cuban music widely acceptable, providing the most recent and daring dance steps and an erotic milieu. With large mambo clubs, including the Palladium, shutting down in the 1960s, the latest manifestation of

"Latin music" was now challenged by a lack of access to innovations from Cuba, with which much cultural contact had been banned by the postrevolutionary embargo.

This created a space for a stripped-down package of from-below musicians playing for a from-below audience, mostly in Harlem and the Bronx. Urban salseros, including downwardly mobile mambo bandleaders and working-class emerging talent, were steeped in a postcolonial drive for Afro-Latin populism and authenticity. Most musical genres at the time were beginning to repackage themselves as part of the globalized spectacle of rock and later hip-hop, with most of the traces of populist, local, and nationalist narratives discarded by the increasing use of kitsch and pastiche (although the authenticity and politics of the hegemonic African Americanist narrative of hip-hop is subject to continual debate).

Salsa and salseros shared the stripped-down format that predicted hip-hop: small clubs, young and unknown performers, balky sound systems, edgy discordance. But in its postcolonial identity project, salsa retained a modernist narrative, avoided nihilism, and served as a galvanizing force for the cultural nationalist politics of Nuyorican New York. Because it developed in a community setting, in venues that predominantly served a poorer social class, and because culture and politics tend to become linked within marginalized groups, salsa can be interpreted as a manifestation of the same impulse that produced the radical politics of the Young Lords.

While the Young Lords clearly influenced the Latin Americanist "nueva trova" songwriting of Panamanian singer Rubén Blades, who became an honorary Puerto Rican through his collaboration with Willie Colón when he replaced Héctor Lavoe as the lead singer of his group, many of the major figures on the salsa scene were swept up, in one way or another, by the political energy that drove the Lords. Brothers Jerry and Andy Gonzalez, for example, who began playing with the Ray Barretto orchestra and later invented a new kind of Latin jazz with their group the Fort Apache Band, were politically radicalized. And the Jewish bandleader turned Santería devotee Larry Harlow composed a proto-nationalist "La Raza Latina: A Salsa Suite" in 1977. But the most prominent intersection between salsa and the Young Lords came through one of its core members, who also happened to be a poet.

In 1971, pianist and bandleader Eddie Palmieri played a concert at Sing Sing Prison in upstate New York that featured a poetry reading by Felipe Luciano, one of the core members of the Young Lords. Ostensibly the lead-in to Palmieri's major hit "Azúcar," itself a play on the sugar plantations that enslaved blacks in the Caribbean for much of the seventeenth and eighteenth centuries, Luciano's poem is significant in the way it continues the evolution of the jíbaro figure, further distancing it from its whitened origins in the early part of the twentieth century. With "Jíbaro, My Pretty Nigger," Luciano describes the transformation of the jíbaro from an idealized white peasant of the Puerto Rican countryside to the modern-day black, urban Puerto Rican, whose racial identification was a major part of a political radicalization project:

> Jíbaro, mi negro lindo
> De los bosques de caña
> Caciques de luz
> Tiempo es una cosa cósmica.
> Jíbaro, my pretty nigger.
> Father of my yearning for the soil,
> The land,
> The earth of my people.

Luciano's part in the formation of the Young Lords is telling. Having grown up in New York strongly identifying with African Americans to the extent that most of his early organizing was done in Harlem, Luciano was also one of the original Last Poets, an ensemble of bards whose take on poetry fused elements of Beat poetry—a mostly white genre with two prominent black contributors: LeRoi Jones, later Amiri Baraka, and Ted Joans—street rhyming, and Afro-Caribbean percussion in the form of conga drums. The Last Poets recorded in the late 60s and early 70s and are widely acknowledged as one of the progenitors of rapping technique in hip-hop.

As Luciano tells it, Guylan Kane, one of the Last Poets, suggested to him one day that even though his contributions to the black movement were appreciated, it was time for him to do something for his "own people." By that, Kane meant Puerto Ricans and, more generally, Latinx in New York (indeed, much of Nuyoricans' formation included other Latinx groups in a similar socio-historical moment to Puerto Ricans, as well as the substantial involvement of African Americans).

The core of the Young Lords, in fact, included Pablo Guzmán, a half Cuban and half Puerto Rican Afro-identifying Minister of Information; Miguel "Mickey" Meléndez, part Cuban and part Puerto Rican; Denise Oliver, who is African American and participated in the group because of her close working relationship with Puerto Ricans; and Puerto Ricans Juan González, Iris Morales, David Pérez, and Richard Pérez. This racial crossover of membership even extended to the Black Panthers, who counted several Afro–Puerto Ricans in their New York branch. (Saeed "Shariff" Torres, the over-zealous FBI informer who appears in the 2015 documentary *[T]error*, was an Afro-Latino ex-member of the Black Panthers.)

The Young Lords were originally formed in Chicago by former street gang member turned political organizer Cha Cha Jiménez, but quickly grew into a major movement in New York through a group of college students and community workers. The core membership of the group was motivated by local community concerns, such as the infrequency of garbage collection, the lack of access to tuberculosis testing, and the impact of lead-based paint used in tenements that housed the children of the urban poor. Like the Black Panthers, it functioned as a national liberation movement with a strong focus on culture and identity, while remaining committed to the radical political debates of the day, including the Maoism that predominated in the late 60s and early 70s.

The Young Lords, like their Chicano counterparts, were also laying the groundwork for the intersectional movements and discourse that developed later in the 1970s. The group openly addressed sexism and homophobia in its weekly newspaper *Pa'lante*, and members Iris Morales, Denise Oliver, and Sonia Ivany played central roles in the group's efforts. Member Richard Pérez's essay "On Machismo" critiqued the male supremacy that was common in that era. Unfortunately the Young Lords found their dissolution in ways that paralleled the Black Panthers, subject to FBI informants who stirred up internal dissension and arguments over which socialist tendency to follow. They also found themselves overextended by chapters that were formed in cities up and down the East Coast, as well as in Puerto Rico itself.

The rift between the Young Lords and their counterparts in Puerto Rico over the independence movement was representative of a conflict that continues to emerge between US Latinx and Latin Americans from their original countries. Once the new, hybrid identity is created, the question of authenticity, with racial overtones, arises. As most Latinx immigrants tend to be on the darker side of the spectrum (mulatos, indios, cholos), their language and manner begins to reflect more of that side and deviates from the Hispanic values of Latin America. The Young Lords may have been perceived as arrogant for setting up shop in Puerto Rico to collaborate or lead the independence movement, but the Puerto Rican independence activists may have acted arrogantly as well, reacting to the Nuyorican Young Lords' apparent blackness or mulato-ness, as well as their relative inefficiency in speaking fluent island-style Spanish.

In keeping with their masterful present-ness during a period that included the Panthers, the Weathermen, SDS, the Paris of May '68, and the dawn of the women's movement, the Young Lords were also

extremely media savvy, capturing the attention of edgy journalists at the *New York Times,* the then-liberal *New York Post,* and the
Village Voice. One of the quintessential moments in Young Lords
history was captured in a documentary made by the fledging Third
World Newsreel, which filmed their takeover of the Spanish Meth-
odist Church in East Harlem in December 1969. The film showed
the famous free breakfast programs and a musical performance by
nueva canción folklorists Gema & Pavel. But arguably the film's
most riveting moment came when Pedro Pietri, one of the founders
of the Nuyorican Poetry movement, read his classic "Puerto Rican
Obituary," a paean to the Island migrants who, as in this excerpt,
suffered long lives of working at low-paying, subservient jobs only
to die in obscurity:

> Here lies Olga
> Here lies Manuel
> who died yesterday today
> and will die again tomorrow
> Always broke
> Always owing
> Never knowing
> that they are beautiful people

Pietri's poem memorialized the sacrifice of countless laborers with
dignity, but he sounded the death knell for a generation that lacked
self-awareness. He relinquished the myth of melting-pot assimilation
for New York Puerto Ricans and allowed Nuyorican to be born.

Though Pietri's words outwardly evoked strong emotions about
the past, moving the youthful audience to mourn the fates of their
parents or grandparents, he also hinted at what was in store for them
in the future. Our generation, he was saying, knows it is beautiful,
and won't hang its head in shame and misery. Our generation will
change this town so that Manuel and Olga may rest in peace.

Influenced by doo-wop music, Langston Hughes, and Federico García Lorca, Pietri once worked as a shelf-stacker at Columbia University's Butler Library. He was aware that he was black, but felt that it lent an air of absurdity to his work. One of his stack reports contained a scribbled poem called "Malcolm's Corner":

Last

One

Down

The

Stairs

Is

A

White

Man

Although he was one of the earliest Nuyorican poets and would ultimately write Nuyorican classics like "The Spanglish National Anthem," he was not part of the core group that ran the Nuyorican Poets Café on the Lower East Side. That group included Miguel Piñero, a Jean Genet–style junkie thief who became wildly famous when Joseph Papp staged his play "Short Eyes" about a child molester in prison at the trendily prestigious Public Theater. Piñero's goal was to plumb the turmoil inside himself that stemmed from his past abuse and how he longed to abuse others. He mined the deep vein of tortured memories dating to his own time in prison, wallowing in regret, searching for justification and for a way to explain the unexplainable: the motivation for unspeakable crimes. His famous wish to have his ashes scattered across the Lower East Side so he could be closer to the "stabbing and shooting" was a refusal to abandon his community for upward mobility, a testimonial to the colonial wound.

But the central guru of the Nuyorican poetic movement was Miguel Algarín, who founded the café in his living room on Sixth Street and had a day job as a professor of Shakespeare at Rutgers University. He edited the first anthology of Nuyorican poetry and was the proprietor of the café space until he relinquished it to the board due to failing health in the early 2000s. Algarín and Piñero, as well as Sandra María Esteves, Papoleto Meléndez, Victor Hernández Cruz, and Lucky Cienfuegos, mastered the art of bilingual poetry and the unique flow of Spanglish rhyming. Walter Mignolo called this bi-languaging, from which a national language inevitably emerges. Nation-building, as Mignolo argued, is an essential process of modernity; Nuyorican poetry, like salsa, was building a national consciousness for a nation that was no longer defined by a national territory.

But rather than return to the Spanish language, Nuyorican poetry chose to engage in a radical form of multivocality famously suggested by Bakhtin and consequently adopted by theorists of hybridity, just as salsa had turned away from the African American hybrid bugalú. Nuyorican poetry employed a discourse between multi-positioned subjects, a language that could only take form in the interaction between speakers—in this case, urban postcolonial migrants—rather than in an individual utterance. Miguel Algarín explained this idea in his introduction, "Nuyorican Language," to the first anthology of Nuyorican poetry:

> The poet blazes a path of fire for the self. He juggles with words. He lives risking each moment. Whatever he does, in every way he moves, he is a prince of the inner city jungle. He is the philosopher of the sugar cane that grows between the cracks of concrete sidewalks. The poet studies Che, Don Pedro Albizu Campos, Mao. He carries the tension of the streets in his mind and he knows how to execute his mind in action. The past teaches the young to juggle all the balls at the same time. The poet juggles with every street corner east of First Avenue and south of 14th Street at the Brooklyn Bridge. Poetry is the full act of naming. Naming states of mind. The rebellious, the contentious, the questioning personality wins out. And poetry is on the street burning it up with its vision of the times to be.

Algarín was suggesting that Nuyorican poetry anticipated the post-modern future while reserving the right to inscribe the nationalism of the streets. Bilingual poetry and letters disrupted linear thinking, engaged in multivocal discourse, and restored call and response as the central logic of internal dialogue. Nuyorican discourse came from the dark side of modernity of which Mignolo spoke, the marginalized groups using a different rhythm in their speech and syntax. As with Pedro Pietri's "Puerto Rican Obituary," the discourse buries the helpless passivity of those marginalized by the hegemonic appropriation of Latin culture that was modernism's totalizing project. It uses the modified language of two colonizers to express the conscience of a conquered race, a raza, by prioritizing its main raíz: the mestizo/mulato/black body.

Nuyorican poetry expressed Latin American cultural tradition as refracted through Puerto Rico's unincorporated territory status and Andalucía's ambivalence toward its estranged Moorish self. Miguel Algarín's "A Mongo Affair" proclaims, "I belong to a tribe of nomads/That roam the world without/A place to call home." Yet its most important message was the element of blackness detached from mulatez, like Bauzá's blackness restored in Harlem, rearticulated in the fusion of African American and Latino voices. The unconscious mestizo/mulato comes to New York with a racial naïveté, only to be required to go through a process of reconstruction and increased racialization; in the end, however, he or she forms a voice in an act of decolonization from both the colonizer to the North and the one to the South.

This decolonization takes place through the primacy of the local over the global. The neoliberal project is an ordered division of labor of the world economy in which pure English and Spanish and pure white and black are forced and unalterable identities. In what Homi Bhabha would call savage hybridity and Cornejo Polar an antagonistic alternative to hegemony, Nuyorican and other hybrid identities undermine the positions of identity and difference. In other words, you is black, you ain't black, so what is black, and when I get back to you, you're still, there, black, but not quite black, yet undeniably black. It's not so much that my subjectivity is defined by a certain grammar, it's that while one can see oneself inside the object yet also outside of it, the identity becomes located in the space of that perception, and difference disappears somewhere outside of its range. How would Noam Chomsky diagram a Spanglish sentence?

> Though worker is simple/Simple though worker is/Though worker we consider simple/
> Simple, though worker we consider/Lo amaremos/hasta que llega la revolución/porque el obrero siempre ha sido raza.

Almost an afterthought to the spheres of salsa, cultural nationalism, and bilingual poetry was a curious, New Age–inflected construction of what would become known as the Spirit Republic of Puerto Rico, a space for this new identity that didn't need a physical national territory.

In 1976, erstwhile Young Lord member and industrious theatrical entrepreneur Eddie Figueroa founded the New Rican Village, a bastion of experimental, activist-inspired culture that opened in 1976 around the corner from the Nuyorican Poets Café. Feeling that the Lords had lost sight of their identity, Figueroa decided to take the radical politics of the 1970s home to Puerto Rico, or the Puerto Rico he found inside of himself and his surroundings: a rapidly tropicalizing New York.

Figueroa was typical of his Nuyorican generation in that he was a man of the street, a picaresque figure whose narrative combined the hustler's *pregón* and the pseudo-intellectual air of the counterculture. He was symbolic of the escaped slave culture that had migrated away from Spanish control in various corners of the island since the sixteenth century. He was moved by what he felt was a profound awakening of consciousness in the 1960s and 70s and absorbed influences from New York bohemia and radical politics, but soon he embarked on a deeper understanding of Puerto Rican consciousness. He was a strong reminder of the sociological coincidence of the United States' baby boomer generation and the coming of age of the children of Puerto Rico's Great Migration.

By the late 70s, Figueroa had been influenced by Gestalt psychology, Pedro Albizu Campos's nationalist movement, and informal New Age methodology, which impelled him to focus his energies on self-transformation and found the New Rican Village. In what later became the gender-bending Pyramid Club on Avenue A on the Lower East Side, Figueroa's great experiment was a showcase for the cutting edge in Puerto Rican theater, music, and poetry, featuring names such as Puerto Rican traveling theater director Miriam Colón, Latin-jazz pioneer Jerry González, and poet Pedro Pietri.

Figueroa was driven by what he called "botánica awareness," a time-shifting worldview he formed during his childhood in Puerto Rico while visiting botánicas: Afro Caribbean pharmacies that dispense religious medicine and counsel and serve non-Western others in barrios from the Bronx to Brooklyn. For Figueroa, botánica awareness was more than just organic self-healing—it was a mystic state essential to Puerto Rican culture, a way of knowing formed by the conscience of blackness and indigenousness and not defined by Western rationality, despite being part of a syncretic system that might include it. As Figueroa put it, botánica awareness was

> the belief in magic, the belief in a multidimensional universe, the belief in simultaneous eternal time, that what we're seeing is only a part of what it is, and that this is inside of something else, and that the real mystery, the real point of all of this is the investigation, the navigation of the self, of the heart, the spirit, because that is where the truth is.

Echoing Cuban theorist Fernando Ortiz's idea that transculturation was connected to the spiritual communication between the living and the dead, Figueroa was a devotee of *espiritista* beliefs: "I was fortunate enough to be raised in a home where we believed in a world that you don't see through your eyes, that you see through your heart when you close your eyes in your sleep."

Most of the leaders of the Young Lords joined Figueroa in helping to open up a liberated space for Nuyorican self-expression in which succeeding generations thrived, working in journalism, community organizing, Latin music, and other cultural production. Figueroa's focus on Pedro Albizu Campos seemed to indirectly make up for the Lords' imperfect involvement in the Puerto Rican independence movement, emphasizing a sense of spiritualism and culture. Like Albizu Campos, who fused Christian morality with national pride, Figueroa strived to understand an essence of *puertorriqueñidad* that transcended political-economic analysis. He conceived of his "Spirit Republic" as a permanent solution to the colonial problem, substituting his hybrid pastiche of Eastern religion and psychology for Christianity, and an imaginary nationhood for Albizu Campos's sense of *patria* (homeland). His work anticipated what Benedict Anderson would eventually call the "imaginary nation," a space in which transnational identity could flourish without the need for an actual physical presence in the home country. "The Puerto Rican Embassy is a concept, it's an idea, it's not a physical location," Figueroa has said. "We're dealing with concepts that are beyond geography, beyond three dimensions. With the Puerto Rican Embassy and the conception of the Spirit Republic of Greater Puerto Rico, we're declaring our independence."

This independence Figueroa envisioned would transcend the island's debate around commonwealth, statehood, and independence. "The spirit republic is a free place," he argued. "So we can do away with plebiscites and voting, because the only person that you should be voting for is yourself. To win this we don't need weapons, *this* is the weapon that's going to win." He pointed to his heart. "The revolution is *here*, man."

Aztlán as a Spiritual Home of La Raza

> when raza?
>
> when …
>
> yesterday's gone
>
> and
>
> mañana
>
> mañana, doesn't come
>
> for he who waits
>
> no morrow
>
> only for he who is now
>
> to whom when equals now
>
> he will see a morrow
>
> mañana la Raza
>
> la gente que espera   `
>
> no verá mañana
>
> our tomorrow es hoy
>
> Alurista, "When Raza?," 1970

In the 1960s, Mexican Americans—who had lived through the conquest of the Southwest Territories, the further usurpation of their
land through unscrupulous practices that stole titles and land grants,
school and residential segregation, Mexican-only days at local swimming pools, thousands of lynchings, the Greaser Act, the Bracero
Program, and Operation Wetback, which deported many US-born
Mexicans, and which most of the contemporary Republican Party
hopes to enforce today—became Chicanos. They claimed an ancestry from the Mexica tribe and no longer hoped to be categorized as
white in the US court system. They began to believe, like Nuyoricans, that they had an imaginary homeland.

Rather than the transplanted Spirit Republic of Puerto Rico
transmitted to the island archipelago of New York through tropicalization, Afrocentrism, and bilingual rhyme, Chicanos of the late

1960s looked to Aztlán, a mythical territory. Although it had been abandoned by their ancestors and had murky formal boundaries, it nevertheless represented an ancestral space due to the hybridism gestating in the border space of the Southwest over more than 500 years, a "homeland" whose presence still rankles the Southwest's Anglo residents.

There is no consensus about the exact location of Aztlán, from whence the Mexica or Chichimeca tribes migrated southward early in the second millennium, most likely because of a drought. Some writings place Aztlán in the northern part of the Valley of Mexico, which extends into the US Southwest; others place it in the current Mexican state of Sinaloa, where the majority of present-day narcotrafficking is centered; others claim that it was as far north as what is now Vancouver, British Columbia. In a 2016 article in the *Sacramento Bee*, an activist historian named Alfredo Acosta Figueroa claimed he had found geoglyphs that located Aztlán in the lower Colorado River basin near the border between California and Arizona.

Yet the lack of a precise location hardly matters; the existence of Aztlán is grounded in the fact that it was a physical space that housed the ancestors of current-day Chicanos, or Mexican Americans. In the late 1960s, according to Arizona State professor Lee Bebout, Aztlán was "mapped onto the geographic territories colonized by and ceded to the United States under the Treaty of Guadalupe Hidalgo." There were so many layers in the construction of Aztlán that it is a classic empty signifier: a space and place with a multitude of meanings, a mythical territory that served as an imaginary nation for the development of cultural and spiritual identities, and a site for the land-grant battles led by Reies López Tijerina, who sought to reverse the process by which land was stolen from Mexicans following the Mexican-American War.

While, as Rodolfo Anaya has written, Aztlán was a place of prophecy, it was also a border zone, analogous to that between Northern Africa and Andalucía, containing the traces of history of both the migration south by Chichimecas and the sixteenth- and seventeenth-century post-conquest migration north by Aztecs, mestizos, mulatos, Africans, and creole Spaniards. In the present day it is still the site of continuous migration, the hot spot of border crossing and vigilante paranoia such that the myth of Aztlán has been claimed by a rabid right-wing xenophobia, whose adherents include Pat Buchanan, ex-sheriff Joe Arpaio, and the authors of the infamous Arizona Senate Bill 1070, otherwise known as the "Papers Please" bill. Aztlán is now invoked not only by nostalgic Chicano nationalists but also by the far right, who want to spread white suburban fear of a Reconquista by Mexicans in the twenty-first century.

Central to the myth of Aztlán, or rather its existence as a "state of mind" or imaginary homeland, was a crucial turn during the civil rights era in the use of the word *raza* towards embracing the non-white and connecting racial indigenous identification with class oppression.

Raza, as symbolized by organizations like La Raza Unida, news-papers like *La Raza*, and ultimately National Council of La Raza, made a point of elevating the identification with indigenousness as paramount. Ruben Salazar, a *Los Angeles Times* journalist who was later martyred during a contentious protest in 1970, suggested in one of his columns that "a Chicano is a Mexican American with a non-Anglo image of himself." Organizations such as the Brown Berets, who were, like the Young Lords, modeled on the Black Panthers, began encouraging the use of slogans like Brown Is Beautiful.

Of course, as Gloria Anzaldúa writes in her classic book *Border-lands/La Frontera*, Chicanos were not pure indigenous people but the products of mixing that went beyond what had taken place in Mexico:

> For every gold-hungry conquistador and soul-hungry missionary who came north from Mexico, ten to twenty Indians and mestizos went along as porters or in other capacities. For the Indians, this constituted a return to the place of origin, Aztlán, thus making Chicanos originally

and secondarily indigenous to the Southwest. Indians and mestizos from Central Mexico intermarried with North American Indians. The continual intermarriage between Mexicans and American Indians and Spaniards formed an even greater mestizaje.

Sometimes called "La Raza Nueva," or the New Raza, Chicanos used Aztlán to develop a racial and folkloric appreciation for their indigenous past. As a new syncretic territorial object, it was also a space that rejected discrimination, injustice, and economic inequality, a space of contestation between the "adaptive" identity of English-speaking mestizos using the existing tools of civil rights law, political organizing, and protest, and the racial, cultural, and spiritual aspects of an emerging national identity. While Corky Gonzales's famous poem "I Am Joaquín" insisted that the former boxer turned activist was "Aztec prince and Christian Christ"—in other words, "both tyrant and slave"—he invoked this identity as a way to reject "that monstrous, technical, industrial giant called Progress and Anglo success."

Gonzales, the poet Alurista, Reies López Tijerina, and many of the original Chicano activists attended the first National Chicano Youth Liberation Conference in Denver, Colorado, in 1969 that produced a formal document of Aztlán-based radical political activism: "El Plan Espiritual de Aztlán." The organizational goals gave class struggle a central role, calling for local control of economies, ethnic studies and bilingual education, restitution for economic slavery, and redistribution of wealth. While the document was less specifically Marxist than the Young Lords' twelve-point platform, it did argue that Chicanos were an internally colonized people, consciously or not echoing Fanon's rejection of "non-being."

Chicanos also came to embrace, with varying degrees of enthusiasm, the label "brown." Brown has become a problematic term in today's race discourse—something that will be covered in Chapter 8—because of its potential use to distance Latinx from black, because of its current, completely distinct use by South Asians, and because "brown" can leave out Afro-Latinx, Asian-Latinx, and lighter-skinned off-white Latinx. Yet its initial use by Chicanos evoked a powerful, internationalist signifying force that jelled with the internationalist class struggle themes of other national liberation movements.

The Brown Berets were formed by Chicanos in the late 1960s, embracing "brown" as a symbol of their mixed-race identity while privileging the indigenous root. Reaching back into the history of North American indigenous people descended from tribes that crossed the Bering Strait from Asia, Brown Beret founder David Sanchez asserted in 1968 that the Viet Cong fighters in Vietnam were "our brothers."

A year later, in 1969, a conscientious objector named Manuel Gómez wrote a letter to his draft board explaining his refusal to serve in the US Army's efforts in Vietnam: "In my veins runs the blood of all the people in the World … I am a son of La Raza, the universal children, and cannot be trained and ordered to shoot my brother." While the idea of la raza is contentious in that its concession to mixture can betray the most harshly oppressed identity—that of indigenous people—and even deny the historical presence of Africans in Mexico, it has the unique ability to turn cultural nationalism into internationalism. This seeming democratization of the racial spectrum, however, would slowly vanish with the radical aspirations of the national liberation movements, in some cases dissolving into squabbling between brown and black factions, demonstrating the strength of the binary in US racial discourse.

In a way that was even more explicit than in Nuyorican nationalism or the idealized Spirit Republic of Puerto Rico, Aztlán represented an unproductive essentializing of Chicano-ness, reducing it to "mixed-blood," while also opening the door to debate about intersecting interests. For all the inevitable clashes between class-based politics and cultural nationalism, raza became a way to understand that the self-perception of belonging to a racial category opens up the question of complicating additional identities. This was clearly evidenced, not only at the historic National Chicano Youth Liberation Conference in Denver, but with the Young Lords as well, by the emerging voices of women.

In *Borderlands*, Gloria Anzaldúa—who did not attend the Denver conference in 1969—made a compelling case that at once strongly disrupted yet reaffirmed the tenuous existence and symbolism of a dynamic mestizo raza. By tracing the history of the consolidation of the Aztec empire that Cortés encountered in Tenochtitlán, she locates the historical moment, just decades before the conquest, when the society militarized and ossified into an exploitative class structure. This was also the moment when matrilineal succession among nobility was interrupted and, in her telling, earth-based agricultural deities were abandoned. The transition from "wandering tribe" to "predatory state" alienated the masses of Tenochtitlán, undermining the ruling powers and making the Cortés conquest much easier. In this way, the founding myth of La Malinche's betrayal is revealed to be inaccurate, and clearly designed, along with the construction of the syncretic Virgen de Guadalupe, to marginalize women and their history. As Gloria Anzaldúa writes in "Entering into the Serpent":

> Thus the Aztec nation fell, not because Malinali (la Chingada) interpreted for and slept with Cortés, but because the ruling elite had subverted the solidarity between men and women and between noble and commoner.

The stirrings of intersectionality are present in Anzaldúa's writing, as is the burgeoning discourse of feminism of color and queer theory. This would be continued by playwright Cherríe Moraga, whose critiques of Chicano theater legend and UFW collaborator Luis Valdez's male centrism were prominent in the 1990s. Anzaldúa's "border thinking" stemmed from her gender critique, revealing how raza language was weakest when it relied on a flattened and vague

notion of brown mestizo-ness. Perhaps the strongest critique of the
racial binary is that it so strongly resembles the sexuality binary,
minus hypodescent. Various anthropological studies have shown that
categories of sexuality or sexual preference in Latin American and
Native American cultures are more on a spectrum than adhering to
the polarities of male and female, straight or gay.

Counterculture Begets Postmodern Latinx Modernisms

As the 1960s turmoil gave way to 1970s fragmentation and dissolution
for both the mainstream counterculture and the national liberation
movements of blacks, Latinx, Native Americans, and Asian Americans, intersectional critiques from women and LGBT groups
proliferated and the cultural manifestations of these movements
began to eclipse the political activism, which was under siege by a
new authoritarian right wing. Nuyoricans and Chicanos (as well as
Latinx from other groups who were drawn to their movements) had
attained an elevated level of consciousness, feeling the electric charge
of an identity that had begun to clarify the contradictions of their
existence as internally colonized yet self-aware, bilingual, bicultural,
and developing a sophisticated dialogue about race, class, and gender.

On both coasts, Latinx were entering a period of creativity that
coincided with the onset of postmodernism. Yet while postmodernism for the "counterculture" was characterized by the breakdown of
certain modernist story lines, increasing fragmentation, nihilism, and
a tendency toward cutting and pasting that demonstrated dissatisfac-
tion and self-destruction, Latinx cultural production had more to do
with the socioeconomic determinants of postmodernism: the crisis of
industrial capitalism. It used stripped-down tools or instruments and
subversive mimicry that embraced global events while reconfiguring
them as powerful symbols of affirmation.

The involvement of Nuyoricans in the creation of hip-hop in the
Bronx paralleled the key participation of Chicanos in the early years

of Los Angeles punk rock, and both groups played significant roles in the development of experimental and alternative visual arts scenes as well. Flowing directly from the innovations of Nuyorican poetry, which was taking on an increasingly performative character, hip-hop began to blossom in the Bronx. While there was some crossover with theatrical works such as Nikki Giovanni's "For Colored Girls Who Have Considered Suicide/When the Rainbow Is Enuf," the architecture of Nuyorican poetry performances helped to institutionalize street poetry as a spontaneous and natural expression of New York's Latinx subculture. As mentioned above, the work of Young Lord Felipe Luciano in the performance group The Last Poets, Tato Laviera, and Pedro Pietri clearly prefigured rap.

As historians of and participants in the early years of hip-hop agree, hip-hop itself was constructed around four elements: rapping, MCing, breakdancing, and graffiti writing. It was a multicultural movement in which blacks, Latinx, whites, and Asian Americans all participated, but because of the consolidation of hip-hop culture into an archetype that only rappers could represent, the art form took on an Afrocentric character that was not entirely representative of its origins. While the turntable element of DJing was dominated by Caribbean talent such as Grandmaster Flash and DJ Kool Herc, Nuyoricans were strongly represented if not dominant in breakdancing (or b-boying) and graffiti writing (also known as spray-painting). Two films by downtown filmmaker Henry Chalfant (an Anglo-American) called *Flyin' Cut Sleeves* and *From Mambo to Hip Hop* place Nuyoricans close to the center of the emergence of hip-hop.

Flyin' Cut Sleeves includes the story of influential Nuyorican Benjy Meléndez or "Yellow Benjy," a secretly Jewish Puerto Rican and member of the Ghetto Brothers, a street gang. In the summer of 1971, Meléndez's trusted lieutenant, Cornell Benjamin (also known as Black Benjie), was killed during an altercation with a rival gang. But instead of violently lashing out in revenge, Meléndez called for a peace summit with other gang leaders, and the Ghetto Brothers were transformed from roughneck turf protectors to political organizers who helped set the stage for the dawn of hip-hop. In *Flyin' Cut Sleeves* and a personal interview with me, Meléndez describes how the peace summit began a politicization process for gang members. Meléndez himself became associated with both the Black Panthers and the Puerto Rican Socialist Party, which had been doing work that at times complemented, at times contested that of the Young Lords.

Meléndez's own story illustrates the multicultural intersections at the core of hip-hop. Along with the multi-positional subjectivity of a Latinx, in this case a Nuyorican, Meléndez integrated street gang membership into his identity, a protective necessity during a period of extreme disinvestment in the South Bronx, which had prompted white flight to the suburbs. Although hip-hop has evolved into a genre seemingly disconnected from rock and mainstream American culture, its roots were at least partially affected by a New York Puerto Rican whose family secretly practiced Judaism.

"My family were descendants of marranos from Spain," Meléndez recalled, *marrano* being the derogatory word used to describe hidden Jews in Spain and Latin America. "My father would draw the curtains and read from the scriptures; then he would send us to the streets to play on Saturday, so no one would get the impression that we were Jews." In the 1980s Meléndez became active in a synagogue in the South Bronx:

A woman in the synagogue asked my name and I said, "Meléndez," and she said, "That's not Jewish, that's Spanish." And I said, "What's your name?" and she said, "Epstein," and I said, "That's not Jewish, that's German." She came up to me and apologized later.

Meléndez was at once a practicing Jew racialized as a Puerto Rican person of color in New York and grew up immersed in American pop culture, picking and choosing what he could reformulate into something that represented him. Meléndez's fascination with California

Benjy Meléndez was a visionary
Nuyorican gang leader in the 1970s.

motorcycle gangs inspired him to wear specific colors that set the
standard for inner city youth gangs of the 70s:

> One day I saw a film with some friends of mine called "Hells Angels on
> Wheels." When I saw the Hells Angels and I saw their colors I said, "I
> can do that!" I went to the fabric store and bought some felt. I cut out
> rockers. I went to Harry's on Southern Boulevard, bought the letters,
> ironed them onto the rockers, and then painted a logo on the felt and
> then everything was sewed onto the jacket. From then on, a lot of groups
> started to do the same thing. A lot of the old guys had leather jackets.
> They had the colors but they were on leather. So since I wasn't riding
> motorcycles, I said, "Let's put them on a Lee jacket."

Meléndez attributes the phrase "Flyin' Cut Sleeves" to Black
Benjie, who was referring to the act of wearing denim jackets with
the sleeves cut off, sporting the colors of one's gang. But Meléndez's affection for the Hells Angels dissipated when he went to their

headquarters in New York's East Village to try to join. "I found out later that they don't accept black members. When they told me that, I was shocked and I just left."

Soon after the gang peace summit, Meléndez was visited by a Black Panther organizer named Joseph Mpa:

> He told me, why don't you take all this energy and do something constructive in the community—brothers can't be killing brothers. I had a meeting with the presidents, vice-presidents, warlords of all my divisions and I said I'm going to change the platform, brothers. We're going to take off our colors, we're going to start wearing berets, and we're going to start cleaning our community, taking out the drug pushers, start giving out free food.

Meléndez began working with United Bronx Parents, a social service organization run by local community activist Evelyn Anotinetty, and with activists working for Puerto Rican independence. Unlike many Nuyoricans, Meléndez had a strong command of Spanish that allowed his band's music to anticipate the political edge of much of 70s salsa.

But although Meléndez was a central force in the street collectivity and party atmosphere that inspired hip-hop, he did not have a strong connection or understanding of the genre:

> The Ghetto Brothers used to play every Friday night after the peace treaty, after the death of Black Benjie. Afrika Bambaataa saw this and took it to the next level. When I saw it for the first time, guys dancing, I looked at my brother, and said, "They look like the Pentecostals," because I saw them turning in circles, that's the way I saw them in church. So my brother said, "No, Benjy, that's called hip-hop!"

Afrika Bambaataa, the progenitor of Zulu Nation, had been present at the peace summit. He began promoting weekly parties at his home in Soundview in the Bronx as a way to shift the aggressive and violent tendencies of gang members toward cultural competitions in rapping, DJing, breakdancing, and graffiti writing. His efforts, along with those of DJ Kool Herc, began to generate a new cultural movement with strong roots in African American and Latinx culture. Bambaataa and another collaborator, Fab Five Freddy, were also influenced by European and Downtown trends including electronic music pioneers Kraftwerk, punk music priestess Debbie Harry of Blondie, and East Village Fun House Gallery impresario Patty Astor. The rock legacy of hip-hop is carefully hidden but evident in Bambaataa's "Planet Rock," one of hip-hop's first classics, which samples Kraftwerk's "Trans Europe Express," and The Treacherous Three's "Body Rock," as well as The Strikers' lesser-known "Body Music," which urges you to "rock, rock to the punk rock."

Chalfant's *From Mambo to Hip Hop*, Juan Flores, and Raquel Z. Rivera in her book *New York Ricans from the Hip Hop Zone* all document the often hidden ways that Nuyoricans contributed and were essential to the development of hip-hop. The context of widespread poverty was crucial, as massive cuts to public school music education programs made the cultivation of a newer generation of salsa musicians, like trombonist/arranger Willie Colón, who grew up on hard South Bronx streets, all the harder. Instead, the environment favored the flourishing of musicians such as Carlos Mandes, who changed his name to DJ Charlie Chase to obscure his Puerto Rican ancestry and blend into the seminal hip-hop group the Cold Crush Brothers. Mandes has suggested that his family hoped he would become a salsa musician or radio DJ, but his true self was best represented in hip-hop. His new surname "Chase" referred to him "chasing" the greatness and originality of technique exemplified by Grandmaster Flash, whose family came from Jamaica. The strategy of name-changing, employed by many European entertainers to pass for white, allowed several Puerto Rican hip-hop artists, from Charlie Chase to Big Pun and Fat Joe, to avoid disrupting the market forces that helped make hip-hop solely identifiable with African Americans. Just as commercial concerns encouraged the end of salsa's emphasis on Latin American political solidarity and the musicianship of instrumentalists and the commodification of the "telenovela idol"

Puerto Rican photographer and visual artist Adál Maldonado uses an out-of-focus self-portrait in his spoof Nuyorican passport (1994), a surreal take on the desire for a national territory and identity.

lead singer, hip-hop morphed from a four-element set of artistic practices that were a conflict resolution strategy for urban youth into
"urban" pop music with the MC as the central commodity.

Latinx also played hidden roles in the development of avant-garde
visual arts scenes in New York and Los Angeles. Nuyorican Rafael
Montañez Ortiz participated in the first Destruction in Art Sympo-
sium in the mid-1960s, a gathering of artists inspired by Fluxus-style
"Happenings" that focused on the element of destruction that
appeared so prominently in the Vietnam War. Having made his name
by destroying pianos in Europe, Montañez Ortiz turned from the
mainstream avant-garde to become director of the community-based
Museo del Barrio in the 1970s, an institution that was essential to
preserving the Taíno identity of Puerto Ricans by establishing a permanent exhibition of Taíno objects. With subsequent director Marta
Moreno Vega, who did most of her work on African spirituality in
the Caribbean, the museum promoted a vision of New York Latinx
culture that foregrounded African and indigenous tradition as well
as community-based, US-born Latinx artists. Nuyorican artist and
curator Geno Rodríguez co-founded the Institute of Contemporary
Hispanic Arts, En Foco, and the Alternative Museum, the latter a
pioneer of the SoHo/Tribeca scene of the 1980s. Papo Colo's gallery
Exit Art in SoHo was primarily as a space for alternative political
art—an outgrowth of the East Village scene whose art became
rapidly commercialized by Wall Street money in the middle of the
decade. All of these spaces showed the work of photographer Adál
Maldonado, who did all the graphic projects connected with the Spirit
Republic of Puerto Rico, including the passport pictured above.

In Los Angeles a group of artists formed around the nexus of Patssi
Valdez, Harry Gamboa Jr., Willie Herron, and Sylvia Delgado. They
called themselves Asco, which, roughly translated, means revulsion.
Like Montañez Ortiz, Asco was originally motivated by revulsion at
the violence generated by the Vietnam War, but soon moved toward
a critique of the art scene in general, not sparing the nationalist

conformity of agitprop Chicano art that dominated Southern California's Latinx tastes in the mid- to late 1970s. Their focus on gender issues and the restrictions associated with binary notions of gender identity also coincided with the work of musicians such as Teresa Covarrubias, lead singer of The Brat, an East Los Angeles punk group that predated much of the Los Angeles punk scene. Covarrubias explicitly criticized Chicanx gender roles in a postmodern reexamination of Anzaldúa's analysis, and strongly influenced Exene Cervenka, the lead singer of seminal Los Angeles punk group X.

Tense Negotiation of New Hybrid Identities

In these many ways of creating new identities as part of establishing their residency in the United States, Latinx have disrupted many binaries, dualistic oppositions, and conventional notions of dialectics. Prominent among these binaries is race, but once the racial binary is contested, others are not far behind. Yet another binary, or dualism, is central to Nuyorican and Chicano identity that relates to perception and thinking, or epistemology.

Latinx identity has transcended the organic mestizaje of Latin America; it's not necessarily about miscegenation, despite the fact that many Latinx have chosen to intermarry and reproduce with Anglo-, African, and Asian Americans. In the middle of arguments about the dark side of modernity and whether the history, institutions, and socio-cultural ethos of modernity are inseparable from colonialism and patriarchy, hybridity is framed in terms of globalization and Latinx identity is a site of contestation between the global and the local. Latinx are equipped to engage in a project of globalization and universal values while carrying huge amounts of cultural information that reinforce the essentially "local" content of human cultures. This information is carried through intact cultural traditions that date back to the introduction of African and indigenous people to Europeans, as well as several already hybridized or synthetic traditions that appear to be African or indigenous but are, in fact, already charged with elements of or responses to European civilization.

What Latinx are doing when they "become Americans" is not simply an assimilative process. It is a critique of what "American" is, or at least an unmissable opportunity to launch such a critique. The way in which this tension is resolved will be fundamental to determining the American character of the twenty-first century.

5

Border Thinking 101

Can La Raza Speak?

We only ever speak one language. We never speak just one language.

Jacques Derrida

By writing in English I'm already falsifying what I wanted to tell you.

Gustavo Pérez Firmat

I don't belong to English
Though I belong nowhere else

Junot Díaz

For the first several years of my life, my mother would often refer to me as "mi negro," and I would translate it as "my dear." It took many years before I perceived that this phrase had any racial content, which is common for Puerto Ricans and perhaps other Latinx and appears at the very end of Pedro Pietri's poem "The Puerto Rican Obituary":

> Aquí to be called negrito
> means to be called LOVE

But if only it were as simple as that. When my mother called me "mi negro," my conception of the word did not include blackness. It simply implied closeness, caring, pronounced "neh-gro" and not "nee-gro," the latter a word that was in the process of becoming obsolete in the lacunae between the civil rights movement and the black nationalist movement. There was a subtle subversive quality to my mother's use of the word, just as there can be when it is used among (Caribbean) Latinx to signal a certain solidarity that need not be spoken with formality.

The complicating factor here is that my father was significantly lighter-skinned than my mother and his command of English was significantly better. He never called me negro, although my mother called *him* negro. The divisions between my parents in terms of language use and pigmentation, and the contrast between my father's mostly white, Catholic family and my mother's mixed, Afro-Taíno, Protestant clan, were not discussed, but yet they were always somehow clear, subtextually, in my own view of myself.

They were present, for instance, in my father's story about being stationed in Kansas City when he was in the Army and being questioned by a hotel owner when making a reservation about whether or not my mother was white. Without necessarily implying to me that she was black, he signaled that she might be suspected of it, as the owner had seen my father's last name and racialized him as Hispanic. Despite being called negro by my mother, my father was also called "güero," an epithet meaning white, by Mexican soldiers in his unit.

Submerged in the racial text of everyday Puerto Rican-ness, which in my childhood was transforming into Nuyorican-ness, was the language and ritual of dance music. Afro-Cuban cha cha chas and pachangas, translated through modern Latin orchestras like Tito Puente's, reinforced the message that mixed-Afro mulatas were desirable sexual partners. "Oye cómo va mi ritmo?" asked Tito's lyrics. "Bueno pa' gozar, mulata," came the response. Like a beneficently boastful Q-Tip, the vocalist confidently asks how well the band's rhythm flows, directly addressing a hip-swaying mulata drawn to his shamanic magnetism.

Never did the idea that mulata was a racially derisive term enter my mind, even less so when the song was reconfigured as a San Francisco psychedelic bugalú by Santana at the height of the Woodstock era. I most likely translated *mulata* in this case as the dear negra implied in my family discourse, perhaps somewhat darker but cast in terms of a "look"—like a brunette, in a land where blondes don't really have more fun. The dance and its music, of course, became emblematic of "Latin" music as well as Latinx culture, not just because of its rhythmic essentialization, but because of its representation of racial ambiguity, when race was explicitly present yet invisible.

It is tempting for me to attribute this view of *mulata* to slippery identity, the heterotopic space of mixed identity that emerged from my cultural background. But somehow in the exchange of language that occurred in my childhood, and the translation of my parents' island culture to the metropolitan island archipelago of New York, I sense movement and negotiation. In Spanish, *traducir* means to translate, but in English, *traduce* can mean to degrade or humiliate, implying that this space of understanding is perhaps shameful. But let's for the moment think of it in the original Latin sense, "to carry across."

In a 1982 article called "The Evolution of the Term Mulatto: A Chapter in Black-Native American Relations," the insightful Native American writer Jack Forbes rightly points out that the meaning of *mulatto* necessarily changes over time. Racial mixes of the sixteenth and seventeenth century are not equivalent to racial mixes of the nineteenth or twentieth century. The difference lies in the periods of migration to the New World and the state of existing populations of Europeans, Africans, indigenous people, mestizos, and mulatos in the Americas. But the bodies that were marked as mulatos were of course not the same, depending on degrees of blackness, brownness, and whiteness, and how their identity construction played out.

Forbes digs deeper into the etymology of mulato, revealing not just an added meaning, or technical caveat, but a suggestion of how religious identification in Spain gave way to racial terminology and identity. While *mulato* did refer to the mule as an example of a hybrid offspring, he argues, there is considerable evidence that the word may have derived from the Hispano-Arabic word *muladí*, which was used to describe a Christian Spaniard who renounced Christianity and adopted Islam. This usage in turn mostly likely came from the Arabic *muwallad*, which meant a non-Arab who had adopted an Arabic and Islamic identity. *Muwallad* was also used by the Sudanese to refer to Egyptian-Sudanese marriages as a way to disparage the lighter-skinned offspring.

At the same time, the many Muslims in Spain who had become Christians were referred to as *mozarabes*, as outlined in Chapter 1. According to Forbes, "These mozarabes ('almost Arabs'), as Christians living in Andalús Spain were called, were soon outnumbered by the muladís or converts [to Islam]." The upshot was that over time, after the Spanish conquistadors had traversed the Atlantic, the meanings of these words were conflated, and *mulato* simply came to mean mixed. Eventually it referred specifically to African-European or African-(Latin) American mixes, without any built-in descriptor about which side was dominant and which was adoptive. So when Forbes describes a "Spaniard writing from Puerto Rico" about "one of Sir Francis Drake's pilots in 1595," categorizing him as an "ysleño de nación mulato," there is only the mix, the New World, and the vague concept of a mulato nation whose internal dynamic is largely unknown.

I could imagine then that my father's perpetual insistence that he was a "cocolo" at heart, which not only referred to his preference for hardcore salsa but also alluded to a blackness he saw in himself, was merely a reenactment of the desires of a muladí, while my mother's inability to convey the blackness of her use of "negro" made her a kind of mozarabe. And in the New World, the old dynamic of religious persecution and passing had rendered cross-racial identification relatively meaningless, leaving us with the empty category of mulato, which had an even more negative meaning in Anglo-America, and therefore should be erased completely.

The lack of useful ways to describe this process is at the core of how Latinx construct their racial identity in the United States. While the activity is still there—the human searching through utterance, movement, the desire to organize politically—there is a profound lack of language and categories from which to draw, the result not only of the inadequacy of the racial binary, but also of the flattening of identities that happened in the process of Latin American mestizaje ideology.

Language's effect on Latinx identity stems from bilingualism's effect on consciousness. W. E. B. Du Bois's fundamental contribution to the understanding of African American consciousness was the phrase *double consciousness*, which roughly describes how, in order to live coherent lives in Anglo-American society, African Americans live, breathe, and know their own African American identity, language, and traditions as well as those of "mainstream" society. Yet this seeming "unity of opposites" is a bit of an oversimplification. Du Bois's idea was considerably more complex because he posited a "veil" that acted as a "one-way mirror" on which the dominant "white" perspective projected its racialized view of the "other," making black people invisible. Blacks therefore have a unique, enlightened perspective on their own dehumanization and the dominant white perspective. Whites, on the other hand, cannot "see" blacks, and therefore are unable to perceive their subject position.

The achievement of African American culture in the United States is accordingly spectacular if one takes Du Bois seriously. Reformulating aspects of African culture as they adapted in often highly fragmented fashion to a colonizer's language and institutions made them a dominant force in the co-creation of American culture. Double consciousness allowed blacks to see through the illusions of America's benevolence while incorporating its technical achievements as the leading edge of modernity in the age of industrialization. Being able to perceive the ironically tragic nature of America's international emergence allowed black people to shape their cultural character.

The "two warring ideals in one body" that characterize Du Bois's double consciousness are challenged to survive as "the sole oasis of simple faith and reverence in a dusty desert of dollars and smartness." Hypodescent and the racial binary created an enlightened-ness and a forging of consciousness under duress that have been central to the African American nation. Yet the white American is blinded by the imposition of the racializing veil and unable to perceive blackness, making black identity a relatively private affair.

Double consciousness, then, serves black people by allowing them to develop their awareness and take actions in the world that reflect their direct understanding of blackness and white hegemony. But the binary of American society serves to reinforce uninterrupted binary thinking. The black-white separation inhibits mixing, logically providing Du Bois with a model for explaining African American reality through the categories of race and class. Bilingualism, race mixture, and border thinking create a different kind of identity, a different form of adaptation or acculturation.

The rhetorical clash between nationalist (or race-based, Afrocentrist) politics and politics based on class struggle is quite old, but was renewed again during the 2016 presidential campaign. Writers such as Ta-Nehisi Coates expressed their discomfort with Bernie Sanders's class-based politics and his relative subjugation of race issues to the problems of class conflict. But the political ground that is the base of Du Boisian double consciousness was designed take on both a Marxist and a black nationalist perspective. In many ways Du Bois predicted Gloria Anzaldúa's intersectionalist "border thinking" in its illumination of new areas of contestation and representation of an emerging conflict to be resolved in this century.

Moving from Du Boisian double consciousness to Gloria Anzaldúa's border thinking, a path long traveled by academics and literary critics, is represented best as a shift from the race plus class argument to the race plus class plus gender intersubjective argument. In some ways this was the crux of the tension between African Americans and Latinx, but it was also an intersection between radical cultural nationalism and feminism. The literal meaning of the racial binary, in which black and white are "separate but equal," is transgressed by the uncontrollable border, where the other is both inside and outside and, like migrant workers, allowed in briefly to provide essential labor but always subject to expulsion.

History is quite clear on this dynamic. On the one hand, African-descended people became part of Anglo-America through slavery, where they were unambiguously commodified, and after emancipation, even more strictly categorized as "outside" through Jim Crow laws and the explicitness of hypodescent-based segregation. On the other, the landmass that was once part of northern Mexico and its people, who were Mexican, Native American, mestizo, Afro-Indian, Afro-Mexican, and even crypto-Jewish, were literally absorbed like a foreign antibody that by the early twentieth century was often classified as "alien."

So as African Americans crystallized their identity behind the veil, with whites increasing their surveillance of bodies that could literally dematerialize from view, Latinx, in the border regions, the fragmentary archipelagic apocalypse of the Caribbean, and the Bolivian outskirts of the Andes and the mysterious Southern Cone, were present as visible alien invaders, simultaneously polytheistic and monotheistic, entrepreneurial and collectivist, most often on a nomadic pilgrimage northward across the desert, the most unknowable and alien part of the United States. The valleys and rivers of the Southwest, which run through what the Chicanos called Aztlán, are, for Anzaldúa, the physical territory of a gaping colonial wound.

All the drama and contentiousness that spring out of Corky Gonzales's "I Am Joaquín," the fraught nature of the clash between the colonizer and the colonized, are contained within one body space, which Anzaldúa conceives as a new feminist liberation that can ultimately dispense with a fixed gender identity. Her famous tenet that the "new mestiza" is capable of tolerating contradictions and "turn[ing] ambivalence into something else" suggests rebirth, but can also be nebulous. In her attempt to defy essentialization, she creates a space that no one knows quite how to navigate, but with a freedom that allows for transcending the narrow limits of nationalism and its male, binary premises.

"In a constant state of mental nepantilism, an Aztec word meaning torn between ways, *la mestiza* is a product of the transfer of the cultural and spiritual values of one group to another," writes Anzaldúa in *Borderlands: La Frontera*. She sees the knowledge derived from this translation of cultures as a "counterstance" that rejects dominant cultures and "cross[es] the border into a wholly new and separate territory." "In our own very flesh, (r)evolution works out the clash of cultures. It makes us crazy constantly, but if the center holds, we've made some kind of evolutionary step forward."

Anzaldúa suggests a syncretic unity of opposites, a kind of yin-yang model that explicitly evokes race, class, and gender. Here in the border region, the liminal space, or what Foucault imagined was a heterotopia, is the place of pure change that Anzaldúa called Nepantla. It is a safe shelter from colonial hegemony, defined by an openness to the process of change, and an enabling zone of transition between social classes, spiritual yearnings, racial identifications, and sexual desire. It is through Nepantla that queerness emerges, and can be understood not just as a positioning through sexual preference but a kind of baseline orientation that attempts at all costs to defy categorization and prescriptive normalcy.

The core of Nepantla, or any imagined in-between space, is its defiance of categorization and essentialism, which is particularly important in an era when commodification has reached far beyond commodities that are being distributed and sold to the reactive behavioral processes that are used to purchase them. The seductiveness of the Internet's "call and response," in which web-surfing and auto-corrected keystrokes are compiled by cloud-based servers equipped with algorithms that track consumer profiles in real time to predict the next purchase, is coaxing individuals to create profiles that will be used to track them. Marketers are in the business of claiming to possess the fleeting knowledge of the categorized consumer-subject, and the anathema to such a system is the liminal eros of Nepantla, a loosely defined in-between space whose untrackability is subversive and sexually charged.

Border thinking, as suggested by Anzaldúa, can be located in something she calls "La Facultad" (the Faculty, as in "thinking ability"), which implies that a mysterious form of knowledge emerges from a nexus of different, non-Western thinking (that can still be part-Western) that ostensibly challenges the rules of the game. Of course La Facultad can also act as an ambiguous and potentially empty description of a "state of mind" or a way of being that happens to carry an unknown force conditioned by centuries of traditional knowledge. In Anzaldúa's argument, that traditional knowledge includes the practices of several tribes in northern Mexico/southern Aztlán as well as repressed matriarchal forms of thinking, spirituality, and knowledge that preceded the abrupt patriarchal takeover of the early second millennium.

Anzaldúa's shift to border thinking involves moving away from narrowly defined patriarchal nationalisms to mixing spaces that are vaguely defined yet brimming with possibility. As Cristina Beltrán says in her essay "Patrolling Borders: Hybrids, Hierarchies and the Challenges of Mestizaje," Anzaldúa has migrated the project of Mexican American identity from Aztlán to Borderlands, from the static to the dynamic. With a reinterpretation of mixed-race Mexican history, she evokes the North African past by suggesting subliminally that this border movement is one from scarcity to abundance. In this way we can reimagine the mass migration of mixed-indigenous-African people from Central America and Mexico as not (just) an attempt by impoverished people to "live the American Dream" but rather the movement of multiply identified subjects towards a new zone of even greater knowledge. In the United States, a mestiza Chicana, through meditation on her multiple differences, finds her own queer past through encounters with an Anglo-American gender politics that was not sufficient to include her.

The implications of border thinking are strongly political in nature. Conceiving of oneself as being on the border, or in that border space, resists the drawing of borderlines, which in itself is a colonial act of power. Awareness that one's self possesses multiple possible subjectivities or identities resists categorization and disrupts traditional power relations. In today's world of instantaneous marketing through social media and other now-inevitable acts of living on the Internet, multiple subjectivity undercuts the marketer's goal, which is to assemble a coherent profile of one's consumer preferences.

Invoking "border thinking" as a political strategy is not unique: such claims to "secret" or "superior" subaltern knowledge have been used even in Marxist considerations of the working class, as well as in contemporary debate around the use of the word *woke* to symbolize a general awareness of systemic racism shared by blacks, other people of color, and white sympathizers. Latinx seem to be capable of all the Western subject decentering mechanisms Stuart Hall tracks from the nineteenth century onward. Yet while drawing on outsider-ness as a strength—something even mestizaje idealists like Vasconcelos tried to do—is an invigorating, necessary ploy, all kinds of messy essentialisms come into play. Despite her revolutionary proclamation that she was a "third world lesbian feminist with Marxist and mystic leanings," Anzaldúa was not beyond assigning labels when identifying enemy oppressors. As Beltrán points out, Anzaldúa made generalizations about "the natural storytelling powers of Mexicans," seemed to think men were incapable of trust, and painted the varying Spanish-speaking ability of Chicanas with one broad brush.

Yet it is counterproductive to take such pronouncements literally. Matriarchal taboo codes expressed universal distrust of men long before the Spanish conquest, storytelling is rapidly becoming a lost art, those in touch with a more traditional sense of culture are probably not losing it as rapidly, and it's true that Latin Americans deriding the Spanish-speaking skills of US Latinx is elitist and counterproductive, reflective of the standardization of language that was essential to the colonialist nation-building of nineteenth-century Europe. It's Anzaldúa's critique of nationalism, primarily through the lens of gender relations, that is the most important space she has created.

In this way we can see the importance of a multi-subjective consciousness, or awareness, of Latinx primarily derived from racial identity and further elucidated by reconsidering sexual boundaries, a powerful intervention in the hegemony of Anglo-America. Despite the Faustian "benefits" of the United States' racial binary for African Americans, who have drawn on a clearer awareness of race discrimination as a strong organizing tool, the continued ability, over generations, to perceive race as a varying spectrum is innately corrosive to the imposition of a national identity. In the case of the United States, this identity produces an exceptionalist justification for all forms of postcolonial exploitation, proxy wars, and corporate hegemony. No wonder Samuel Huntington was worried. But while it was imperative for him to advance the idea that Latinx immigrants are unassimilable intruders, it is equally imperative for us to adopt a unified stance against increasingly looming threats of anti-Latinx violence, stoked by the white supremacist populism of Donald Trump. Still much can be said for the strategic embrace of the idea that, on an ideological level, and perhaps at the level of consciousness itself, a Latinx awareness can provoke a needed re-examination of long-held assumptions about self, identity, and nation.

Hybrid Language as a Defense Against Class Prejudice: La Raza's Counter-Nationalism

For some, the "linguistic terrorism" or intolerance of foreign languages described by Anzaldúa that goes along with American xenophobia seems to have an expiration date: the ugly intolerance and physical violence toward Spanish speakers should dissipate as Latinx become fluent in English by the second generation and as their use of Spanish outside of informal code-switching diminishes over time. Yet the oppressive shame Latinx may feel over their inability to speak English in the first generation dissolves into another, subtler shame over inability to speak Spanish when visiting their ancestral homeland, or, perhaps more shamefully, in encounters with Latin American native Spanish speakers in professional settings.

Even as globalization encourages Anglo-Americans to learn Spanish (or other languages) to better "compete in the global economy," it tends to punish US-born Latinx for their imperfections in Spanish, revealing an important aspect of hemisphere convergence. Bilingual forms of communication and Spanglish code-switching among US Latinx are denounced as degradations of pure language, and their rejection is part of a growing perception that elite Latin Americans who migrate to the United States to work as professionals are better suited for advancement in US society. Yet while the goal for US Latinx should be a strong command of both languages to facilitate hemispheric unity and better contact with origin national cultures, the majority find that goal impossible due to economic and educational marginalization.

Although speaking "perfect" Spanish and English can be a formidable weapon on both sides of the border, enforcing nationalist ideals regarding the correct form of speaking reinforces the colonial system of elites. The power of hybrid languages, dialects, creoles, and pidgin is in their representation of several subject positions, allowing for different forms of subaltern utterance. These Spanglish extravagances of speech employ various signifiers to suggest Latin American origins, practices, customs, flora, fauna, even food. They are tropicalizations of the temperate zone through language, but their greatest impact often occurs through evocations of race.

This Spanglish emerged from Piri Thomas's metaphoric phrase "between two sticks" to describe his unstuck racial identification, Tato Laviera's "broken Spanish," referring to the black Spanish he transferred from urban San Juan to urban New York, and Sandra María Esteves's description of speaking a racialized "alien tongue." Further along in the era of transnationalism and globalization, the prose of Junot Díaz contains a greatly expanded sense of multiple subjectivity designed not so much to take its place in Anglo-American letters as to reinvent it.

In an interview with Paula Moya in the *Boston Review*, Díaz reveals that he is strongly influenced by women writers of color, precisely because of their ability to move the needle of the narrative by adding gender to the equation, "fundamentally rewriting [Franz] Fanon's final call in *Black Skin, White Masks*, transforming it [from: 'O my body, make me always a man who questions!'] into 'O my body, make me always a woman who questions ... my body.'" This is the setting for Díaz's attempt at unironic distance from naked machismo while inhabiting multiple subjectivities: vaguely mulato Dominican (or, as the Trujillo-imposed fantasy would categorize him, *indio*); Ivy League professor in Cambridge conversant in the Western canon; victim of Boston-area racism; hip-hop head and Afro-Futurist Negro Nerd; and returning diasporic transnational Northeast Dominican not yet completely estranged from campo Quisqueyano.

When Díaz's surrogate character Yunior proclaims, "I'm not a bad guy," in the first sentence of "The Sun, the Moon, and the Stars," the first story in the collection *This Is How You Lose Her*, he is telling us that he is all of the above, including a long-suffering machista. He seems to know, like many overeducated Latinos of his generation, that the very basis of our masculinity, at least the way it was handed down to us by conquistadores and esclavos alike, is unsettlingly perplexing. He speaks in this case for Dominican men specifically, but Boricuas, Colombianos, Cubanos, and Chicanos are all implicated —a very postmodern attempt at Latinx unity—and isn't sure about whether he wants to joke about it or beg for forgiveness.

Díaz's recontextualization of machismo, or its self-destruction, is done with the precision of a nineteenth-century Spanish zarzuela channeled through De La Soul and Samuel Delany, breaking down such thorny issues as intra-Latino racism ("they beat the anti-Pura drums daily: Ella es prieta. Ella es fea"); the awfulness of the fall semester in Boston, and the quiet desperation of newly arrived immigrants. His use of the second person is an invitation, a way of saying "hey you" to someone who is not sure there are stories, much less published fiction, about their point of view. The point of view is multi-subjective: Dominican/American, Dominican, American, black, Latinx, mulato, young, urban, suburban, bilingual, bicultural.

Trading in the tired travails of tragic mulattos for the high-yellow hijinks of comic book nerds transformed into aging, jaded professors of creative writing, Díaz constructs a hybridism that privileges blackness, erasing the last vestiges of the failed mestizaje ideology that is his Dominican legacy. It is an internal dialogue among staggered selves that staves off madness rather than allowing the diasporic imagination to fall into it. When his narrator utters the phrase "Negro, please," he is at once invoking African American vernacular and the irony of the use of the word in Latin America. Yet negro is filled with a new content, the discovery of African-ness engendered by the passage to the North.

Díaz's bold use of Spanglish is an act of defiance, a way to impose difference on monolingual Anglo-America. At times, it allows for cognate translation, as when he says about Yunior, "Dude was figuerando hard," or that "Homegirl had fly tetas." Other times, it requires the knowledge of common idioms, such as when he describes the difficulty of wrestling with lost love—itself a trope found in the corta-vena (wrist-slashing) ballads of Latin America—"Clavo saca clavo. Nothing saca nothing." With this phrase he evokes the visceral image of using a nail to displace another, and the pain of lost love becomes a piece of splintered wood.

His evocations of Boston-area living, whether in Cambridge or working-class Mattapan, evokes the migration of many Dominicans there. His inclusion of a best-friend character who is a more typical working-class Dominican engaging in a double life in the Dominican Republic speaks to the quintessentially transnational nature of that group. When the two travel together to the island to see his second family, he takes the reader deep into the countryside—called the Nadalands, with no lights and no running water—away from any idea that Díaz is an elite voice, a migrant from a bourgeois family who moved northward to take his rightful place of honorary whiteness in the *New Yorker* world of letters. This is where the real bridge is built between the dispossessed of Latin America and the underclass of Latino USA, where the Spanish is not forgotten, and it's spoken with homeboy rhythm, rhyme, and caesura.

Díaz also attempts to inhabit female characters through his narration, with mixed results. *This Is How You Lose Her* describes the struggles of a recently arrived undocumented immigrant, and Díaz's massive novel *The Brief Wondrous Life of Oscar Wao* includes a rebellious, sexually ambiguous punk rocker who prefigures members of actual punk rock group Downtown Boys, a band that uses Spanglish lyrics to describe what they call a bi bicultural aesthetic. *Oscar Wao* also tells the story of Belicia Cabrál, whose physical abuse at the hands of the henchmen of the infamous dictator Rafael Trujillo symbolizes the original sin that is the basis of moving forward with an awareness, rather than an erasure of racial marginalization. The assault on Beli's body is the climax of *Oscar Wao*, brutal in the vein of slave-beatings in narratives such as *Twelve Years a Slave*. Her confrontation with Trujillo, whom Yunior calls a pig-eyed mulatto who bleached his skin, is a necessary step for black consciousness to emerge in a transnational Dominican psyche trained to reject it. In Trujillo, Díaz identifies the self-hatred in whitening mestizo and mulato myths. Overlooking the darkness of appearance cannot erase the pigmented truth; the tragedy of the Caribbean mulato can be excised with memory and truth telling. Díaz accomplishes this though his legend of the *fukú*, a Yoruban word for the curse that the colonizer has placed on his people, embraced by denial until finally dispelled with Díaz's science fiction-cum-Tolkien take on the literary hero.

When we consider the work of Díaz, the Nuyorican poets, novelists such as Sandra Cisneros and Cristina García and Chicano poets and prose writers, we see evidence of a new bilingual discourse that has arisen from the popular sectors. Waves of newer writers, nurtured by the nationwide institution of poetry slams and spoken word performance, have reveled in bi- and multilingualism, incorporating not only English and Spanish, but standard English and Black English, as well as Urban English, arguably a combination of the three and other emerging subaltern influences. Recombinations of previous innovations by immigrants and first- and second-generation Americans are charged with a level of creativity that might be other manifestations of border thinking.

There is a growing preponderance of studies within the field of psychology, mostly focused on Asian bilinguals, the fastest-growing group of biculturals worldwide, that try to measure in somewhat objective fashion these higher levels of creativity. They do so by measuring the "blendedness" of their biculturality: that is, how efficiently they correlate both cultural perspectives in evaluating tasks, setting goals, and engaging in creative activity. Individuals whose biculturalness is more "blended" are capable of greater creativity. Another way to look at this idea is understanding how creativity can increase through bicultural-ness or multicultural-ness because of the way it escapes constraints. As Patricia Stokes puts it, the essential idea behind constraint is derived from the economic idea of scarcity.

Border thinking, in its manifestation as a thought process that moves through or crosses a desert to find abundance, escapes the limitations, or constraints, of a national culture or tradition.

The idea of escaping constraint is highly developed in feminist Chicana writing, documented at length in studies of Los Angeles punk pioneer Alice Bag, who borrowed the style of punk rock to reformulate Chicana identity in a way that allowed her to escape the constraints of male-dominant and heteronormative Chicano nationalism. In African and indigenous traditions, these patterns are customary—new ideas are often formed by drawing on the teachings of ancestors to selectively replace or modify a particular contemporary tradition. The blendedness of Alice Bag, or Gloria Anzaldúa for that matter, accounted for their ability to find the connections between ancestral innovations and combine them with whatever progressive activity was taking place in the 1970s and 80s.

While recent research can reveal how some of these processes are occurring as a direct outgrowth of globalization, contemporary ideas about hybridity are relatively undeveloped and market-driven. The "organic" mestizaje that emerges through Latinx mixed-race identity has been in practice for several centuries and is strongly grounded in bodies and spiritual tradition. Border thinking has always been present across the Americas, but as the twenty-first century unfolds, it is poised to take on a more prominent role.

How then, does "blendedness" or constructive correlation between cultural, creative, or simple thought processes play out in the dialectic between local and global for US Latinx? In marketing and advertising, there has been a tendency to limit the amount of blending, and instead craft messages for one side or the other. The effect is that Latinx who become English-dominant are added to the general pool of Anglo-American consumers, ignoring or erasing the dynamic aspect of their blended mixed-race identification. Recent Latinx immigrants or migrants, or those who for one reason or another perpetuate Spanish-dominant language patterns or other cultural manifestations that keep them separate from the mainstream, are marketed to exclusively in Spanish, and are not associated with multi- or intercultural orientations.

As I will explore further in successive chapters, these marketing exigencies, which have become even more salient by the large increase in immigration from Latin America since the mid-1980s, tend to distort this subset of Latinx into the dominant representation of Latinx in the United States. The "family values" of Catholicism, the predominant use of Spanish only, and vestiges of Latin American semi-feudalism are described as perpetual qualities of Latinx, which discounts the reality that cultural borrowings begin the moment one crosses the border and the constant and dynamic cultural and social activity that Latinx carry as a result of their mixed-race identity, further stimulated by this new passage or pilgrimage to the North.

Concerns about the roles of Latinx in the United States should shift from their ability to "adapt" or "assimilate" to whether they will retain their capacity to nurture a constantly evolving border thinking. From this point of view, there ceases to be a question about whether Latinx can adapt or incorporate US norms—we have a long track record demonstrating our ability to do so. The question becomes, then, whether the capacity and tendency to blend one or more cultures will be subdued by the constraints of a monolingual, monocultural imperative that the United States has increasingly attempted to enforce since Reconstruction. Will "becoming" American mean adopting its static, analytic, linear, market-driven ethos, thereby ensuring its claims to exceptionalism?

Claims by Anzaldúa about La Facultad might be dismissed as essentializing, as if it were a special knowledge that Chicanas, Tejanas, queer brujas, indígenas, lesbianas, and feministas who straddle the border might have. This is the essence of the backlash that Supreme Court Judge Sonia Sotomayor faced during her nomination period when Republicans objected to her assertion that as a "wise Latina" she had an indispensable insight into matters of justice. It is more useful, rather than viewing La Facultad as "silencing" or "shutting out" other points of view (mainly, those of thoughtful, progressive whites), to see it as a metaphor. La Facultad is not an amassed knowledge or set of codes; it's the code itself. It is merely a reference to a mental or cultural activity that refuses to situate itself in one particular point of view, or subject position.

La Facultad is a point of view that recognizes the power relation between subject and object. Engaging in border thinking allows one to give up the power of marginalizing an outsider point of view, because nothing is outside and everything is inside. For Anzaldúa, this broad palate of knowledge is readily accessible, yet she is attempting to re-privilege much of what she feels has been lost to faulty memory, and in that way work toward healing the colonial wound. This approach to identity, whether framed by race, class, gender, or sexual preference, can be particularly useful as the centuries of human conflict and contestation persist.

Again, it appears that the science is there to back such an assertion. Studies of bilingual children indicate that bilinguals are "smarter" because of improved "executive function" of the brain. When it is required to switch languages often, these studies claim, the brain must constantly keep track of changes in the environment. In other words, the bilingual brain excels at monitoring, which means not only that its gaze switches more quickly, but that it is able to anticipate changes before they happen. But is it all that important to be smarter? Who is measuring this intelligence and who does this smartness serve?

What seems to be more significant is the finding that bilinguals communicate better and have a higher capacity for empathy. The reason for this is simple. According to a recent *New York Times* article by Yudhijit Bhattacharjee (March 17, 2012), bilinguals "have to think about who speaks which language to whom, who understands which content, and the times and places in which different languages are spoken." As translators of language structure who shift between subject positions, they are constantly involved in "social experiences that provide routine practice in considering the perspectives of others."

The capacity for empathy is crucial to imagining ways in which America's race problem can be efficiently debated, and if not resolved, moved to a place of progress. The case made by Cornel West in *Race Matters*, for instance, is prescriptive in nature when he draws on the idea that prophetic wisdom is essential for humanity to move forward. Such prophetic wisdom derives from spiritual beliefs and a conscious learning of texts, oral history, and religious ritual that inculcates compassion and empathy between selves, drawn from the assumption that those identifying with different races are necessarily estranged as subject positions.

If we take La Facultad, border thinking, and other potential decolonial epistemologies as a model for changing the way we think about subject positions, and recognize that by acknowledging bilingual or multicultural identity we are taking a step towards de-essentializing the subject, then prophetic wisdom becomes second nature. Multiculturalism is transformed from the way it is interpreted by rationalism as a set of self-contained cultures existing simultaneously—in some sort of crowded noisy classroom of clamoring individual subjects—into the idea that all those subjects exist within the same consciousness. Whether this idea about *raza* can hold or not in this era of fragmentation and distribution of digital information is another matter.

6

Our Raza, Ourselves

A Racial Reenvisioning of Twenty-First-Century Latinx

It has repeatedly been argued that, in the case of Latinx, demography is destiny, and in many ways such an assertion is the justification for not only all the attention given to the fact that Latinx as a group have become the United States' largest minority, but also my attempts to speak about Latinx as a group, as incoherent as such a formulation may be. Yet if we are to operate under the premise that the most significant way to measure and analyze Latinx in their demographic, political, cultural, and social aspects is through their unique racial identity or racial orientation, or how race shapes their consciousness, it might be more accurate to say that for Latinx, phenotype is destiny. That's because the phenotypical appearance of Latinx can vary so much as to greatly affect their social standing and class mobility, generating different racial groups or identities and making their racial identity less distinct.

Yet it can also be argued that for Latinx, phenotype has an inverse relation to destiny because their phenotypical appearance can often have nothing to do with how they racially perceive themselves, and such a shift in racial identification is usually more tolerated and less transgressive than it would be among US whites and blacks. For most Latinx, defining themselves by race or assigning themselves a racial category is a daunting task that can bring up a feeling of revulsion, ending in defiantly choosing "neither" black nor white as an identity. This is the reason that many Latinx so often choose "other" or "mixed" as racial identification, or even embrace the use of the labels Hispanic, Latinx, or even "brown" as racial identification, even though, according to the prevailing rules of race classification, those labels do not constitute a defined "race."

So it follows, then, that Latinx's perception of ourselves in racial terms is a considerably more existential proposition than it is for others in the United States' race hierarchy. To look in the mirror often does not create an immediate certainty about a racial identity, and to examine that image more closely can involve everything from an internal debate to creative self-appropriation to insidious self-deception and denial. Yet in the context of the racial binary, what matters most is that lack of clarity, which can and should be a moment of freedom.

In my mirror, at first, it was just me, as it always is for children. Lacanians say that children create their first notion of identity through the mirror, as they come to understand that there is a self outside of it. I assume that this interpretation is part and parcel of the Western fantasy of the unified subject that I'm supposed to be busily decentering; therefore it's useful for me to consider that literal mirror a metaphorical one, in which the faces and subjectivities of immediate family and neighbors acted as ways for me to distinguish myself and begin to think as an individual. Our apartment in the Bronx was frequented mostly by Puerto Rican migrants who had settled in New York during the 1950s and 60s, and that meant they constituted a rainbow of racial types, with hidden or diffuse hierarchies attached to their phenotypical appearance.

I did not consciously go through any racial categorization as a result of this interaction with mirrors, literal and figurative, but there was little to nothing said about race or phenotypical appearance as I was growing up, outside of a vague sense of those who were not Puerto Rican, who were usually referred to by either their European ethnicities or their African Americanness. In that sense, the binary was intact for me from the beginning, naturally enough, but never really within my own family. It was part of my public life more than my private life. This conforms to what writers such as Eduardo Bonilla-Silva have already theorized, which is that Latinx don't talk much about race among themselves. In fact they avoid talking about it.

My father represented my role model, light-skinned and skilled enough in English to deflect a considerable degree of racialization, providing an unspoken notion of normality to which I could aspire. When meeting people in schools or Little Leagues or my neighborhood, I never read into the reactions when people saw me with my father, whose skin is somewhat lighter than mine. If they said, as they often did, "You sure look like your father," it seemed logical to me, as our faces were similar enough. In my first awareness of whether or not I was handsome, I would attribute any such qualities to my resemblance to my father. In retrospect I imagine that such comments might have been designed to encourage me to identify as fully as possible with my lighter-skinned father, so that the off-white privileges he enjoyed would not be interrupted.

The best way I can describe my racial self-identification as a child was ambivalence, a vague awareness that there were racial differences and that I carried one. I had no revelatory moment, as Du Bois did, in some "dark Housantonic wind" when a young white schoolmate refused my attempt to give her a "visiting card." Instead, I sensed veiled moments when race was hinted at, usually in a glimmer of recognition between me and my peers—a young girl with curls and a slightly broader nose than others, smiling at me more quickly, inviting me toward the faint glow of the crucifix that hung around her neck—that connoted group identification.

In that world the word *moreno*—which carried with it a sense of undesired difference—substituted for negro, which still held its meaning of deep, intrafamilial love, and *white* usually meant Irlandés, or Irish. New York's European ethnic hegemony seemed to erase the White Anglo-Saxon Protestants that were the keepers of true whiteness in the United States, saving me from a direct confrontation with the true owners of the colony from which my people came. I could imagine myself as "ethnic" or "black" only through identifying with my schoolmates and neighbors. There were even times when I was perceived as "chinito" for the vaguely Asian cast of my eyes, and some Sicilian families, who were technically "white," seemed to be darker than mine. The Bronx, my immediate location, and New York City, my general location, were in their most dynamic state of multiculturality, with working-class Latinx, African Americans, Jews, Italians, and Irish—and even some German-Americans in peripheral culs-de-sac to the North—pushing up against each other in public schools, subways, pizza joints, Little Leagues, and bowling alleys in ways that, in Marshall Berman's judgment, were significantly eroded by the likes of Robert Moses and his neighborhood-destroying, infrastructure-building Cross Bronx Expressway.

As a child I understood that there was race discrimination, and that African-descended people bore the brunt of it from both white ethnic Europeans and Latinx. While it was clear to me that my family and friends were "different," that difference was framed more in cultural terms—the fact that my parents spoke a different language, consumed a different cuisine, and listened and danced to Latin music—than racial ones. There was never a suggestion that we could be black, but there existed a subtle awareness of otherness, a brownness, so to speak. Yet it was stressed within my immediate and extended family that our Catholicism somehow put us on a par with ethnic whites.

One of my earlier memories was being driven through Harlem soon after the assassination of Malcolm X, and understanding the symbolic force of blackness in such a space, as well as images of the events in Selma, Alabama, and the continuity with baseball heroes such as Willie Mays and Roberto Clemente. But I was not raised with a consciousness of being a person of color, which, while it caused a degree of confusion, also allowed me to imagine that I was somehow free of the constraints of the racial binary and that I could be different things to different people. My bilingualism immediately created within me the notion of a hidden or secret identity that I would camouflage through my facility with English, and my relationship with being a mainstream American and a native New Yorker contained an ironic distance.

In some cases, most notably Tampa, Florida, in the mid-twentieth century, and possibly in the unstated message of the Broadway play and Hollywood movie *West Side Story*, Puerto Ricans were conceived of as a "race," if for no other reason than that their presence was felt but impossible to categorize as black or white. This notion has the feel of the Chicano/Mexican idea of *raza*—and like the Mexican model, it tried to take advantage of honorary whiteness where possible. This off-whiteness was buttressed by identification with Latin American Catholicism, the general rejection of blackness—though it was highly ambivalent among darker Puerto Ricans—and the privileging of lighter-skinned women with straight(ened) hair as desirable sexual and romantic partners.

While there were also many Puerto Ricans who aggressively sought to identify with blackness, their acceptance as black would often be judged by African Americans, who were often skeptical of the honorary white privileges that many Puerto Ricans would pursue or receive. In typical Caribbean mulatez-inspired fashion, Puerto Ricans often claimed blackness through the Afro-Caribbean basis of music and dance, including the natural gravitation to R&B and soul music actively played out through the bugalú era of the early

1960s. Terms like *cocolo*, used in Puerto Rico to identify with a shade called *trigueño*, or wheat-colored, carried cultural cachet in some senses, appropriating a racial-cultural route toward authenticity or coolness. The intersection between Afro-Caribbean religions like Santería—a syncretic union between Yoruban and Congo religions and Catholicism—and espiritismo—a Spanish Caribbean variant of Allen Kardec's spiritualism, which was an essentially European mystical religion similar to Kabbalah—gave Puerto Rican spirituality racial overtones.

My father's side had more explicit aspirations to whiteness, both in their affiliation with Catholicism and their seemingly greater accumulation of wealth. They saw themselves as closer to Puerto Rico's creole elite and had a seeming preponderance of lighter-skinned family members. My mother's side seemed to be more mixed, with less of a concern about preserving whiteness, and were often devotees of Baptism, a religion popular among black Americans in the South. The small barrio where the family was based is still deeply immersed in evangelical Pentecostalism, as well as Jehovah's Witness worship. An evening's drive through the area where my mother grew up reveals several churches swarming with mixed-race practitioners wearing white, a common Afro-Caribbean religio-spiritual expression.

The Luquillo Mountain Range is my spatial origin, as both my mother's and father's families operated small farms on the western and easternmost sides of the range. The mountains in Puerto Rico, as they do in Cuba, signify a powerful intersection where the idealized inputs of Spanish, African, and indigenous peoples came together to create an illusion of racelessness. Spaniards carried their original mix from Iberia but also merged with Canary Islanders, who had their own creole elite mixed with both Arabic and pre-Arabic Berbers, given that the islands are located off the coast of Northern Africa, as well as Africans, enslaved and free. The preponderance of Galicians, or Gallegos as they are known to Spanish speakers, also created an interesting synergy with Africans in the Caribbean and the legacy of whatever Taíno culture existed. Gallegos, although racially closer to Gallic and even Celtic origins, were fiercely independent and never really part of the Castilian elite. Their metal-making culture, called Castro culture, had been in existence since the first millennium before Christ, and had an affinity for mountain living, in part to affirm their freedom from centralized authority, and also to take advantage of metal- and mineral-rich rivers that flowed from the mountain to the coastal plains below.

It was that affinity for the mountains that allowed Gallegos, who were often heavily exploited as indentured laborers, to meld or intersect with Africans hoping to escape slavery and form an uneasy coexistence that still featured considerable white-black racism while enabling a commingling of cultures that in places like Cuba, and less famously in Puerto Rico and the Dominican Republic, produced the Spanish/Arabic/African folkloric music that prefigured "Afro-Cuban" or "Latin" music. The uprooted yet panopticon-free jíbaro, whose racial identity has waxed and waned between whiteness and blackness over the decades, was gestated in a continuum of Spanish coffee and tobacco farming, as well as a sugar industry that came to be dominated by US corporations after possessing Puerto Rico in the early twentieth century.

Yet the Luquillo Mountains are ground zero, as it were, for the Taíno origin myths of Borikén (the Taíno name for Puerto Rico). Luquillo is the Spanish corruption of the name for a human/god figure known as Yucáhu, one of a pantheon of intermediaries between "high" gods like Yayá and mere mortals below. While they are widely agreed to have become extinct as a social group in the late eighteenth century, Taíno presence is supposedly reflected through phenotypical features like straight black hair and high cheekbones, characteristics that are usually feminized, particularly owing to the unique way that Latinx women signal their racial identity through hairstyle. Romanticized notions of the sudden eruption of Taíno "traits" can occur to me when I'm back on the mountain range, which in legend is ironically called "the white lands," evidenced in some of my relatives and locals. And there are days, in the middle of a chaotic *aguacero* or tropical rainstorm in the mountain range, when I find it easy to imagine inhabiting the spirit of Yucáhu, whose presence there serves to shield the surrounding lowlands from hurricanes (*huracán* is the original Taíno word) from the Eastern Caribbean, and whose ultimate origin is, of course, Africa.

Yet a fierce debate has been going on for several years now about the significance of identifying as Taíno in Puerto Rico, involving several movements, including one called the United Confederation of Taíno People, that encourage Puerto Ricans to participate in Taíno rituals, practices, and customs, alluding to the possibility of claiming Native American status. Parallel movements exist in other Spanish-speaking Caribbean island nations, but while it is laudable to find ways to connect to such a past, some academics including Gabriel Haslip-Viera and Miriam Jiménez Román argue that Taíno movements tend to elide the greater importance of African roots, and are based on unscientific assumptions about some empirical data about DNA content in genotypes. Although a study of genes that passed through a single female line of ancestry indicated that 61 percent of Puerto Ricans had a minor trace of indigenous DNA, Haslip-Viera writes, he points out that "a study examining a male line showed that 70 percent of Puerto Ricans had European DNA, 20 percent African and 10 percent Amerindian." Haslip-Viera feels that groups like the Taíno Confederation are angling to claim territories and tribal status, with no continuity of history in their experience and claims. "The Puerto Rican Neo-Taínos cannot point to anything like the broken treaties, the massacres, the forced migrations, the 'Trail of Tears,' Geronimo, Little Big Horn, Sitting Bull, and the reservation experience of North American Amerindians from the sixteenth to twentieth centuries," he argues. "Neo-Taínos," in fact, are potentially a "politically divisive force."

The Taíno debate in Puerto Rico reflects the dangers of over-reaching through phenotypical appearance and ignoring distinctions between appearance and actual genotypic information. While there is no harm in feeling the spirits in the wind during an archetypal rainstorm revelry, straight black hair may well be an indicator of Gitano or Romany blood from Spain, which itself can be traced back to the Indian subcontinent. This confluence of imagined race and real racial identity as measured by DNA content allows me to theorize about a phenotype-genotype rule for the practice of constructing Latinx identity: There's no harm in imagining what may be inside you, just as long as you insist that there are empirical grounds for it, and that such an identification should not always be taken literally for socio-political purposes. While it's obvious that diverse racial origins exist for Latinx through genetic code, social and cultural practices, phenotypical appearance, or shared collective memory, it can be counterproductive to make the leap from fantasy to what can amount to a variation of Anglo-American "playing Indian."

It would be short-sighted of me not to acknowledge the possibility that since my family can trace it ancestry to Spain, that Jews were early inhabitants of the Iberian peninsula, and that many Jews of Middle Ages Spain chose either to convert or conceal their identity, there is a reasonable probability I have some Jewish ancestry. Any illusions about Gallego, Madrileño, or Andalusí I might claim would undoubtedly contain some Jewishness, perhaps hidden just prior to the Inquisition, or perhaps mixed with Ladino-Mozarabic linguistic crossover. The Jews predated the Arab invaders in Spain and actually preferred them and their Berber surrogates to the oppressive Visigoths. The "speculative mysticism" of the kabbalah might inform some parts of my thought processes, and there are times that the flamenco singer sounds like a cantor to me. While this lost essence is primarily Sephardic, I developed a sense of connection with the Ashkenazi New York Jewish world, which expressed an alterity that I didn't find through my connection with Catholicism.

After collecting my various racial guises, including chino, negro, blanquito, and mulato, and examining the way they have been translated into my New York City youth, the one that is perhaps most occluded is moreno, which means different things depending on who you ask. For Puerto Ricans in New York, as well as other Latinx groups, *moreno* is a pejorative word; whomever is tagged with it is clearly "black," as in black or Afro–Puerto Rican or Afro-Caribbean. Yet in Mexico and other parts of Latin America, it is an ambiguous term that could refer to both light and dark Moors. As Latin American race scholar Edward Telles explains of the Brazilian use of the term, "The ambiguity with the term moreno allows persons who might not have the option of calling themselves white to escape the more stigmatized nonwhite categories." Yet the ambiguity of moreno allows me to claim aspects of African identity (though not in order to escape identification as African) and embrace blackness as much as my essence objectively generates it. This of course is a tricky space to occupy, given that the historic treatment of sub-Saharan Africans by Arabs and North Africans is inflected by widespread racist beliefs.

But when I locate my affinity for moreno, or Moor-ishness, there are many contextual threads. First, my appearance is best described as moreno/mulato, with the fond flourishes of chino I never seem to outgrow. My genetic mix is apparently largely southern Spanish (that elusive mixture of light and dark Moor, despite any quixotic imaginings of my father as a Gallego, which sticks to me stubbornly whenever I eat at one of the few remaining Spanish restaurants in Manhattan's Chelsea neighborhood, the same one my father landed in first after arriving from the island) and African, whether free, indentured, or enslaved. The chino might be explained by a trace of Taíno or a mix with some nineteenth-century Asian immigrant to the Caribbean. Yet when I am in the presence of people from the Middle East, or when I watch a documentary about Palestine, or exchange glances with a hijab wearer in a Brooklyn café, I get the sense of belonging to this raza árabe I see before me.

The crossover between my Latinx identity and the Arab world goes back centuries, as I have described, through the Berber-surrogate Islamic caliphate of Spain, the presence of thousands of Arabic words in Spanish, and even the possible interaction between Arabic peoples and the indigenous people of the Americas before Columbus. I have described how the movement of Arabic and Berber peoples northward into southern Spain and Italy repeated with a different set of "mixed-race" peoples from southern Mexico to the Southwestern United States, and how that movement has been accompanied by a methodology of translation and acculturation that is also a search for knowledge. There is even a feeling of being at a major intersection of world history by identifying as moreno —the translations of Arabic knowledge by Jewish philosophers in Spain incubating precious sciences like mathematics as Western Europe suffered from plagues and the Dark Ages, a buffer between Western and Eastern knowledge, bordering the vast African continent to the south, all in the spiritual flash of a nomadic culture on metaphorical horseback.

So today it is no accident that race-baiters like Donald Trump have identified Mexican immigrants and Muslims as America's greatest enemies of the twenty-first century—an argument that comes almost word for word from Samuel Huntington's liberal hawk script, progressing from his pre-9/11 *The Clash of Civilizations* to 2004's *Who Are We?* In some ways, the non-whiteness represented by Latinx and Arabs can be even more threatening than the patently obvious non-whiteness of blacks and Asian Americans because there are hints of Europeanness in Latinx and Muslims—they are seen as Trojan horses, or human-horse chimera, capable of crossing borders stealthily and silently and plotting and corrupting from within.

Like McCarthy-era Communists, Trumpian alarmists believe Muslim extremists and Mexican Reconquista fanatics might be living unnoticed next door, planning for that fateful day when a terrible violence might strike against a sea of innocents in suburbia. And like conversos and moriscos in fifteenth-century Spain, they may not be immediately recognizable and may require extensive testing to determine the "purity of their blood," which would now be measured by "loyalty to America." So it is that in Trump's America, Puerto Ricans who "look like" Mexicans might be subject to deportation if they are lacking state-issued identification, and non-Muslim South Asians who wear headgear mistakable for hibabs can be massacred by demented white supremacists.

Ironically it is from our moreno appearance that most Latinx achieve whatever honorary white privilege they have in the United States, as few Latinx have British-Irish Germanic or Scandinavian phenotypical traits. Yet, true to its ambivalent light/dark Moor context, the moreno aspect is a negative racial marker as well, perhaps the primary racializing agent that affects Latinx aside from the indigenous appearance of many Mexicans and Central and South Americans.

Being assessed exclusively through my phenotype is only one—if very significant—layer of my racial identity. The moreno has an ambivalent racial identity in Latin America, but is black in the United States. In New York my identity seems to exist on that axis, extend from that vector, flow from that radiated spectrum of colorism. In US moreno mode, among other morenos, prietos, chinos, indios, and blanquitos, I exist practically, in social and cultural worlds, as a Latinx mixed-race set of codes. But as the Spanish and Spanglish chorus of conversation becomes muted and the angular binary urban stance predominates, a curious slant rhyme incorporating high yellow Harlem and blackness at the edge of downtown emerges. Mofongo can become motherfucker right quick. With a turn of phrase, the language of racial reasoning is revealed less as a set of signifiers than a collective call to conversation, a continual set of revisions, Monk-like bop-prosodic critiques of purity.

The blackness of the Puerto Rican-ness I grew into was already built in to my New Yorkness, like the Savage Nomads logos stitched into denim gang jackets, the no-look passes after spinning to the hoop invited a double-team, the short steps and swivel turns of Eddie Palmieri's well-oiled guaguancó justicia mambo machine. It praised the ham hocks and corn grits soul food of bugalú and shadowed the Caribbean moment in the creation of hip-hop. Abuelas in faded black and white photos suddenly became black and not merely negras. Yet once all the love became one love, did I forget to feel the anguish of the past, accept it as a pretty story of intermarriage with a mixed stew of overt and subtle racism?

If recent DNA studies are taken at face value, and genetic mapping conclusively shows that the European content in African Americans' genetic makeup can be traced to a few decades leading up to the Civil War, one can draw the inference that most of this racial mixing occurred under the coercive practices of slavery. This removal of the ambiguity of how African Americans came to be of mixed race creates a clear antagonism toward the idea that a mixed-race person of Latinx descent could "imagine" different "racial" characteristics existing within their identity and consciousness. Such a revelation reduces much of what I have mentioned previously to the level of dilettante musings. My "black" feelings could be mere "play" in the context of historical violence that is beyond my naïve Nuyo-Caribbean worldview.

Yet as I openly acknowledge the cruelty of Spanish and Portuguese slavemasters, the massive slave trade that dwarfed the one in the United States, and the continuing racism, overt and subtle, in Latin America today, there are still some distinguishing factors that need to be taken into account. As mentioned previously, there were more free blacks in Latin America, which was supported by colonial laws; intermarriage was encouraged, even if it was not the path toward upward social mobility for all; African tribal traditions were kept more intact at a much greater level than in the United States, and negotiations between different tribes in the acculturation process were a salient feature of Latin American blackness. Finally, the wild card in all of this is "European." Just as Spain's European-ness has always been questioned, we must also question what the European percentage of DNA found in such testing means. Most likely there is a predominance of Northern and Western European DNA in the US testing and more Southern and Eastern European DNA in the so-called European component of Latinx.

So, when studies come up with the widely accepted percentages of European DNA in Latinx—around 60 to 70 percent, with the remainder divided into African, Asian, and indigenous DNA, there is no accounting for the mixed nature of said European DNA. This refers back to questions posed earlier, about what Latinx whiteness is, whether it is qualitatively different from Anglo-American whiteness, and what implications that has for the multiracial way that Latinx perceive themselves and are perceived by others.

Whiteness has been the subject of much speculation over the last fifteen years or so, and it plays a double role as both the antithesis of racial marking and the persistent basis of racial discrimination. In her book *The Future of Whiteness*, Linda Martín Alcoff calls all racial categories, including whiteness, social constructions: "If race is a myth, whiteness is, some argue, the driving plotline," she writes. This is obvious enough to academics and philosophers, but less so to mainstream Americans who tend to believe that racial categories are fixed, if not by gross stereotypes, than by socially agreed-upon characteristics that produce clear distinctions.

Latinx identity allows for a lack of fixity through a commonly shared belief that even when the overt phenotypical appearance of one race or another is present, difference is assumed somewhere within. The problem is that in daily life, Latinx tend to seek white privilege rather than critique it. This is a root of the tension between Latinx and African Americans—the apparent embrace of black-ness, indigenousness or some form of otherness by Latinx, and yet the desire to skirt the issue by accepting white privilege when it's convenient.

I've already brought up how identifying as white, including

through the conscious efforts of advocacy groups and individuals, has been a strategy for lighter-skinned Latinx to avoid discrimination in the United States. There have also been times, such as the case of *Gonzalez v. Texas*, in which courts have granted Latinx (in this case Mexican Americans) a white identity if only to prove that they were not discriminated against on racial grounds. (The court averred that Mexicans were white, which meant that the lack of Mexican American jurors chosen in this particular Texas county did not indicate discrimination, given that almost all of the jurors chosen were white.) Among Puerto Ricans in New York, identifying as Spanish was not only a reaction to acknowledging their racialization through the use of a foreign language, it was also a strategy to claim a kind of whiteness through ethnic European identification, although the privilege gained was an "off-whiteness" similar to Southern or Mediterranean ethnic European groups—enough to distance oneself from blackness and gain a position of relative privilege.

The curious position Latinx are in now—in some way shared by people from Arab countries and Asian Americans—is one in which the definition of white seems to be changing again, as it did following World War II when other Southern and Central European groups were granted white status. What's different now is that whites are beginning to confront their own whiteness in ways they never had before. The embrace of white "identity politics" by alt-right figures such as Milo Yiannopolous and Richard Spencer is not only a cynical take on subaltern empowerment strategies but also a way for white people to construct a content-laden identity. In the modern age, whiteness has most often been considered the absence of racial or ethnic characteristics, a kind of default state of humanity that established whites as superior by equating them with rationality, impartiality, and the standard from which other groups would deviate. This non-value-laden status of whites is the basis of American exceptionalism, the hidden reality behind notions of America's superior political and economic system.

Even though whiteness can be defined, as Martín Alcoff quotes
Adrian Piper, by an inability to imagine the other's behavior, because
hybridity itself so threatens its own self-conception, whiteness also
has empirical characteristics associated with certain phenotypes, a
historical construction that is inseparable from the evolution of the
West and the United States, and a kind of imaginary that organizes
and informs the social sphere through so-called respectable lifestyles
and ethics. Whiteness is in a crisis of self-perception, but may choose
to solve that crisis by magnanimously including new members whose
phenotypical appearance may be somewhat deviant, but who buy
into the historical weight and social imaginary of whiteness.

In this racially charged time when Latinx are racialized as potentially violent immigrants, and when the overwhelming majority
of Latinx are US-born, a great deal of rhetorical energy is being
channeled toward proving that Latinx are not in conflict with much
of the white social imaginary because of our "family values" and
desire to be "good Americans." Yet there are strong countervailing
forces of identification among Latinx with something "other" than
white, sometimes an imaginary that is explicitly black or indigenous,
often accompanied by a desire to assert an Americanness and a lack
of desire to either leave the country or identify strongly with their
country of origin. It's unclear how much of a concession to whiteness
this process will entail. If some Latinx believe, as Baldwin writes in
The Fire Next Time, that white people are the "slightly mad victims
of their own brainwashing," will they also be willing to "accept them
and accept them with love"?

It comes down to whether Latinx are capable of making an
informed assessment or engaging in an effective critique of their
own understanding of race. In the process of writing this book, I
distributed a questionnaire to various acquaintances, strangers, and
students of mine to talk about how they perceived race and what role
it played in their lives. One student of mine, who describes herself
as an Afro-Indio Trinidadian from a mixture of Indian, Venezuelan,

Portuguese, and black people, says she is seen as black, Dominican, or Cuban in New York. She strongly identifies as black and doesn't "see Latinx as an in-between, special zone where identity is more fluid because of ethnic mixtures."

In fact, there is much evidence that no matter how one perceives one's own identity in the mirror by assessing one's phenotypical appearance, many geographical and political-economic factors play a role as well. In telling the story of Felícitas Méndez, the matriarch of the Méndez family that brought the famous desegregation case *Méndez v. Westminster* in the late 1940s in Southern California, Jennifer McCormick and César Ayala discuss how she was perceived racially in three different ways during her life. The case, in which the Méndez family sued their local school board because they were told their children could not attend the white-only school in their neighborhood, is a source of pride for many Mexican Americans—ahead of the civil rights era curve, as it preceded *Brown v. Board of Education* by seven years.

Yet although the Méndez family was Mexican American and living in Orange County with a patriarch of Mexican descent, Felícitas was actually born in Puerto Rico, having migrated to Arizona in 1928 to pick cotton in part because the Arizona Cotton Growers were becoming exasperated with Mexican migrant labor. As McCormick and Ayala explain, Felícitas was called "La Prieta" in Puerto Rico, a way of establishing a colorized identity for her on the racial spectrum. When her family arrived in Arizona, Puerto Ricans were often perceived as "Negroes" (as they were in Louisiana, where Aunt Jemima–like caricatures advertised yams from Puerto Rico).

But when Felícitas's Puerto Rican family moved to California rather than return to the island, they found themselves assimilating into the Mexican and Mexican American communities, where they shared a language and some cultural similarities. In an interview, Felícitas's daughter Sylvia (who won the Presidential Medal of Freedom from President Barack Obama in 2013), explained that her

Lody Knows (2000), Miguel Luciano. Puerto Ricans were racialized as black in the deep South in the early twentieth century.

family, as well as other Puerto Rican families in Southern California,
spoke English and Spanish in typical Mexican and Chicano accents.
When their case came to court, there was no reference made to the
fact that the children were half Puerto Rican. The final irony is that
some of the arguments used in the case employed the strategy that
Mexicans should be considered white, although the ultimate ruling
ended discrimination against not only Mexicans but other disenfranchised black and Asian American groups in California as well.

Most Latinx are well aware of the distinction between how they
see themselves and how the rest of America sees them. It's not
merely a matter of ambiguity and inconsistency, but an exposure of
the uncertainty of racial categorization. Living that contradiction
exposes the fallacy of racial identification in the first place, and leads
to a particular kind of indignation. The majority of the respondents
to my questionnaire, like most Latinx nationwide, see themselves
as "mixed," and for the most part are very reluctant to identify
themselves as white. In my own extended family there is generally
a disdain for blackness, with some of the stories about blackness in

the Luquillo Mountain Range characterized negatively, as something in the past. If there are remaining vestiges of blackness, they are presumed to be fading.

In one search of my ancestral records, a woman identified as a "mulata" in the 1920 census was part of my family tree. In another, my great-uncle, who according to some relatives was one of the barrio's central figures, owning the only general goods store in the mountaintop community, with a reputation of being extremely well-read and a poet, while at the same time having an insatiable sexual appetite—a picaflor, if you will. The absence of narrative about the black members of my family is not unusual and the ambivalent morality yet obvious agency and creativity of the second man has parallels in my own life and actions. I look in the mirror and try to find them, as well as the other silent black women who tirelessly worked and nurtured enough to instill the idea that negra was not a description of a color but of family ties, warmth, and love.

Yet the racism of Puerto Rican and other Latinx cultures relegates blackness to historical memory, with the unspoken imperative to erase it. Women seem to carry most of that burden, subtly erasing the blackness of their appearance by straightening their hair and adopting an air of white presentability in the hopes of finding a lighter-skinned husband. Much of the mythology of blackness is transferred through the phrase "Y tu abuela, donde está?" (and your grandmother, where is she?) often rewritten in Black Spanish as "Y tu aguela, aonde ehtá?" Taken from a poem by Fortunato Vizcarrondo, the line describes the gradual whitening over generations that is standard practice in Puerto Rico and elsewhere—you can imagine this disappearing act today as a family selfie with the black grandmother cropped out of an Instagram post.

Proud blackness among Puerto Ricans and other Latinx is often a political decision. An irony in Puerto Rican politics is that José Celso Barbosa, often referred to as the "father" of the Puerto Rican statehood movement, was black; he even helped found what was known as the Puerto Rico Republican Party. Yet his interest in state-hood was most likely fueled by the naïve notion that association with the United States would be better for black Puerto Ricans than an independent Puerto Rico ruled by white elites. To this day the Inde-pendence Party in Puerto Rico, while considered the furthest to the left, is criticized as being a vehicle for an aging white elite out of touch with most of the population.

Yet as I have touched on previously, the political decision around race identification for Puerto Ricans, and certainly for the Mexican Americans who identified themselves as Chicanos, involved moving toward blackness or at least mixed-ness as a way of associating with left values or forms of decolonial resistance. A Lehman College pro-fessor I interviewed named Andrés Torres told me that although "I perceive myself as being both Euro- and Afro-descended, these are not mutually exclusive, they are overlapping." Defying his fami-ly's tendency to elide his Afro side, he says, "I embrace my 'black' side and feeling; I don't embrace my 'white' because of the negative connotations I associate with this racial identity in the US context." Melissa Valle, a sociologist who teaches at Rutgers University Newark, noted:

> It's interesting to see the way people perceive me at different points in my life. My father is African American with some Italian blood, my mother Puerto Rican. When I was a kid my Puerto Rican cousins, who did not look like me, would see a black girl and say, "She looks like you."

Despite the fact that her mother was a fairly dark-skinned Puerto Rican, her peers would ask if she was white. In Colombia, where she does research, she is seen as both Latinx and (US) American, a gringa:

> Multiple identities can be convenient at times. I'm very African Ameri-can, very Puerto Rican. I'm very much a mainland Puerto Rican as well.

But I get ambivalent about being Latin American even though I speak Spanish well. I'm part of LASA, the Latin American Students Association and I don't feel like going to the convention. They're in love with their whiteness, but they want to say they're different from American whites, they like to play up the sexiness of Latinidad.

This comment of Valle's blew up a fantasy-myth that had been plaguing me for some time—a strong theme of my first book, *Living in Spanglish*, that is at the root of much of the media imaging and marketing of Latinx in the United States today. Although they are obscured, the roots of this view goes back to nineteenth-century Uruguayan writer Enrique Rodó, who in his essay "Ariel" argued that Latin America, with its superior European culture (essentially a Romance-language or Mediterranean culture), was the higher civilization of the Americas. Latin America was Ariel, Prospero's delicate and introspective slave in Shakespeare's *The Tempest*, while the United States was symbolized by the brutish Caliban. This of course flipped a nascent white supremacy script: Caliban is supposed to symbolize the untamed African slaves of the New World, invoking both the Caribbean and the cannibals that supposedly inhabited it.

Rodó's vision of the cultured, intellectual Europeanized American as opposed to the United States' anti-intellectual imperialist lout lives on in US Latinx marketing and media through Latinx identifiers that draw on the "off-white" construction of whiteness. It's a smarter white, an earthier white, a more sensual white, one informed by black and indigenous people whose labor and bodies have been effectively controlled by the love/hate embrace of Catholicism, whose "higher purpose" obscures centuries of exploitation and racism. It is the embodiment of the hidden racism in Latin American mestizaje norms, and allows millions of people to feel that they embrace blacks and indigenous people in theory while the society they rule systematically excludes them.

Visual artist Cristina Tufiño's extended
family in the early twentieth century.

Yet even though this conception of Latinx exists, it doesn't necessarily condemn all Latinx who consider themselves mixed as
stubbornly racist. The interaction between the US racial binary
and the three-sided model of Latin America (white, mestizo, black)
creates a number of reactions and adaptations, and is in the midst of
a crucial process of negotiation.

Visual artist Cristina Tufiño, for example, like many younger
Latinx, is more clearly aware of the different racial strands in her
identity and actively seeks to move past some of the white privilege
her family acquired in favor of stronger ties with their black or indigenous selves. "My mother is white Hispanic from a liberal elitist class
very proud of their Catalonian roots, educated, a little bit lefty but
still conservative Spanish," she said. "Her family always treated me
with a little distance maybe because I wasn't blonde like my mom. My
grandmother adored me she was pale white and freckly and had red
hair and always reminded me I looked European as if to console me."

Tufiño's grandfather was the legendary Puerto Rican painter Rafael Tufiño, who was known as the "Painter of the People" and often focused on Afro–Puerto Rican subjects and cultural traditions. "I wasn't really around the Tufiños as a child so I grew up with a lot of what I view as white Puerto Rican entitlement," said Tufiño. "But I wasn't white enough or rich enough for the elite island crowd and have a rebellious resentment against class culture in Puerto Rico— maybe it's a general Tufiño family malaise."

Cristina, who would just as soon listen to Drake or the latest in Miami Beach trap music as traditional Puerto Rican or Cuban sounds, was spurred by her alienation from white privilege to seek affinity with the collective black consciousness as a way to develop inner strength as she navigates a competitive visual arts market. "I identify with my mixed-race family because I inherited a lot of my talent and resilience from them and some of their wiliness too, and always felt maladjusted and I think they did, too. As a teenager I got closer to the Tufiños and I remember my aunt lamenting, 'the problem with this family is that we are attracted to foreigners,' it's true. My grandfather had children with women from Mexico, Sicily, and America, a Jewish woman. His daughter Nitza had her own half-Japanese son and half-Jewish daughter. It's created a lot of issues for sure, but I think it's healthy to look for the 'other.'"

Dilemmas of Latinxty

The anthropologist David Jenkins wrote in a 1994 article that racial group membership is a product of both internal and external definitions. This means that we all have an idea of what our racial identity is, but it doesn't always coincide with how others see us. With the way that US norms about racial identification and classification are set up, Jenkins's theory doesn't mean all that much to those of us who fit into clear categories of white and black. But it does tend to hold true for most Latinx, who come to the United States with an identification of off-whiteness or mixed-raceness, which in Latin America grants them a degree of privilege.

The sociologist Nicholas Vargas presents evidence that Latinx perceive themselves as white at a much higher rate than they are perceived as white by others. He cites a Portrait of American Life Survey, whose numbers strongly parallel the 2010 census, revealing that when asked to name their race when there was no option for Hispanic/Latinx, 42 percent of Latinx chose white, while 50 percent chose "other." But out of that 42 percent, only 6 percent reported being regularly perceived as white. This seems to indicate a split in how a Latinx will identify when confronted with the ambiguity of their off-whiteness.

Theorists of race in Latin America such as Edward Telles claim that socioeconomic status can influence how one is perceived in Brazil, particularly those who are phenotypically ambiguous. This can be increasingly translated into contemporary US experience: if your social standing is higher because of educational achievement, wealth accumulation, and intermarriage with a "white" US citizen, it is easier for you to claim white status. This allows many Latinx to enjoy certain off-white privileges of white status while maintaining casual affiliations with non-white "root" cultures.

These sorts of observations are central to the idea that the definition of whiteness is changing in the United States and that the white category is expanding as it did in the post–World War II era to include Jews and southern and eastern Europeans. At first sociologists posited that a "beige/black" binary or a "non-black/black" binary would take the place of the white/black binary, but Eduardo Bonilla-Silva's model of the three-tiered racial system may be most appropriate—a transformation resulting from encroaching globalization, which has made it difficult for the United States to hold on to its exceptionalist self-image.

Bonilla-Silva also proposed that the United States' delusional "post-racial" society of "racism without racists," with its discomfort about discussing race and desire to move away from systems of racial categorization completely by eliminating affirmative action and other race-based social policies, closely paralleled race discourse in Latin America. As Bonilla-Silva's work implies, the increasing plague of violence towards racial and sexual minorities by law enforcement, private citizens, and, more recently, mass murderers armed with assault rifles has almost completely done away with the post-racial rhetoric.

Yet even as America grapples with the overt racism encouraged by the Trump presidency, the reality of its urban centers still reflects neo-liberal models of increased racial tolerance. As Trump's policies are increasingly revealed as failing to address the needs of the working and middle classes, neoliberal Democrat-influenced states, cities, and municipalities will continue to push society towards tolerance. Outside of marginal activities and spaces, overt racism will probably be much less sustainable in the United States than in Europe, where the original xenophobic nationalist party chic originated.

In the first half of this decade, one of the major race debates in the United States had major participation from Latinx, yet the nuances of their identities and positions in the binary were vastly overlooked. The first was the shooting death of Trayvon Martin at the hands of George Zimmerman, the case that helped spark the Black Lives Matter movement and put the targeting of black urban youth in the media spotlight. Zimmerman is half-Peruvian, which was cited by conservative commentators as proof of his incapacity to be racist in his actions toward Martin. But there is a history both in Peru and in South Florida of Latin American and Latinx discrimination against, if not outright racism towards, black people. Although the government of Peru issued a statement in 2009 apologizing for the "abuse, exclusion, and discrimination" against black Peruvians, one of its highest-rated television shows is a comedy in which a central character dresses in blackface. And despite the perception that South Florida is a haven for Latin Americans, particularly Cuban exiles, poor relations between Latinx and African Americans and Afro-Caribbeans have stemmed from a series of riots in Miami suburbs in the 1980s, as well as an incident in 1990 when Cuban American politicians snubbed visiting freedom fighter Nelson Mandela.

That Zimmerman could be perceived as white by some African Americans in South Florida was revealed by Rachel Jeantel, Martin's friend, who said during an interview about her testimony at the trial that referring to Zimmerman as a "cracker" referred not to his race but to someone who acted like a policeman. By inappropriately taking on a police persona, Zimmerman was, for Martin, symbolic of white privilege, making it harder for him to see his "multicultural" background. After his acquittal, Zimmerman moved even further to the fanatical right, allying himself with white supremacists and spouting dogma indicating that he identified as white, despite the fact that his mother and uncle, who both testified in his defense at the trial, possessed unambiguously indigenous phenotypical appearances. Undoubtedly they were whitened by his mother's marriage to a white American. An extreme case, it is also an example of the process through which many Latinx come to identify as white Americans.

Another tabloid TV race drama that dominated headlines for a week or so was the controversy that forced NBA owner Donald Sterling to relinquish ownership of his team, the Los Angeles Clippers. Sterling was indicted by public opinion after a secretly recorded conversation with his supposed girlfriend, V. Stiviano, who says she is half Mexican and half African American, was released. While there is an important intersection between racism and patriarchy here, eighty-something Sterling's main motivation seemed to have been preventing his twenty-something girlfriend from posting photos of herself with Magic Johnson on Instagram. Happy to make millions in philanthropic contributions to African Americans, Sterling insisted that he loved black people, but didn't want someone close to him to be seen with them.

Embedded in the dialogue are clear representations of a central dynamic in the evolution of whiteness and racism in America. Stiviano presents a dilemma that threatens her relationship with Sterling: "I wish I could change the color of my skin," she says, but "I can't be racist in my heart." This is a problem faced by many Latinx who aspire to "pass" as white in American society. But passing is something best accomplished through silence—the tacit approval of mainstream white racism embodied by people like Sterling. Stiviano refused to silence herself.

"I am flexible," she says, alluding to Latinx's ability to reach in either direction of the black/white racial binary. But, Sterling insists, "You're perceived either as a Latina or a white girl ... You're supposed to be a delicate white or a delicate Latina girl." In this way Sterling explains how he could be involved with Stiviano despite her dark complexion. For his purposes, she is "either" Latina or white. Then comes the bombshell of the conversation, a revelation that confuses and/or repels Sterling to the point that he considers breaking off their relationship. "I'm a mixed girl," says Stiviano. "Black and Mexican ... Whether you like it or not ... You're asking me to remove something that is a part of me and in my bloodstream."

Stiviano's testimony points to the choice Latinx have in determining America's racial future. Will she consent to being perceived as a "delicate Latina or white girl," or will she claim blackness? Being half African American tilts the equation, but there is African blood in most of us who claim Spanish and/or indigenous roots.

In the introduction to *Dog Whistle Politics*, Ian Haney López cites his Harvard Law professor Derrick Bell—who was also President Obama's professor—who said, "Black people will never gain full equality in this country. Even those herculean efforts we hail as successful will produce no more than temporary 'peaks of progress,' short-lived victories that slide into irrelevance as racial patterns adapt in ways that maintain white dominance." These patterns are indeed changing, says Haney López, who confesses that after disagreeing at first, he has come around to Bell's logic.

Bonilla-Silva's tri-racial structure shows how an approximate model of Latin America's mestizaje racial categorization system keeps intact the essential truth of the US racial binary, but in a more nuanced way. His model is roughly as follows:

- Whites, composed of traditional whites, new immigrants, lighter-skinned children of mixed marriages, and "assimilated Latinos."
- Honorary Whites, composed of the majority of Latinx, Japanese, Koreans, South Asian Indians, Chinese, the majority of mixed-race Americans, and Middle Easterners.
- The Collective Black, composed of African Americans, Vietnamese, Cambodians, Laotians, and (possibly) Filipinos.

In the aftermath of the Zimmerman and Stiviano events, and a subsequent series of articles in Slate and the *New York Times* theorizing that Latinx could be in the process of becoming white, there was some indignation expressed by Latinx-oriented media. How could it be that after almost ten years of extremist anti-immigrant politics directed at Mexicans and Central Americans, Latinx would become white? How could we identify as white after Puerto Rico had never been considered a candidate for statehood in the early twentieth century for fear of its mixed-race population?

The practice of Latinx identifying as white has a long history, and its more recent manifestations may only amount to an exercise in either self-delusion, erosion of potential political power, or merely returning to or re-establishing a whiteness that had already been cultivated in Latin America. But the Trump era has created the surprising phenomenon of some Latinx who actually identify openly with extremist white supremacy. As outlined by journalist Gabriela Resto-Montero in a post for Mic.com, young men such as Alex

Michael Ramos, of Puerto Rican descent and from the Bronx, took part in the beating of an African American man, DeAndre Harris, during the disturbances in Charlottesville, Virginia, in August 2017. Resto-Montero's piece goes on to cite Christopher Rey Monzon, a Cuban American, and Nick Fuentes, a Boston University student who hosts a white supremacist podcast. These Latinx are emblematic of the racism embedded in Latin America's ambiguity about its mestizaje project, and even Spain's original authoring of modern racism. But by embracing white supremacy they are trading temporary agency for inevitable cultural suicide.

These questions are posed at a time of great contradiction in the way that Latinx view their racial identity. Some, as I stated earlier, openly move towards whiteness as a way of solidifying their position in a society where racism still clearly exists: blunting any non-white aspects of their bodies, cultural activities, and speech, attaining wealth and homeownership and acculturating to majority-white communities, openly discriminating against blacks. Others are drawn to the suggestion of a new "racial" category in the census for Hispanics, despite the reality that this might disrupt coalitions against racial discrimination by separating Latinx, many of whom are black, from blacks.

Yet there are those who maintain or increase their identification with blackness even as their lives move more towards the material trappings of white privilege. Is it possible, then, that the idea of blackness could expand enough for many Latinx to claim it, regardless of social class? There is also the possibility of choosing the "brown" middle, but is it too ambiguous in light of the overt racism in the black-white binary? One Latinx professional I interviewed, Loren Carvajal, reported, "I have recently been grappling with the possibility that I am a white Latina because of my appearance, but I honestly refuse to accept that possibility because I have definitely experienced racism and completely feel dissonance with white privilege/culture." Carvajal feels uncertain about claiming the "brown" middle.

However dubious her credibility after her obvious attempts to capitalize on instant celebrity status, V. Stiviano still manages to point us in the direction of seeking membership in the Collective Black body. It's a philosophical imperative, a question of ethics. In this new era of intersectional resistance, let us propose the idea that we claim blackness until there is no longer a stigma associated with it, no matter what degree of blackness is apparent in our appearance. In this way, we avoid the dubious destiny of honorary whiteness.

As a "mixed" child of a "Latin American" couple, I could be seen as socially undetermined—part of a mestizo/mulato muddle, yet embraced as part of a national identity. In the United States, it appears my fate has been to be inexorably drawn to the identity of my lower-status parent. Like Pedro Pietri penning the obituary of the passive Puerto Rican, I accept and cherish that embrace, but hope to bury the dear negro in me. It's time to let go, and embrace the blackness that, as I've always known, is at the core of my being.

7

Towards a New Raza Politics

Class Awareness and Hemispheric Vision

Latinx have been interpreted as a political force in various ways, but the point is to show how the act of being Latinx is political and personal. One way to do so is to conceive of the Latino political condition as grounded in our racialized bodies, borrowing from the body politics of black thinking as well as groundbreaking work by feminists. But perhaps more importantly, Latinx have the greatest potential for exercising political power when we consider how, as the relentlessly exploited lower half of the American hemisphere, our historical condition has been determined by our geographical position, and the racial imprint it has left on us.

If the passage from East to West for Europeans has been charged with forgetting, exemplified by the name-changing practices of Ellis Island or the forced Anglicization of the Germans and the Irish, the passage from South to North has, more often than not, refused to suspend historical memory and the collective consciousness of José Martí's Nuestra América. Retaining that historical memory allows us to cope with how we are racialized, constantly reminded of where we come from because of what we look like. Avoiding our history would make us ineffectual political actors or dysfunctional people. Finding ways to nurture those memories goes a long way towards defining our political existence.

As has been suggested by some writers, the "strategic essentialist" strategy proposed by Gayatri Chakravorty Spivak regarding women is quite fitting when thinking, talking, and acting on Latinx political power in the United States in the twenty-first century. Some form of strategic essentialism allows our diverse assemblage of characteristics to agree on some common ground so as to seek political power while allowing the boundaries of the group to remain open and fluid. While this may seem impractical and dubious on some level, it's a terrific fit for Latinx, whose incredibly diverse nature needs flexibility for definition. The lack of strict boundaries, in fact, allows for the development of a set of positions outside the Democratic/Republican binary.

We've seen that the Latinx, Latina/o, Hispanic, and "Latino" categories are problematic because they tend to erase national, racial, and ethnic difference in a way that is strikingly parallel to the mestizaje/mulatez model from Latin America. While this criticism is valid because of Latinx's diverse national, ethnic, and racial manifestations, as an organizing principle the label still conveys significant meaning and a narrative of shared experience, though more so in the United States than in Latin America. Although Mexican Americans on the West Coast may have sharp differences with Puerto Rican migrants in New York and with Cuban Americans in Miami, Latinx have in common, besides a shared language and parallel cultures, a history marked by US intervention that has in turn driven immigration northward. While the hemisphere's future will be determined by the continuously evolving political relationship between the United States and Latin America, there is a marked disconnect between US Latinx politics and the United States' role in Latin America that doesn't translate into setting a national political agenda.

In the 1960s and 1970s, the term *Latino* was embraced by a growing constituency of US-born Latinx who identified with the civil rights and national liberation movements of the era. They saw the term as an alternative to the Nixon administration's use of *Hispanic*, a European-identified term with assimilationist connotations. But over the years, the "Latino" activist charge has waned. Largely as a result of perceptions created by corporate media and consumer marketing, Latinx are now often cast as recent arrivals, imperfect English speakers, and "others" from *el otro lado*. This contradiction is reflected by the changing nature of US Latinx politics, in which crucial concerns around immigration policy have eclipsed, at least in public perception, the other class-based concerns of working people who historically have occupied a larger role in the Latinx political agenda.

The traditional view of US Latinx politics holds that the three dominant groups wielding political power are Mexicans, much of whose country was absorbed after the Mexican-American War in 1848, and Puerto Ricans and Cubans, whose countries were ceded to the United States after the Spanish-American War in 1898 (with Puerto Rico still a US territory). In the twentieth century, the political and cultural power and awareness of these groups matured, staking out three distinct regions of influence. Mexican descendants, who make up almost two-thirds of the US Latinx population, are concentrated in the West and Southwest; Puerto Ricans, who are born US citizens and are therefore not technically immigrants, are concentrated in the Northeast; and Cuban Americans are concentrated in South Florida.

In terms of political orientation, Mexican Americans are probably the most diverse. Although their political history has been anchored by citizenship and civil rights struggles and has produced a considerable left-liberal intelligentsia, the long-term experience of Mexican Americans in the United States has resulted in a slight uptick in conservative and libertarian tendencies among class-ascendant Mexican Americans in various parts of the country. Puerto Ricans—because of factors ranging from their rejection of their colonial status, to their exposure to harsh discrimination in Northern cities, to relatively low levels of wealth accumulation—are mostly liberal-left. And Cuban exiles in South Florida, propped up by government entitlements for individuals and small businesses since their mass arrival in the early 1960s, form a bastion of right-leaning Latinx that has been crucial to the Republican electoral victories enjoyed by Ronald Reagan and both Bushes. Because of the Cold War politics surrounding the Castro Revolution, the Cuban migration came largely from the whiter upper and middle classes, made several ties with covert US military operations, and was supported by right-wing Republicans in Congress who signed on to their attempts to lay legal claim to property lost when they went into exile in anticipation of the fall of Cuba's socialist government.

The absolute predominance of Mexicans, Puerto Ricans, and Cubans began to change from the mid-1960s through the end of the century. However, when a new wave of immigration from the Dominican Republic, Mexico, Central America, and South America introduced several new variables to the Latinx equation, it in some ways forced the increasing adoption of the tenuous labels *Latinx* and *Hispanic* to describe this growing demographic constituency. During this period of transition there was much debate about these labels, mostly defined by the preference for *Latino* among left- or Democrat-oriented Latinx, who felt that *Hispanic* whitewashed Latinx as comparable to ethnic Europeans. This was borne out by the fact that Mexican and Puerto Rican groups tied to civil rights and social justice rhetoric preferred *Latino*, while Republican-leaning, business-oriented groups and even the US government preferred *Hispanic*. *Latino* represented an assertion of mixed-race, African, or indigenous identity and a rejection of whitened Spain as the motherland.

Yet with the addition of these new immigrants and migrants, as well as the simultaneous emergence of marketing efforts led by growing Spanish-language print and broadcast media, the old political debate between *Latino* and *Hispanic* began to fade and the terms became almost interchangeable—a stark contrast to the development of *Negro* and *black* or *African American*. The perception of Latinx began to change, with neoliberal discourse eliding the civil rights era identifications made by Chicanos and Puerto Ricans and focusing on new immigrants as the "face" of twenty-first century Latinx America. Latinx immigrants were racialized through doubt about their citizenship; citizenship status became the primary marker of otherness, somewhat eclipsing racial difference.

Much of this book so far has promoted the argument that any working definition of Latinx is essentially derived from an identification with racial difference. In some cases that racial difference is expressed through the perception of Latinx as black or brown, in others through the vagueness of mixed race as a marker. We've also seen how whitening, while integral to Latin American identities, tends to remove Latinx from a sense of Latinx identity. This whitening involves not so much appearance but rather the taking on of characteristics associated with whites in order to gain access to white privilege, such as wealth accumulation, intermarriage, and educational achievement.

Given the incredible diversity of Latinx in terms of culture, dialect, racial mix, geographical location, and other factors, the most effective way to define Latinx politics in the United States seems to be to outline a strategic essentialist commonality among us that recognizes racial difference as an organizing principle. While there is an understandable debate about whether sympathetic heterosexuals can be considered queer, the operative principle of queerness as one that continually subverts binaries and nationalism—found in the diaspora as well as Western normativity—suggests that Latinx identity can potentially include "white" or "off-white" Latinx who identify with racial difference through their affiliation with Latinx culture, political agendas, and communities of color. This is already a dynamic that is operational in Latinx and other marginalized communities and would only formalize what, to a large extent, is already in place, given that Latinx who wish to disassociate themselves from racial difference (i.e., identify as white) are likely to avoid identifying as Latinx at all.

Clearly any such coalition would require arduous intersectional work with African-, indigenous-, and LGBTQ-identified Latinx necessarily pursuing rights and grievances at times in conflict with the often myopic nature of Latinx identity, which marginalizes them in favor of ambiguous mixed-race, heteronormative hegemony. This kind of double-sided effort—which might strike some as contradictory—is similar to the need for Latinx to continue to focus on issues that affect their immediate national communities (Mexican, Puerto Rican, Dominican, and so forth) while at the same time engaging in a strategic essentialist project aimed at accruing national (US) political power. Hayes-Bautista and Chapa suggested in 1987 that the basis of Latinx solidarity should be the common experience of having been invaded or interfered with in some way by the military or economic power wielded by the United States. A majority of Latin American countries, from Mexico to Argentina, have been exploited economically or repressed militarily, through either direct invasion or US-backed military dictatorships.

By using race as a referent less to a specific racial identity and more to racial difference in general alludes to the functional definition of what Chicanos intended raza to be, and perhaps what New York Latinx of the early twentieth century imagined Hispanos to be. Moreover, stipulating an affiliation to racial difference severs any connection to reactionary tendencies that have gestated among some elitist Latin American and proto-fascist Iberian sectors over the last hundred or so years.

The problem with this approach to Latinx identity is that it doesn't quite mesh with the demographic studies that political scientists, sociologists, and policymakers use to identify the Latinx effect on politics—studies based on Latinx as defined by national origin, or just a "Hispanic" last name. Such studies, however, can be extremely useful to effectively organize voters and natural constituents in political campaigns and around various issues. In fact, huge sums of money from both government and philanthropic sources are apportioned according to demographic information.

The current demographic figures claim that Latinx are 17 percent of the population and 39 percent in California, and that by the year 2050 the figure nationwide will increase to almost 25 percent. The growth in these numbers from 4.7 percent in 1970 has been largely fueled by changes in the immigration laws beginning in 1965, and have led to many pronouncements of a new Latinx era in the United States, starting with *US News & World Report*'s 1978 declaration of the 1980s as the Decade of the Hispanic.

Such pronouncements led to great expectations for the future political impact of Latinx in the United States through the metaphor of the Sleeping Giant: as our numbers grew, despite a lack thus far of large-scale political reverberations from Latinx, it was presumed inevitable that a mighty constituency would soon emerge with a bold agenda. This has not happened, and the following section explores why.

Why We're Still Not Woke: The Empty Cipher of Latinx Political Power

Because such a sizable percentage of Latinx in the United States are not currently citizens, fulfilling the promise of the Sleeping Giant would entail acquiring citizenship through either traditional methods, which are prohibitive, or significant immigration reform, which—if you believe that Trump-style nativism is the last gasp of an aging white population—might come as soon as the next presidential term. The awakening would also require the development of charismatic political leaders to enact a nationwide agenda that includes the different Latinx constituencies, and instilling the drive towards political engagement beyond simply campaigning or protesting for immigration reform.

Yet the much ballyhooed surge in the Latino population in the last fifteen years has resulted not in a burst of civic participation, but in relentless targeting as consumers by everyone from auto insurance companies to fast food chains and disposable diaper manufacturers. Moreover, it has helped make Spanish-language network Univision the second- or third-largest television network in terms of viewership, creating a kind of hegemonic vision of consumerist ideology. And most significantly, the population burst has meant that racist anti-immigration forces—which were working as far back as the mid-1980s to make English the official language of the United States—have become, as in nationalist movements of Europe, almost mainstream. The failure of Latinx to organize an effective political machine has allowed these groups, at least for the moment, to disable the Latinx Sleeping Giant. The Republican/Fox News strategy to overexpose this point of view has resulted in the Trump fiction that these represent "the views of the majority." Yet poll after poll has shown that a majority of Americans of all stripes support immigration reform that allows the undocumented a path to citizenship.

Latinx do have a problem with the perception that immigration reform has become a hegemonic single-issue "ethnic empowerment strategy." But while it's true that, especially since 2006, it has been a dominant issue, resonating strongly in the West and among Mexicans and Central Americans, it may not be an immediate concern to all of the millions of Latinx citizens—with high voting eligibility rates— who have been citizens for generations.

Latinx advocacy groups, in the hopes of creating a softer landing for undocumented people, seem focused, unfortunately, on trying to highlight immigrants' lack of difference from mainstream America at a moment when nativist racist rhetoric makes clear that Latinx's most potent organizing tool is a political identity based on their marginalization through racial difference. By insisting that Latinx share "American" values, these groups are not critiquing the long-standing white supremacy embedded in institutions, policies, the economy, and globalized capital. It is precisely the racist rhetoric that comes out of the "paranoid" white supremacist minority that moves the immigration issue beyond its stated goal of a path to citizenship for the undocumented. The atmosphere created by intolerance of immigrants has already generated a series of laws in Arizona and California that threaten to subject a majority of Latinos to stops and searches based on their phenotypical appearance even if they have been citizens for generations. The uptick in high-profile ICE deportations as the Trump era progresses has not only paralyzed many immigrant communities with fear but also emboldened racist attackers.

While the Trump victory has put this trend in the spotlight, the systematic attack on Latinx goes back to 1990s California and its Republican governor Pete Wilson. The notorious early 2000s Arizona law SB 1070, which had a few of its provisions cut by the Supreme Court, had several predecessors in both states that aimed to create what the American Immigration Council calls a criminalization of immigration and, by extension, a widening suspicion of Latinx and Latinx culture in general. Many of the facets of this criminalization run parallel to systemic mass incarceration, with shared roots in the War on Drugs. An additional factor is the creation of ICE in the first place, which took immigration enforcement out of the Department of Customs and made it a priority in the Department of Homeland Security following the reorganization of national security organizations after 9/11.

The hate speech that arises from this form of politics serves to remind many Latinx—even the relatively successful ones—that institutional racism, whether it stems from intolerance of immigrants, continued residential segregation, job discrimination, the income gap, unequal access to education, or restriction of voting rights, is alive and well and needs to be addressed, of which Republicans seem far from capable. The broad-based Latinx opposition to Donald Trump has arisen overnight because he epitomizes the condescension of a majority culture that is uncomfortable with a "foreign" language or a community made up of largely mixed-race people of color.

Rejecting Trump to the tune of 75–80 percent in the election has not necessarily given Latinx much power in the Democratic Party, despite the election of Thomas Perez, of Dominican ancestry, to the leadership of the Democratic National Committee. Yet Latinx options in the two-party system are few. They could threaten the Democrats by considering affiliation with Republicans, but the increasing lurch of Republicans to the racist right makes this extremely untenable. So Latinx are left again with the uncomfortable truth that there is slow growth in their political representation and more often than not they are represented by elected officials who do not make effective criticisms of the Democrats' neoliberal agenda.

This agenda betrayed Latinx on several important issues. President Obama was dubbed Deporter in Chief because of the record numbers of undocumented immigrants deported during his tenure. This policy, intended to show "good faith" to anti-immigration Republicans through "enforcement" of immigration laws, has not produced any significant effect in Congress, not even in the flip-flopping Senator Marco Rubio. This has led to a dependence on Obama's DACA initiative and has not created the conditions for real immigration reform, which under Trump's presidency seems even more unattainable.

Meanwhile, the Democratic Party's solution to the debt crisis in Puerto Rico has resulted in the imposition, pushed by Republicans, of an onerous fiscal oversight board with colonial powers to enforce further austerity on the non-incorporated territory. The Obama administration's diplomatic gestures toward Cuba were clearly intended to open the island to investment in order to take advantage of low wages and extract profits as in other islands in the Caribbean. The cheaper availability of Cuba's labor market has undercut Puerto Rico's growth potential even further.

The continued free trade neoliberal policies in Latin America, the coup in Honduras, and the ramping up of military spending in Mexico in the guise of combatting drug trafficking have created conditions that encourage more illegal immigration to the United States. Yet Latinx have, for the most part, immersed themselves in the myopic worldview of US politics, of local victories and incremental progress, and continued to pursue the strategy of loyalty to the Democratic Party—even though, given the party's disarray in the wake of Trump's victory, it would seem an even less effective vehicle for the Latinx political agenda, if one existed.

Still, Latinx attempts to engage in their nation's electoral politics have not been entirely ineffectual. If Obama didn't deliver immigration reform, is that the fault of Latinos attempting to organize political power by electing him? Didn't they deliver votes to a candidate who promised what they asked for? Is it unreasonable to expect that organizing around a major election guarantees that a candidate will not renege on his or her campaign promises?

While there is an obvious conflict between Democratic Party–loyal National Council of La Raza (NCLR; now UnidosUS), Mi Familia Vota, and the Eva Longoria–driven Latino Victory Project and conservative groups such as the Koch brothers–backed Libre Initiative, the Latino Partnership, and the Hispanic Leadership Fund, the Trump phenomenon has essentially rendered it meaningless. Hispanic/Latino conservatives have an impossible chore convincing voters that the Republican Party will welcome or at least tolerate them, and the hopes that Latinx Democratic loyalists had for power through a Clinton victory have left them in a shambles.

The more crucial political battle faced by Latinx today seems to be between Democratic loyalists, who dominate the Congressional Hispanic Caucus, and groups that are closer in communication with and driving the needs and agenda of urban Latinx. In 2016, a progressive nonprofit called Presente, which had previously been involved in successful efforts to remove anti-immigration news commentator Lou Dobbs from his CNN show, openly criticized HUD

secretary and one-time potential Hillary Clinton running mate Julian
Castro for being too chummy with financial institutions involved
with buying distressed mortgages, thus encouraging gentrification
of poor neighborhoods. Another example of progressive advocacy
was Arizona Representative Raúl Grijalva's complaint that HUD's
Distressed Asset Stabilization Program had been involved in selling
homes that once belonged to poor families to Wall Street "entities."
As a result, the National Hispanic Leadership Agenda, a coalition
of forty Latinx groups, threatened to excise Presente from its membership. Separately, Democratic Party loyalists including ex-NCLR
director Cecilia Muñoz have had to take the heat for the Obama
administration's increase in using the tool of deportation. Some
of this opposition played out during Bernie Sanders's challenge to
Hillary Clinton for the presidential nomination, and, in a crucial
development, some Latinx challenged Democrats' loyalty to neoliberal policies and began to make connections between US foreign
policy in Latin America and immigration as well as the ineffective-
ness of Democratic domestic policy and the growing inequality gap.

Devising a US Latinx political agenda must involve a perspective that looks at the hemispheric implications of US policy. Even
the media framing of immigration reform as a "single issue" is misleading. Free trade policy weakens workers' rights, depresses wages,
and erodes the environment on both sides of the Rio Grande, and
is therefore the driving factor behind much of the immigration
surge, leading to the collapse of civil societies in Mexico and Central
America and widespread human rights violations.

The immigration issue is an aspect of the battle surrounding
workers' wages and rates, the protection of the environment, and
the safety net provided by federal entitlement programs. Latinx
must decide whether to seek out a government that protects those
hard-fought gains, or to gamble on neoliberalism's anti-regulatory,
pro-business agenda, which may advance the lives of an elite sector
of Latinx who would most likely avoid using racial difference as

a sign of unity. It's also a battle centered on the emerging world of PACs and 501(c)3 organizations that channel so-called "dark" and not-so-dark (labor union) money in the post–Citizens United elections-for-sale era. So far Latinx leaders in the Democratic Party have done little to address this issue; instead they merely engage in the same mania for fundraising at any cost that has created a lack of trust in party leaders.

Where Are the Leaders?

The issue of leadership is a difficult one, and becomes an unpleasant conversation when one compares the political leadership of the African American community and that of the Latinx community. We can return to Christine Hickman's argument about the benefits of the racial binary for African Americans, whose racial difference is so clearly defined that it gives them an automatically universal constituency and an unambiguous agenda aimed at overturning racial injustice. Add to this indisputable circumstance the nature of African American migration in the United States, which shares a common origin point: the Jim Crow South, from which blacks fled to all points North, Midwest, and West.

The primary stumbling block to Latinx unity is the diversity of Latinx racial, class, and national origins. The twenty-plus countries that comprise Latin America have different experiences of race-mixing, which, as discussed earlier, has led to different national ideologies emphasizing indigenous or African aspects of the national identity. This is most clearly seen in the opposition between the Caribbean, Mexico, Central America, and the Andes region countries and Southern Cone countries such as Argentina, Chile, and Uruguay, the latter which have de-emphasized mixed-race ideologies despite having sizable mixed-race populations. National cultures, dialects, speaking accents, and relative orientations towards European and Anglo-American influences differ as well.

So, while African American leaders from the past and present such as Jesse Jackson, Al Sharpton, Andrew Young, Tom Bradley, and even Marion Barry hail from different cities and class backgrounds, their collective political voice is not limited by regional difference. They all speak to an African American political identity and experience that shares the same take on hundreds of years of slavery, Jim Crow, and neoliberal forms of discrimination like mass incarceration. Although there have been flareups between "leftist" and "neoliberal" black politics, sometimes involving Black Lives Matter and traditional black Democrats, and Cornel West's recent controversial critique of Ta-Nehisi Coates's glossing perspective on the presidency of Barack Obama, there is still a strong sense of black unity in African American politics.

Latinx political leaders, however, are most effective when speaking to and for their regional constituencies, which are associated with whatever national identity is predominant there. Antonio Villaraigosa made history when he became mayor of Los Angeles, but he has little resonance with Latinx on the East Coast or in the South. The struggle of Puerto Ricans for the office of mayor of New York is not on the radar of Chicanos or Miami Cubans. The two Latinx leaders with perhaps the broadest progressive reach are two representatives, the Puerto Rican Luis Gutiérrez from Illinois and the Mexican American Raúl Grijalva from Arizona, both of whom have been outspoken on both immigration reform and the Puerto Rico debt crisis.

The need to base Latinx political power on an assertion of racial difference is made clear by the controversy in 2016 over whether senators and presidential candidates Ted Cruz and Marco Rubio were really Latinx. The primary argument that they were not was that they were "white" oriented and identified through phenotypical appearance and Cuban origin, which signals whiteness because of the nature of Cuban migration and the lack of racial discrimination Cubans have faced in South Florida. But most commentators overlooked that Cruz's and Rubio's "whiteness" was aligned with not only their origins but also their political agenda, which was essentially in line with the Republican Party's move towards white supremacist rhetoric. Both men were also associated with the Tea Party, which had its beginnings in the not-so-subtle racist reaction to the presidency of Barack Obama in 2008.

Many objections to the Latinx identities of Cruz and Rubio included the argument based on the different circumstances surrounding Mexican and Cuban immigration. As I've detailed earlier, thousands of Mexicans were violently absorbed into the United States in 1848 and then endured decades of economically forced migration and the withholding of citizenship to build a pool of exploited workers. Because of the Cold War–era propaganda value to the United States of accepting Cuban exiles from the Castro regime, Cubans have had very little difficulty obtaining citizenship, and built a major urban area in South Florida by escaping the marginalization and persecution that hounded other Latin American immigrants. Even if Cubans are not all white, they have been effectively whitened by federal policy. This creates an immediate gulf between the Mexican American and Cuban American experience, as well as those Latinx voters with a self-consciousness of their racial difference.

To characterize Ted Cruz and Marco Rubio as the "sons of Latin American immigrants," therefore, can be misleading. Because of the privilege of having virtually no problems with immigration status, they do not share the experience of the majority of Latin American immigrants. Branding Cruz and Rubio as "traitors," as some have done, is a bit ludicrous, but privileged Cuban immigrants arguably do not represent the interests of the majority of Latinx. This includes Puerto Ricans, who despite having no issue with citizenship status, suffer similar racialization and discrimination to that of Mexican immigrants. Cubans' claims to representing all of Latinx relies on the argument that our inherent social conservatism—a fallacy—can be absorbed into the white hegemonic mainstream.

The phenomenon of Latinx conservative political organizations and figures in the United States cannot be ignored. The core of political activity in South Florida is oriented towards a rightist Republican view of foreign policy as well as fiscal conservatism, and there are several groups and representatives of Latinx in California, Texas, Florida, and the Northeast who represent a broad range of ideological and fiscal conservatism. Claiming that their progressive counterparts define themselves by "pandering" to a regressive desire by Latinx to be "dependent" on government entitlement programs, they are actually more dependent on the center-right mainstream. Like the Koch-funded group called Libre, conservative Latinx paint a picture of Latinx as having conservative family values. In fact, Latinx become more like mainstream Americans the longer they live in the United States, which means that religion and the nuclear family become less important to them. Since the ultimate goal of conservative Republican Latinx is to prove that there is little difference between them and mainstream conservative values, they adopt a mindset oblivious to racial difference, which in the long run defeats the purpose of their organizations.

The Sleeping Giant narrative is fitting because there is no national agenda for Latinx, and not enough effort has been expended on creating one that will unite disparate groups living in different geographical areas. Because Latinx in conventional politics have yet to develop a national agenda, at times even regional agendas are marginalized, and the primacy of loyalty to the essentially neoliberal Democratic agenda disrupts our political power. For instance, while Congress devised a law that would restructure Puerto Rico's debt, the Congressional Hispanic Caucus did little to acknowledge the unfairness of the debt accumulation and the blatant exercise of colonial power by the US government over its non-incorporated territory in imposing an unelected fiscal oversight board. This blind spot made it much easier to accept the narrative that the debt was the Puerto Rican government's fault, and that there was no way to correct the situation besides imposing austerity on the territory's citizens.

Early in the process, the Congressional Democrats' leadership on the Puerto Rico issue appeared to devolve into holding news conferences in Washington that featured *Hamilton* creator Lin-Manuel Miranda standing around with Senators Schumer and Gillibrand, making chummy offers of free tickets to his off-the-charts Broadway smash to Congressional Republicans in exchange for any bill to come out of the House that might "save" Puerto Rico. The stance adopted by the Congressional Hispanic Caucus was that because Puerto Rico was not eligible to file for bankruptcy protection and defaulting on its debt payments threatened to create administrative and fiscal chaos, a colonial fiscal oversight board was a necessary evil.

Even Raúl Grijalva, so strong in his immigration reform rhetoric, felt that when "measured against the worsening crisis," the legislation as written was necessary. Luis Gutiérrez, who at first seemed sympathetic to the pseudo-intervention by playwright Miranda, ultimately took a strong stance against the legislation, parting ways with the caucus. Similarly, Democratic Mexican American leaders and elected officials rarely engage with the policies of military buildup in which the United States is involved as part of the drug war along the border and in northern Mexico.

The end result is another example of the meaninglessness of the Sleeping Giant narrative. Latinx did organize enough, regionally at least, to elect several representatives to the US Congress that would ostensibly represent their interests, but this leadership either coalesced to support deleterious policy, or had its minor objections ignored. The Puerto Rican economic crisis will affect over 3 million US citizens living on the island and cause a migration surge to US cities, putting migrants into competition for job and government entitlement resources with current residents. Efforts to enact immigration reform or stem the increase in deportations have been barely affected by Latinx representation in Congress, and US government backing of free trade policies and military governments in Latin America has further spurred immigration northward, straining resources in the United States and adding even more undocumented and nonvoting Latinx to the paralyzed Sleeping Giant.

The Rise of Philanthropy, Latinx Meritocracy, and Progressive Technocrats

Political campaigns are increasingly determined by money, and candidates must compromise to an extent according to who donates what. On the local level, elected officials are often following the lead of unions and nonprofit organizations who owe their existence to corporate-backed philanthropic institutions. Nonprofits advocating for Hispanics often back corporate positions (most famously net neutrality) that are in conflict with the needs of Latinx.

It hasn't been easy for Latinx to adjust to our increasingly "free" society, in which federal entitlements are called handouts and the common good must always be stamped by a corporate logo. As progressive tax policies become equated with socialism, philanthropy has increasingly become a central player in addressing problems in our society, whether health, education, or welfare. The period that began during the Reagan administration's government-slashing has matured into one in which philanthropy, whose goals are shaped by its wealthy and corporate donors, has replaced government agencies in addressing social inequalities. This is problematic, not necessarily because of the involvement of large foundations, which can act independently in many cases, but because of the increased involvement of corporate money that can have the effect of silencing Latinx advocacy groups on important issues. For instance, the massive contributions by telecom companies have prompted some advocacy groups to come out against net neutrality, which would limit access to lower-income Latinx. A new class of philanthropists, most notably Microsoft's Bill Gates, have funded, on their own or through hedge funds, the creation of hundreds of charter schools designed to undermine teachers' unions while subtly attaching pro-corporate ethos to basic educational curricula. Prominent advocacy groups such as LULAC and the Hispanic Federation have taken millions of dollars of contributions from Herbalife, a nutritional supplement company and Ponzi scheme that has preyed on the Latinx community.

As the economic policies of the neoliberal era have increasingly abandoned or discouraged government-sponsored solutions to the problems of marginalized communities, the unhealthy dependence on philanthropic solutions has greatly increased. Even worse, Latinx receive less of a share of philanthropic contributions according to their percentage of the population. A 2014 report by the Foundation Center, "Foundation Funding for Hispanics/Latinos in the United States and for Latin America," done in cooperation with the foundation affinity group Hispanics in Philanthropy (HIP), showed that between 1999 and 2009, Latinos received only 1.3 percent of funding dollars from major foundations and corporations, despite having grown to around 16 percent of the US population. In addition, the globalized philanthropic agenda aimed at addressing inequality and lack of opportunity has introduced original ways of marginalizing US Latinx by diverting funds to Latin America. One report found that between 2007 and 2009, about five times as much foundation money was donated to Latin American countries than US Latinx, most of that going to "environmental giving" and "international affairs."

The nonprofit/philanthropy community argues that the solution is to increase funding of dynamic organizations that would attract more funding to foreground or prioritize the role of leadership in addressing social justice. This seems to make sense, given that small nonprofits would naturally have more direct and intimate contact with the Latinx community and better understand its needs. This is the model of the Hispanic Federation, based in New York, co-founded by Luis Miranda, who has used the success of his son

Lin-Manuel's *Hamilton* to stage various *Hamilton*-related fundraisers for Democratic heavyweights such as Andrew Cuomo and Hillary Clinton.

The Hispanic Federation has not been universally welcomed in New York's Latinx community as the vanguard force they purport to be. The federation acts as an intermediary group that, in addition to running voter registration drives and technical assistance programs, funnels money to smaller nonprofits. Yet critics point out that, as is the case with the corporate world from which groups like the Hispanic Federation draw their funds, they seem to provide large salaries to their leadership while getting mediocre reviews from their supposed constituency. One-time Hispanic Federation director Lillian Rodriguez, who in 2010 made over $230,000 a year, left abruptly for a position at Coca-Cola in Atlanta.

Recent trends in philanthropy tend to focus on a "meritocracy" that focuses on class disadvantage, disregarding the fact that race largely corresponds with lower social class. Funding also tends to go to groups that demonstrate statistically a need for resources or a technocratic game plan, not goals based on long-term trends that take into account historic patterns of systemic discrimination. Meritocracy is a hallmark of neoliberalism in that it marketizes the idea of equality, putting individuals in permanent competition with each other. These positions echo the debate on affirmative action and other arguments that a level playing field exists in terms of race and access to housing, educational opportunity, and employment.

The rise of new technocratic leaders under the umbrella of progressivism is a central trend in Latinx politics. They fill a need to distance Latinx from the old civil rights tenets and engage in a project to increase representation in government, pushing for diversity while ignoring fundamental critiques of neoliberalism. They emerge from national organizations such as Latino Victory Project and its offshoot Latino Victory Fund PAC, bringing together labor leaders, the business community, entrepreneurs, and the star power of people such as actress Eva Longoria. Longoria and Henry R. Muñoz III were major bundlers—individuals who bundle together large campaign contributions—for Obama and Hillary Clinton.

Progressivism among these new Latinx electeds can involve a subtle erasure of their identifications with racial difference. For example, Joaquín Castro is often open about his inability to speak Spanish. For Latinx, speaking Spanish can be a marker of racial difference as speaking Arabic is for immigrants from the Arab world. These languages, unlike other foreign languages spoken on the streets or in the suburbs of America, heighten an anxiety in monolingual Americans that they are being spoken about behind their backs and threatened.

Language preference is a complicated issue. Many Latinx feel that they are being ostracized by Latin American elitists if they don't have a proper command of Spanish. Yet the curious emphasis on lack of Spanish use as a way to solidify a nonthreatening identity is an unnecessary concession to racially charged ideals about who constitutes a true American. The potential goal for an organized Latinx political agenda could be to demonstrate how Americanization does not necessarily increase political power.

Latinx political power could not only organize through the recognition of racial difference, but also a positionality acknowledging that intelligence should not only be measured in terms of standardized testing or the ability to master Western rational thinking. Groups dedicated to political advocacy for Latinx could strive to make changes in the electoral system that would enhance democracy and levels of participation while also fostering political discourse whose efficacy does not rely on traditional electoral politics. This would take advantage of the "in-between-ness" of Latinx identity: What kind of fusion can be made between electoral politics and direct-action community organizing?

There has been some hemming and hawing about the decreasing rate of Latinx voter participation. While it is a general trend across all demographics in the United States, the Latino numbers are even worse. Yet these numbers did not prevent the election of Obama or several candidates that favor immigration reform. The drop can be attributed to voter-disqualification campaigns (including requiring photo ID and elimination of early voting) orchestrated by Republicans and their think tanks to disenfranchise voters of color in several states.

Latinx know that the Republicans will never favor immigration reform given the current climate, and that Democratic Party leaders—apart from their indignation over the Trump Muslim travel ban—will hedge their bets on the issue. Many communities struggle with political engagement, and this country is experiencing a moment of generalized skepticism about a political system that is increasingly less democratic. This is evident in the failure of neoliberalism to restore well-paying jobs to average Americans and in the perception that the massive surge in campaign financing, whose origins are often hidden from public view, is dominating the effective results of the political system. In addition, the relative youth of the Latinx population and lack of direct involvement in civic life are obstacles that must be addressed over time.

There is a sense that, having been projected as a major force in American life for thirty years and "anchored" by a high birth rate, Latinx have blown their chance at political power. Yet this is true in only the most superficial way. There are powerful forces at work to disengage most Americans from the full and effective use of their political power. Any action driven by the demographic inevitabilities of this Sleeping Giant must be accompanied by new and innovative political thinking—which is, among other things, capable of confronting the newer tendencies of Latinx millennials (who don't often conform to past political models), the age of digitized global information, and its attendant tweets and self-reproduced images, citizen journalists, and lack of privacy—that will allow us to address our political destiny.

While the large-scale pro–immigration reform marches of the mid-2000s have dissipated, the apparent drop-off in engagement is mitigated by several factors. There may be a sense that immigration reform activists feel betrayed by the lack of action on reform after the 2006 peak in activism and are regrouping. Outlets such as Univision radio, which used several of its morning DJs to swell crowds ten years ago, have refocused on developing the growing consumer market. The escalating criminalization of immigration carried out by anti-immigrant legislation and linking of their detention to the privatization of the prisons brought on by mass incarceration has also had a chilling effect. It may be unreasonable to expect a community that is in many cases subject to deportation to match the intensity of Black Lives Matter protests, whose numbers include not only mostly American citizens but a much larger number of whites than most people care to notice.

While there is mostly a tacit acceptance of white allies in such marches, there have been admonitions that they not be lionized in a way that merely feeds the self-image of white liberals. It's difficult to dismiss the impact of the reality that, moments before she was run over by a car and killed by a white supremacist during the fateful August 2017 rally in Charlottesville, Heather Heyer had been chanting "Black Lives Matter."

The decline of Latinx movements, whether one is referring to those of the civil rights era or mid-2000s immigration reform activism, were not isolated failures caused by internal problems but products of the historical reality of the period. Class-conscious movements have been marginalized and harassed out of existence across the board, and individual neoliberal consciousness, emphasizing Horatio Alger myths, entrepreneurialism, and military service as a path to respectability, has proliferated.

In the Hispanicizing era that began in the Reagan 80s, the individual Hispanic ideal merged with a modified nationalism based around shared artificial myths about both the origin country and the role of Latinx in the United States, and a focus on the consumer as the primary individual. This is also a moment when politically and socially conservative Cuban American elements gained power, creating a successful and efficient bilingualism and bicultural character.

Cubans' bifurcated identity, exemplified by cultural figures such as Gloria Estefan and Pitbull, put the idea of Cuba entirely in the past, a memory inflected with nostalgia and a relatively distorted view of history. Unlike Puerto Ricans rejecting colonialism, Cuban Americans build a non-rebellious norm that served as a theoretical jumping-off point for the idea of the Hispanic. Cubans became the ideal Hispanic Americans because so many were determined to completely detach themselves from the political reality of their origin country. Their identity was also easily de-racialized because so many of them were lighter-skinned, and because the whiteness of American ideology and social mores meshed well with their virulent anti-Communism. The lasting impact of the Hispanic model is crucial because it emerged during an era when many newer nationalities established themselves in the United States through increased immigration, almost all having to do with US military and economic interventions: Central Americans (Guatemalans, Salvadorans, Hondurans to a lesser extent) and South Americans (Venezuelans, Colombians, Ecuadoreans, Peruvians, Argentineans, Chileans).

While the immigration protest era of the 2000s was akin to national liberation politics, its world historical rhetoric resided mostly on its left flank, which had limited influence on its direction. The middle ground behind causes such as DACA and DAPA is constantly trying to prove that assimilation and privileging of immigrants who do not critique neoliberalism or American foreign policy is an essential mode of survival.

While there was always a limit to what electoral politics could do in the past, technocratic progressive politicians as standard bearers of Latinx political advocacy is a phenomenon inseparable from the historical moment: increased money in politics, networks of political power upheld by party organizations working through nonprofit organizations, money coming from corporate and real estate donors. In that sense Latinx are ideal participants because of the ambiguity of Latinx identity in general and Latinx politics in particular. Latinx politicians combine a base built up by corporate donations and philanthropy, and appeal to white liberals while not addressing the systematic inequality that affects the majority of Latinx.

Nuestra América's Politics of Hemispheric Convergence

While free trade policies aim to diminish borders in order to accommodate the flow of capital, the post-9/11 obsession with "national security" has refocused our attention on borders—whether by remilitarizing the one with Mexico, building Trump's wall, or reasserting the class and race barriers that enforce segregation in our cities. Just as US military intervention beginning in the early twentieth century created migration flows to the north, investment capital flows south and displaced populations to move across the physical border, escaping political persecution and economic devastation primarily caused by US economic policy and US support for anti-democratic governments.

The neoliberal free trade era has caused increasing migrations from Mexico and Central America as it imposes ever-harsher conditions on maquiladora and agribusiness workers on both sides of the border. Ineffectual puppet governments in Honduras, El Salvador, and Mexico also have prompted immigration resulting from political violence and added new variations to the US Latinx political landscape. Beginning in the 1990s and accelerating through the 2000s, these new waves of Mexican and Central American immigration created unprecedented population flows to the US South, particularly to Georgia, Virginia, and the Carolinas.

The continuing economic crisis in Puerto Rico, caused primarily by debt speculation in US bond markets, has resulted in a massive migration of island residents of Puerto Rico to Central Florida and beyond. At the same time, mainland-raised Puerto Ricans are fleeing to Orlando from the Northeast, where the traditional base of manufacturing and public sector jobs has eroded greatly over the last thirty years. These phenomena, as well the waning of hardcore anti-Castro politics among newer generations of Cuban Americans, certainly threatens Florida's status as a Republican stronghold.

Other factors—such as increased immigration of middle-class Colombians, Venezuelans, and Argentines to South Florida, as well as a more conservative strand of Puerto Rican migrants, some of whom are retired military personnel or members of the island's rightist pro-statehood party—are significant but unlikely to affect the Democratic bent of Florida's new Latinx voters. But even with this new exploding Latinx population throughout the rest of the South, it will be a generation or two before this mostly immigrant population—most of which is currently not eligible to vote—begins to play a significant role in electoral politics.

Whatever changes the new migrations to Florida and the US South bring, the liberal Democratic political landscape of California and the Southwest has remained constant as a result of its status as the flashpoint of tension between mainstream America and Latinx. Even as Mexican Americans and, increasingly, naturalized Central Americans experience some wealth accumulation and creeping interest in the tax-cutting mantras of the Republican Party, the conservative politics of fear and intolerance that have marked the mainstream response to increased migration to the region have solidified Latinx's anti-Republican leanings. Because most Latinx in the region are intimately connected to an undocumented immigrant, the backlash against them—manifested in discriminatory law enforcement practices and a general increase in anti-Mexican sentiment—has also negatively affected Latinx who have been US citizens for generations.

Disagreement over strategy within the immigration reform movement erupted before President Obama announced an executive action in November 2014 that would allow 4 million undocumented immigrants to live and work legally in the United States. It pitted younger and more autonomous activists—some associated with the "Dreamer" movement—who insisted Obama act more swiftly against more connected advocates with closer links to the Democratic Party, who urged patience so as not to damage the party's chances in the midterm elections. Yet the Republican victories in those elections demonstrated that Obama should have used his executive power earlier. Now, as the reform process has stalled and the desperate move towards protecting sanctuary cities gains steam, it should become clearer that it's just one part of what should be a larger Latinx political agenda.

Immigration reform is often perceived as the most important issue for Latinx in the United States. And for good reason: it is a human rights issue that affects many Latinx directly and indirectly, as anti-immigrant hostility trickles down to all Latinx, citizens or not. The humanitarian crisis of so many people living in hiding, facing the deteriorating climate of the Trump presidency, the threat of separated families, and the lack of basic rights in the workplace, has created a situation dangerously close to apartheid. But many recent polls suggest that Latinx, while strongly concerned with immigration reform, are equally concerned with issues that affect those with citizenship or permanent resident status: the job market, affordable housing, the erosion of voting rights, and access to higher education.

These parallel the issues faced by African Americans, who have been marginalized repeatedly after continuing waves of European migration, as well as those Asian Americans who do not fit into the model-minority demographic and various other marginalized constituencies, including working-class whites. For all the celebrations of contributions that Latinx immigrants make to the United States, as well as the veneration of striving undocumented Dreamer college

graduates—a "talented tenth" of Latinx immigrants—the reality is
that many Latinx tend to be plagued by a pattern of downward social
mobility because of their lack of access to quality education, and are
increasingly vulnerable to entrenched systemic racism.

The growing wealth inequality in core capitalist countries worldwide has created more opportunity for diverse groups of people to
come together in a common political cause. US Latinx can play a
strong role in raising awareness of how labor is exploited across
borders while we also are well suited to exposing the exploitative
and at times savage nature of US foreign policy, and the way it proclaims democratic freedom at home while actively denying it abroad.

As "Americans" with a broader hemispheric perspective, US
Latinx remain a group with much invested in their home countries,
and, theoretically at least, a clear understanding of how free trade
agreements cast a glaring light on wage inequalities on both sides
of the border. Latinx can connect issues like the downward pressure
on wages—a class issue regardless of race and ethnicity—with the
destructive, inequality-creating neoliberal agenda that harms our
home countries. Bringing all of this into focus is a more comprehen-
sive and potentially revolutionary agenda than merely advocating for
immigrants to be allowed a pathway to citizenship solely on the terms
of the status quo—the US hemispheric agenda.

While aligning with the just cause of bringing undocumented
immigrants out of the shadows, Latinx would gain much by joining
with other US Americans to demand reinvestment in public education, the right to unionize and engage in collective bargaining, the
protection of local communities from neoliberal gentrification projects, and economic justice through queer and racial lenses. Latinx
need not only to protect our most recent arrivals from ruthless
exploitation, but also to reignite the legacy of our long history in the
United States and continue to engage in the struggles we embraced
during the civil rights era and its aftermath.

If Latinx can reinvigorate themselves as a national constituency by combining an identification with racial difference with a broader agenda that includes various marginalized groups in both the United States and Latin America, such a power base can not only confront globalization but resonate with a transnational movement of people between North and South as well. In this historical moment, Latinx are uniquely positioned to push American politics toward truly engaging with racial and class differences, the need for a universal living wage, and just foreign policy, taking the politics of intervention back across the borders in both directions, and radically reshaping Nuestra América.

8

Media, Marketing, and the Invisible Soul of Latinidad

Marketing has become the center or the "soul" of the corporation. We are taught that corporations have a soul, which is the most terrifying news in the world.

Gilles Deleuze, "Postscript on the Societies of Control"

Latinos are continuously recast as authentic and marketable, but ultimately as a foreign rather than intrinsic component of US society, culture, and history, suggesting that the growing visibility of Latino populations parallels an expansion of the technologies that render them exotic and invisible.

Arlene Dávila, *Latinos, Inc.: The Marketing and Making of a People*

As if borrowed from Ralph Ellison's famous sobriquet, Latinx media activists and advocates like to describe the state of Latinx in US consciousness as *invisible*, which is another way to explain why the giant is still sleeping. After all, if a giant woke up and no one could see it, would it really have woken up, or was it merely stirring enough to cause a few branches to rustle, only to remain obscure and ineffectual? The jury is still out on whether this is a permanent hindrance—Latinx life to be lived in perpetual invisibility—or an advantage through which Latinx, by virtue of not being wholly absorbed by the soulless machine of neoliberal speculative finance and its attendant fantasies, can remain free enough to pose alternatives.

Just as key Latinx populations on the East and West coasts came of age during a period of social change and countercultural identity formation in the 1960s and 70s, an expanding population of new immigrants became integrated into the fabric of the United States in the 1980s as neoliberalism began to take hold, remapping the field of civil society into a binary relationship between marketers and consumers. With free trade agreements, borders would become blurred and the process of eroding national identity would accelerate. As this new segment of the Latinx demographic settled in, the crux of identity increasingly became defined by the consumer, and the logic of the system became defined by the corporation, replacing the interaction between citizens and government. In a gradual movement, media representation became a significant part of political representation, and the essence of Latinx political ideology became increasingly derived from the soul of the corporation.

Over the last thirty years, the perception of Latinx, as Arlene Dávila writes in *Latinos, Inc.*, her relentless anthropological study of how Latinx came to be marketed, has been constructed as a bifurcated phenomenon that is both a threat to American identity and also the future promise of American prosperity. These two sides correspond to the way neoliberalism has shaped late twentieth-century/early twenty-first-century US and global politics. Because free trade policies have resulted in creating a global competition for labor, favoring lower-wage migrating workers, neoliberalism has spurred the growth of nativist politics as well as the scapegoating of people of color, regardless of whether they are citizens or undocumented and transient.

Both groups are accused of draining government expenses, increasingly provided by middle-class taxpayers as corporate contributions to the tax base vanish, and causing the downsizing and shrinking of the domestic labor market, even though offshoring and automation are the key culprits. The proliferation of the image of Latinx as a threat serves as an organizing principle or galvanizing issue for rightist and Republican elected officials, who preside over increasingly bloated advertising budgets driven by the politics of fear and hate. For Latinx, being perceived as a threat has a long history, going back to early twentieth-century stereotypes of Mexicans as "banditos" and "greasers."

These negative images were softened a bit during the period of the World War II Good Neighbor Policy, US foreign policy that projected Latin Americans as "friends" to ward off the threat of a German recolonization. That era produced the Latin lover stereotype, which provided a lot of work for Latinx leading males such as Ricardo Montalbán and Cesar Romero, while also portraying Latinx women as either harlots or naïve and easily seduced. These stereotypes changed in the postwar era when American cinema went through a period of introspection about US social maladies—Latinx then became juvenile delinquents (*Blackboard Jungle* and *West Side Story* were early examples of this), drug traffickers, and other street criminals.

As the 1980s and 90s arrived, a newer segment of the Latinx population, coming from a more diverse array of national origins, became "criminalized immigrants," folded into a familiar War on Drugs narrative that paralleled the one used against African Americans and precipitated the era of mass incarceration. With the changes in the US worldview in the early to mid-2000s shaped by concerns with national security and an increase in Mexican and Central American immigration to the Southwest (largely driven by NAFTA), the Latinx stereotype regressed to a conception of Latinx as foreigners, poor English speakers, recent arrivals, garden landscapers, and domestic servants. It was fitting that one of the most important Latinx figures on US television became Sofía Vergara, whose character, despite having married an Anglo man, spoke with a thick accent and exhibited some of the stereotyped overemotional impatience associated with 1950s television giant Desi Arnaz in the precedent-setting sitcom *I Love Lucy*.

While most marginalized people of color in the United States are negatively stereotyped, there has always been confusion about Latinx, as I've outlined in previous chapters. Escaping the black-white binary while failing to conform to stereotypes about Asians and Native Americans, Latinx were most often characterized as dangerous, unintelligent, lazy, and sexually hyperactive. Yet as the Latinx presence in the United States persisted through the dawn of the consumer era in the twentieth century, their targeting unfolded in a deliberate and unfocused way, contributing to the invisibility that continues to saddle us today.

Marketers and media programmers have failed to solve the puzzle of attracting and serving Latinx audiences is, in part, because the core of Latinx identity is a multiplicity of racial perspectives, a historical outlier in most business and academic discourse about how race is experienced in the United States. Those perspectives, complicated by the aforementioned language fluidity, an "ethnoracial" experience combining the marginalization of both culture and race and the questioning of citizenship, and inherited self-identification with over twenty different national cultures, makes marketing mechanisms such as data collection and consumer profile construction difficult, if not ultimately irrelevant.

This inability to grasp the object of investigation, making it, in effect, more imperceptible on closer inspection, helps to perpetuate the threat/promise binary that is imposed on Latinx. The threat association moves Latinx into categories and life situations that tend to assign them to an intermediary position between whites and African Americans, with little hope of achieving full equality. Characteristics of this assignment are higher poverty rates, lower access to higher education and quality jobs, and residential segregation in cities, where Latinx tend to live in areas either mostly populated by Latinx or shared with African Americans. While the Latinx incarceration rate is closer to that of whites than African Americans, our poverty rate (26.6 percent) is almost on par with African Americans (27.4 percent).

The new Latinx immigrants of the global era have been labeled as threats, under suspicion for bringing drugs, disease, and terrorist plots across the border and, to a lesser extent, sustaining a cultural presence that refuses to assimilate and thus perpetuates "foreignness," always an anathema to melting-pot American ideology. Yet at the same time, new immigrants constitute a highly desirable pool of consumers for multinational corporations and are less of a threat than unionized labor because they command lower wages and few if any benefits from employers. The targeting of Latinx as a consumer market has been one of the most significant developments in the neoliberal transformation of US advertising and marketing, as the strategies used to target this market have largely been based on culture and ethnicity, and represent a new and unique strategy of totalizing a diverse ethnic constituency for the purposes of the market.

In the past, ethnic markets were local and minimally impactful on multinational corporate advertising. An ethnic group would eventually abandon its home-country culture over time and join the mass of mainstream American media, marketing, and advertising. While this belief has been applied to Latinx from time to time over the last hundred years, the sudden increase in immigration kick-started the sudden and massive growth of the media that would serve them, with national networks such as Univision and Telemundo vying with English-language networks for Nielsen ratings and eventually being swallowed up by the major media corporations, perpetuating an ethnic-focused programming and advertising model in Spanish, yet devising a new monolithic set of characteristics under the label of Hispanic or Latino.

Erasing Stereotypes Through Positive Marketing Images

The vast majority of Latinx characters in mainstream film and television entertainment are criminals and, on news broadcasts, undocumented immigrants and felons. A 2014 report by Frances Negrón-Muntaner of Columbia's Center for the Study of Ethnicity and Race reaffirms the idea that Latinx are relatively invisible in entertainment media. "In 2013, despite being 17 percent of the population," she writes, "Latinos comprised none of the lead actors among the top 10 movies and scripted network TV shows." Latinx characters disproportionately portray criminals or maids compared to the percentage of real-life criminals and domestic workers they actually comprise. In news stories, Latinx are present in less than 1 percent of all media coverage and the majority of these stories feature them as criminals. Alarmists from the late Samuel Huntington to Donald Trump have branded Latinx as un-American as radical Islam, and a certain Latinx phenotypical appearance can welcome scrutiny from law enforcement based on suspicions about citizenship.

Yet marketers, who represent the most potent force in American and global life today—US-based multinational corporations—celebrate and at times salivate over the share of the population that Latinx represent. Varying estimates claim that this group possesses $1.3 trillion in buying power, and, stereotyped as family-oriented Christians, are ripe to be cultivated as prolific consumers, particularly when prudent advertising and marketing strategies are employed to target them. Business is, in fact, booming, as one *Forbes* magazine article asserted: "Between 2010 and 2014, overall expenditures among America's top 500 advertisers only increased by 6 percent. Meanwhile ad spending in Hispanic media jumped 63 percent from $4.7 billion to $7.1 billion."

The two sides of this bifurcated identity are easy to identify in racial terms. The threat is constituted by Latinx whose phenotypical and demographic characteristics associate them with African-ness, indigenous-ness, and even dark mestizo-ness. These include the darker-skinned Latinx in major cities on the East Coast, many of whom have intermarried with or fused into an urban culture that overlaps with African American culture; Mexican and Central American peasants disenfranchised by the lighter-skinned elites who run their countries; and their counterparts from the Caribbean, South American countries such as Venezuela and Colombia with sizable Caribbean coastal cities and settlements, and to a lesser extent indigenous people from the Andes regions and southern Mexico. These people, whose appearance marks them as black, Native American, or even Arabic in appearance, are characterized as the threat.

The absence of a discourse on race is at the center of the mainstream marketer's inability to effectively target Latinx consumers. This is understandable because any race discourse in an advertising message is considered an interruption of marketability. Yet the subtraction of race from the equation induces Spanish language marketers to signal their targeting through obvious markers such as use of the Spanish language, and more subtle ones including in-between racial tones, emotional affectations, and even manners of dress and food consumption. As a response to their exponential growth, Latinx have been invented as a totalizing marketing category that celebrates family, spirituality, and tradition: a new stereotype to battle the old, threatening one.

While Latinx are perceived through the threat/promise binary, the former is more important in political discourse, and marketers find fertile ground in focusing on the promise aspect. Before the emergence of Trumpian rhetoric, the threat association applied more to second-, third-, and fourth-generation Latinx who fall into patterns of downward mobility that often correlate with their inability to whiten themselves (perhaps to the point of disappearing completely as Latinx, per se), and who are then assigned to intermediary categories that hew closer to African Americans than whites.

The simple task for marketers, then, is to determine which Latinx best represents the future promise of America. It is true that the new immigrant diaspora keeps a low profile in segregated neighborhoods, avoiding calling attention to themselves and inviting increased law enforcement/deportation activity. But because of their life outside of mainstream American values, they still constitute a political threat. In addition, a growing number identify themselves as Afro-Latinx, invisible because of their double exclusion: too Latinx to be black and too black to be Latinx.

New immigrants are imminently targetable because they can be indoctrinated into American consumerism through a positive stereotype that celebrates certain superficial aspects of Latinidad (family, spirituality, and tradition), allowing them to escape marginalization to an extent. But there is another group with varying levels of visibility: the part of the Latinx diaspora that are either lighter-skinned or have managed to whiten themselves through educational achievement, wealth accumulation, or intermarriage. They are the Latinx who have been able to maintain a stable economic existence by accepting the terms of neoliberal America, by not drawing too much attention to their ethno-racial identity or doing so only in non-threatening ways, engaging in post-industrial entrepreneurship, or using networks of government, corporate, or academic entitlement to avoid the worst marginalization that is reserved for their darker contemporaries. They are starting to appear more in network television and are subtly alluded to in mainstream advertising, but remain mysterious and unidentified for the most part.

The invisibilizing of Latinx in the mainstream can be attributed to the use of Spanish, which is unintelligible to the vast majority of monolingual America. But when targeting is done in English, it is done through the lens of racelessness, through which subtle signals of ambiguous multiculturalism indicate probable Latinx identity, as well as an attempt to fold it into an emerging tabula rasa of a multi-cultural or mixed-race population. In this way, marketing plays a central role in the Americanization of a significant proportion of Latinx. This kind of identity construction is practically the inverse of the identity and self-awareness that Latinx have created through cultural production in media, literature, visual art, and political activity since the nineteenth century. As the first interactions between Latinx and Anglo-Americans began to bear fruit in this respect, there was a relative independence in Latinx cultural production, whether it be corridos that told the story of resistance to the Texas Rangers, or the early newspapers, founded by Cuban entrepreneurs, in New Orleans, San Antonio, and elsewhere. In fact, Western-style media production by Latinx preceded the establishment of any of the original colonies; as Juan González and Joseph Torres point out in their ambitious history, *News for All the People: The Epic Story of Race and the American Media,* the first printing press in the New World was introduced to Mexico in 1534.

But because of the complexity and diversity of Latinx and their experiences, constructing this identity and devising the appropriate media representations for it has always been something that is best captured from within that experience. The earlier part of this book explored how that task and its attendant techniques arose first within the Spanish language, then through bilingual expression, and finally through an English that, strongly infused with urban dialect, came from the various hybrid interactions along the literal borders in the Southwest and the more ephemeral borders segregating all of the United States' major cities. These are the concrete aspects of Latinx identity that for the most part mainstream media corporations have failed to grasp.

The unique form of Latinx acculturation—in which adaptation was achieved through integrating aspects of the original culture in diasporic fashion—kept nationalist identities intact as adaptation to life in America proceeded. It produced a cultural renaissance parallel to that of African Americans, but proved problematic to the changing world order that wiped away most of the change brought about by the era of national liberation movements. The new superstructure, in which the relevance of government intervention and collective ideologies of community were devalued and the individual consumer came to prominence, required the development of a different kind of identity for Latinx in the United States.

Hispanic Media and Marketing: The Dignified Other

The two main strands that gradually came together to produce the image-making machinery of Hispanic media and advertising came out of the early transnational outreach from US advertising to Latin America by way of Cuba, and a small yet concerted incursion into the US airwaves by a Mexican entrepreneur. As Dávila outlines in *Latinos, Inc.*, the at first unrelated efforts of Emilio Azcárraga, who bought television stations in San Antonio and Los Angeles in the early 1960s because of the difficulty of buying Spanish-language ad time, and a coterie of Cuban immigrants in New York establishing the first Hispanic advertising firm in Manhattan, came together in the early 1980s to create the Latinx marketing juggernaut.

While it seems that Spanish-language or Hispanic media in the United States imported Latin American culture and ethos into the United States via the airwaves, the printing presses, and the Internet, that media was actually the result of transnational processes fostered by a collaboration between elite and corporate interests on both sides. Spanish-language television in the United States created a "standard" Spanish in a similar way that US network television created a non-regional accent that would not alienate viewers in different geographical regions. And, as Dávila suggests, a delicate dance between the way the United States viewed Latin America and the way Latin American elites viewed their own countries led to a "balance of superiorities," essentially an encounter between the US Protestant ethic and Latin America's Catholic, ostensibly spiritual rather than materialistic worldview.

Dávila quotes a 1970s marketing presentation for Colgate tooth-paste in *Latinos, Inc.*, that asserted that Latin Americans were "superior in culture, emotional sensitivity, delicacies of life" while the United States was "superior in technology, modernization, functionality." This worldview is still typical in media and marketing-based identities. While not discarding the idea that Latinx are family-oriented, more "passionate," or prone to emotion, primers and self-help books and seminars targeting Latinx who, say, want to succeed in business, often refer to the need for Latinx to rein in these incompatible-with-capitalism traits and find ways to inculcate US values about methodical, technological efficiency, and amassing wealth through profit-making mechanisms.

In a sense the marketing of Hispanics and their visualization through advertising images, while in many ways the direct opposite of what appears in film and television entertainment and print and broadcast journalism, reflects processes that I've outlined previously: the simultaneous Spanish erasure and nostalgic reminiscence for Moorish culture (the Good Moor), and the way the Catholic Church tried to assimilate and incorporate indigenous people through race-mixing and conversion to Christianity. In that sense, Latinx may actually have been "primed" to become Americanized through centuries of colonial practices, cultural traditions, and archetypes.

The creation of the Cuban American identity between the late 60s and the 80s was a key example of the development of this strategy. As Dávila notes, "Cuban immigration after the Cuban revolution brought key figures of the well-developed Cuban publicity, entertainment and marketing industries ready to tap marketing opportunities arising from the changing demographics in the city." These Cubans were eager to distance themselves from the negative perception of Latinx in the United States, and were successful not only because of their ready-made path toward middle- and upper-middle-class profes-sionalism, but also because they were unable to return to their native land due to political circumstances and were therefore developing an imagined sense of the Cuban nation—nostalgic, frozen in time, and transferred whole, like a house on wheels, to South Florida's sandy shores. Their enemy was not an invading United States but Castro's aggressive and resilient Communism, which alienated them from the pro-working-class, anti-US-imperialism movement that helped consolidate the Latino/a identity for Chicanos and Puerto Ricans during the 1960s and 70s.

Just as Cubans themselves created a fantasy version of the island they had left behind, they were also creating a version of Hispanic identity that was "additive" in the sense that it was proudly bilingual, partially reacting to the late 70s, early 80s nativist US English movements. One fascinating media example of this was a TV show called *Qué Pasa USA?*, broadcast on PBS, a publicly funded network not tied to advertising. The show, which featured Miami Cuban Steven Bauer, who went on to star opposite Al Pacino in the highly stereotypical, Miami-based remake of the drug gangster film *Scarface*, presented a typical Miami Cuban family struggling through the process of acculturation.

One of the sociological realities that *Qué Pasa USA?* depicted was the phenomena of the 1.5 generation, celebrated by writer Gustavo Pérez Firmat and others: those born in Cuba who came to the United States at a young enough age that they retained their Cuban upbringing and added it to an Americanization made easier by the relative welcome Cubans received compared to other Latinx immigrants. This phenomenon created "perfect" bilinguals, who, not tainted by the racialization that beset other groups, were able to Americanize themselves while remaining "Cuban."

Dávila's description of the main players of the Cuban advertising world in the 1980s focuses on their need to address the "shame" of being Hispanic by being "uplifters" of Hispanicity. Many of these earlier participants lived in New York and in large part escaped the intolerance of New Yorkers of Latinx speaking Spanish in private and public spaces, albeit on a smaller scale. In fact, while the creation of

Spanish-language advertising represented a kind of regressive reimposition of US corporate values onto US Latinx, it also represented a liberation as the constant airing of programs and media in Spanish helped relieve Latinx of much of their shame about retaining it as a primary language.

These early models of assimilation through consumerism, or instilling market values through lip service designed to appeal to Latinx's mestizo ideals of Christianity and aspiring toward honorary whiteness, have remained the basis for marketing to this day. The 1.5 generation ideal also pervades corporate preferences for maintaining a hierarchy in the media industry. Everyone from news directors to writers and on-camera reporters are preferred if they have origins in Latin America (thereby retaining their "language purity" through perfect bilingualism, freeing them from hybrid cultural formations like Spanglish and urban-culture contamination), despite the fact that many US-born Latinx speak Spanish well enough to assume key roles in the industry.

These preferences, documented by Dávila in other works, tend to continue discrimination against US-born Latinx today. Latin American novelists, from the Boom Generation of magical realist writers to today's Spanish-language literary stars, are much more strongly promoted and consumed than exceptions like Junot Díaz. Latin American film stars such as Antonio Banderas and Salma Hayek and directors such as Alfonso Cuarón and Alejandro González Iñárritu are much more successful than any US-born Latinx film director has ever been. A museum show featuring Frida Kahlo can put a US Latino art museum in the black for the year, whereas US-born Latino artists are rarely even reviewed in the rarefied US art press. While most of these personalities have ambiguous phenotypical appearances, they are "whitened" by either Latin America's European cultural associations or, in the case of Díaz, approval by the elite publishing world.

While these strategies have generated enormous profits, they are based on the idea that Hispanics are "others" and must be marketed to as such. The exotification of Latinx in a way that suits market exigencies and promotes gradual assimilation has worked on many levels but still fails to create empowering representations in the media. There was an effort in the late 1990s to reflect demographic reality and identify Latinx as a primarily US-born constituency, attempting to address the manifold implications of mixed-racial or even mixed-national identification, but it was quickly annihilated by market forces, a retrenchment of news and entertainment media stereotypes, and changing US foreign policy.

Ricky Martin's infamous appearance on 1998's Grammy Awards telecast, the most remembered performance of the night, signaled a new awareness of Latinx as bilingual and bicultural, with some hints of their mixed-race difference. Although Martin was a classic "white" Puerto Rican with a Hispanic last name indistinguishable from an Anglo one, he did open doors—some say through his some- what apparent queerness—to new media representations of Latinx as partly assimilated, partly Latin American, and somewhat less family- oriented, and an embrace of an "urban" culture that had crystallized around hip-hop, as well as a younger Latinx "reverse-assimilation" throwback to traditional salsa and norteño music and the cultural production of other marginalized urban constituencies.

The new Latinx media stars ranged from Martin, a Puerto Rican who spoke English without an accent, to Marc Anthony and Jennifer Lopez, Nuyoricans who spoke with an "urban" accent, to Enrique Iglesias, the son of a Spanish singing star who grew up in Miami, and Shakira, a Colombian singer who mastered English to the point of recording an entire album in the language, unheard of for Latin American pop stars. This was the period when I published a book called *Living in Spanglish*, the web was just starting to generate lots of US Latinx-oriented content that would not have previously been produced, and major book chains like Barnes & Noble and Borders dedicated sections to US Latinx books and writers.

Yet the market continued to see greater profit in Spanish-language production, rejecting any hint of bilingualness. Although a couple of bilingual cable networks such as MTV Tres and Mun2 were formed, they were quickly overwhelmed by the advertising dollars thrown at Spanish-language-only Univision and Telemundo. As Barnes & Noble moved to the web to compete with the emerging Amazon, it focused on its Libros en Español section, and US Latinx sections disappeared. Then came 9/11, which fell on the same day as the much-anticipated second annual Latin Grammy awards—a show largely built on the strength of Ricky Martin's performance and broadcast on CBS in English—and the United States entered a new phase, reawakening a dormant xenophobia that revived anxieties over racial and cultural purity and even began to draw parallels between Latinx and radical Islam.

The Latin Grammy Awards were moved from English-language CBS to Univision permanently in 2005, signaling the end of a failed experiment to cast Latinx culture as part of the mainstream. Gone were the awkward duets staged between Spanish singer Alejandro Sanz and urban pop goddess Alicia Keys, the occasional mixing of languages during award acceptance speeches, and the attempt to fuse English-dominant US Latinx culture with Latin American pop celebrity. Univision and Telemundo, which was bought by NBC in 2001, became the principal corporate broadcasters of Latinx identity, which was completely informed by the values and consumptive desires of recent immigrants and the 1.5 generation, and of Latin American experts and stars who produced the programming and served as its talent. While the basic content and performance of this identity were apparently derived from Latin America, the packaging and structure of the networks were a reflection of American multinational influence: stereotypes were sharpened, the on-air talent was almost completely whitened, and local ads—such as the ones bought by Puerto Rican bodega owners in the 1970s to air on local Spanish-language TV—were replaced by sophisticated automobile and fast food chain ads, essentially translations of those broadcast to a mainstream US audience, with subtle adjustments.

Spanish-language television became flooded with highly stylized and formulaic telenovelas from Mexico, Colombia, and Brazil (the latter translated into Spanish) that emphasized melodrama and were driven by Mexican and Latin American pop singers whose recordings provided much of the soundtrack. At one point Univision bought up major Mexican regional pop labels including Disa and created its own label to provide music directly to the telenovelas. But while the telenovelas seem to represent an "essence" of Latin American psyche and cultural mindset, their formulas had been ossified and entrenched in a US media profit-maximization feedback loop through repetitions of plotlines and assembly-line production.

Such an "Americanization" of Latin American media has made it obvious why a well-regarded comedy show like *Saturday Night Live* finds it much easier to "parody" telenovelas (which are parodies in and of themselves) than to employ Latinx comedians or portray different kinds of comedic situations involving US Latinx. The content may be vastly "different" but the formulas and stereotypes are easily recognized by US television producers. Mediterranean-hued, African American, and mixed-race actors like Fred Armisen, Tracy Morgan, and Maya Rudolph all become more suitable to playing distorted Latinx roles than actual Latinx.

Globalized telenovela production has become so profitable that the individual cinematic traditions of several Latin American countries —Mexico and Venezuela come to mind—have been vastly undercut; it is now difficult for them to produce the dynamic directors that existed in a brief golden age during the postwar years. Even Mexico's best directors, such as the aforementioned Cuarón and González Iñárritu, have been swept up into the Hollywood machine, and both directors no longer make movies in Spanish, or about Latinx or Latin American lives. Mainstream and independent film and television productions, outside of marginal shows such as *Ugly Betty*, *Jane the*

Virgin, and the Miami Cuban remake of *One Day at a Time,* which still make concessions to American stereotyping and the telenovela tradition, are at a standstill, and there hasn't been a successful film that portrays a US Latinx life to a degree anywhere close to African American TV or cinema for years.

The Conundrum of Latinx's Multiple Identities and Their Incompatibility with the US Market

One of the most surprising things that happened to me as a result of publishing *Living in Spanglish* is that, while I got the expected attention from young people struggling with their bicultural or multicultural identity, I suddenly became extremely in demand with marketers who were trying to do a more sophisticated version of Hispanic marketing, who clamored to interview me and invite me to their seminars. It opened my eyes to the fact that despite my political idealism, I had written a book that was at least in part celebratory of the potential for Latinx to be marketed to as part of our eventual empowerment, a belief many well-intentioned Latinx have fostered.

Yet it was through this experience that I came to understand that the market could not accept or process the idea that Latinx identity was multicultural or sharply African- or indigenous-oriented, had the potential to be fluid, and was incapable of producing the ideal consumer in the terms that the market needed to dictate. Perhaps accelerated by the fragmentation of media itself through the emergence of the Internet, Latinx identity needed narrower definitions in order to be efficiently targeted. The search for these narrower definitions was not only futile, but bordered on absurdity.

In the mid-2000s a media consultant group openly pitching themselves as semioticians presented me with a model of four layers of Latinx assimilation using different tastes and levels of assimilation that would correspond to one of four different hair products being marketed by a particular corporation. While the attempt was somewhat impressive, as it tries to show four different levels of identity that could potentially be a reality for many US Latinx, along with the potential that they might choose to move between them at different times in their lives, what was missing, at least overtly, was a racial narrative. (Some of the actual products featured the ability to either emphasize or control curly or frizzy hair which, for Latinx women, can be a strong signaling of racial identity.)

There have been some attempts at understanding the crossover between Latinx identity, its top-heaviness in youth, and how that youth is growing up in an increasingly multicultural America. Sixty percent of Latinx are under thirty-five, and the median age of Latinx is twenty-eight, compared to the national median age of thirty-seven. Much of the tone for this idea was set by Guy Garcia, a US Latinx journalist and novelist who published a book called *The New Mainstream* in 2004, making the case that American culture, which ultimately bred the consumer culture of the twentieth and twenty-first centuries, had diversity as its essential strength, and that the demographic changes in the population, which would increase the number of people of color and mixed-race people, would usher in the most important consumer and marketing trends of the current era.

By combining the African American, Latinx, and Asian populations, Garcia tries to show that people of color are 35 percent of the population and growing. He wants to expand the multicultural identity associated with Latinx to all people of color, whose needs are being attended to by a growing "creative class" that will nurture diverse expressions of culture that can then be addressed by consumer targeting. In that sense, he was ahead of the curve, yet in many ways he is describing the kind of consumer research that has now been used to describe millennials, who have been assigned a role as a part of this multicultural alliance because of their perceived progressivism in racial, gender, and sexual-preference issues.

By envisioning a growing, young, multicultural segment of the population, marketers and neoliberals are paving the ground for a

new era in which the American character slowly moves away from
the older white European model in terms of mainstream conformity.
Latinx fit into this model as far as they play down "nationalism"
and ethnocentrism in order not to alienate a broader youth culture
with a vague investment in racial diversity. Clearly the multicultural
model mirrors Latin America's mestizaje project in the way it seeks
to de-emphasize local differences and create a universal or global
utopian consumer class less dependent on traditional ethnic cultures
and tied together by superficial "ethno-racial" trends in fashion, art,
and music.

Since then, Garcia has been involved in several consulting groups,
most notably EthniFacts, which on August 22, 2014, announced that
the majority of America's population was non-white, measuring the
"breathtaking scope of America's transformation into a post-Melting
Pot society." (Revised numbers put the new date for the transformation at 2043.) The buying power of this expanded group is now
$2 trillion, significantly larger than Latinx's $1.3 million. In books,
lectures, and media appearances, Garcia has invoked products such
as dulce de leche–flavored Haagen-Dazs ice cream, habanero gua-
camole tortilla chips, and the usual suspects—Coke, Taco Bell, and
McDonalds—to make his point. Partnering with PBS reporter Maria
Hinojosa, he appeared in a documentary series called *America by the
Numbers*, which documents how the gradual population shift calls for
a new tolerance.

Garcia's EthniFact is also behind the publication of a paper called
"The Plus Identity," which says it intends to define a paradigm that
would "replace the notion which Latinos move unidirectionally away
from a culture niche and into a melting pot." In the report they identify trademarked archetypes such as "ambicultural" and "bicultural,"
which represent two different stages of a dual-culture lifestyle, with
bicultural referring to a less-Americanized moment in the transition
to ambicultural. One of the central concepts in this dossier is the idea
that Latinx are best reflected by a transcultural model, which Garcia

names after Fernando Ortiz's coinage, implying that rather than discarding the previous ethnic identity, Latinx create a new synthesis of old and new.

This idea is not new, of course, and seems to elide or forget that the transculturation Ortiz spoke on took place in slave plantations, but the significance in EthniFact's usage is to promote new paradigms that do not question the neoliberal structure and tenets of multinational corporations and consumers. In Hinojosa's adaptation of the New Mainstream's ideas in the *America by the Numbers* series, she does expand this notion to the potential political power of people of color as their population increases and expands to previously unpioneered places such as the South. But, as I argued in the last chapter, the practical activity of democracy remains deeply in question despite this population surge.

The Plus Identity also avers, through its survey results, that Latinx are "coming out of the closet" in increasing numbers by refusing to blunt or hide their identity, and want to become part of the "ambicultural middle," fully identifying as "both Latino and American" rather than erasing their ethno-racial identity or identifying only as "Latino" or with their home country. This muddle in the middle is associated with professional status and wealth attainment, increased travel to Latin America, language proficiency, and multiracial groups of friends. It is ironic that this use of "middle," achieved through an upper-middle class or one-percenter lifestyle, contrasts sharply with the rapid demise of America's actual "middle class."

This concept reflects issues previously discussed with Latin American mestizaje ideology, both the fatal flaws and unrecognized potential. While this desire to be "American" and "Latino" at the same time implies a "cultural parity," it is unclear which culture is hegemonic within this paradigm. The "American" part may very well be dominant, particularly in terms of the way marketing shapes identity and the technocratic influence on measuring political participation. Yet this dominant culture may be influenced by the cultures, feelings, and traditions of "others." The question is whether that force can make a difference in the areas of humanity, spirituality, and real political change, rather than simply providing the "empirical" data used to feed marketing profiles and justify the continued dominance of neoliberalism.

The Problem of Language Purity—Anything but Spanglish

While later generations of bilingual Latinx constitute a measurable portion of the Spanish-language TV audience, the relegation of Latinx to objects of marketing and media production in a language that has gradually become less important to them is an astoundingly irrational development in a culture in which the profit motive is a guiding economic philosophy. To address a group in a language that is not the dominant parlance for the majority of the group is extraordinarily inefficient in terms of maximizing profit. It is a glaring example of how marketing can be affected by an extra-economic methodology that perceives the world through racial binaries and biases.

Forward-looking Hispanic consultancies, although limited by their conception of identity as being completely tied to and subsumed by the marketplace, are at least attempting to grasp the realities of Latinx that are not being addressed by the majority of the Hispanic marketing sector. In the late 2000s an entrepreneur named Robert Rose, who with his partner Renzo Devia started an independently distributed show called *American Latino TV*, accused the Nielsen Corporation of skewing ratings numbers to ensure that investors in Hispanic media would devote almost all of their resources to Spanish-language media. While Rose never got much traction with his HelpChangeTV .com website-based movement, his position—at least in 2007, when his protest peaked—was buttressed by the facts: upwards of 60 percent of Latinx in the United States are US-born, studies show that they become largely English-dominant by the second or third generation, and their buying power is most likely greater than their immigrant counterparts because they have a better chance at higher-paying jobs and developing more sophisticated consumer tastes. My own journalistic investigation in the 90s and early 2000s showed that there were still vestiges of racist resistance to marketing to people of color. For example, in the late 1990s there was a scandal at a local New York radio station involving an ad-buying employee circulating a memo indicating that preferred listeners should be "prospects, not suspects" and ads should not be accepted that targeted people of color. These practices had long been rumored to be as common as residential redlining. Mainstream agencies, television networks and print/online publications seem to prefer to segment their audiences, with the "mainstream" audience being the preferable target and the "minority" audiences relegated to separate networks and publications, served by Hispanic or people of color divisions whose employees are usually paid less than the mainstream workers.

It is probably impossible to prove and seems fundamentally illogical that racism is the reason for the predominance of Spanish-language media, given that it focuses on a smaller segment of the market with substantially lower buying power. It's possible that the advertising media industry tends to be more conservative and less willing to spend money on marketing to a theoretical "ambicultural middle" than the proven Spanish-dominant media and marketing paradigm, particularly when there are US/multinational-owned networks in place to deliver this massive investment. The targeting, again, is tighter, with less ambivalence about the consumer patterns of an ambicultural middle, honing in on the basic needs of a family subsisting at or near the poverty line: fast food, diapers, snacks, cheap auto insurance, and entry-level automobile purchases. It's a more ethical version of the banking industry's focus on exploitative payday loans and mortgages to minority groups and the poor.

Yet the Spanish-dominant marketing paradigm has continued to face challenges, and by the early 2010s, a new set of factors temporarily spurred the development of media for English-dominant Latinx. The passage of time since the 9/11 attacks and the relatively embarrassing failures of the wars in Iraq and Afghanistan as democracy-building experiments had begun to weaken the jingoistic anti-foreign rhetoric that held sway at the turn of the century. In addition, the sobering defeat of the Republican Party platform in the national election as Obama won a second term temporarily suspended the relentlessly anti-Latinx drumbeat against immigration reform—in fact, the party's failure to appeal to Latinx was increasingly seen as key to the conservative right's failure in national politics. The Trump presidency has unleashed a strong countervailing force in the opposite direction. But given the corporate media's hostility to his presidency, as well as loyalty to their bottom line, which includes marketing and selling products to recent immigrants, it appears even increasing anti-immigrant sentiment will not reverse the momentum of these changes.

In another seeming indication of the corporate media's true concerns, the peak years of the pro-immigration reform agenda (2005–7) had been strongly driven by Spanish-language networks focused on enhancing the legal status of a rapidly growing consumer group: recent immigrants and their children. In 2006, the year that some observers cite as the birth of a new Latino politics, radio DJs at Univision-owned stations were crucial in helping to draw huge crowds to immigration reform rallies in Los Angeles, Chicago, and other cities. At this time Univision was owned by Jerrold Perenchio, who is not only not Latino but a major Republican donor. While there was considerable anti-immigrant sentiment among Republicans in California and Arizona, the Bush presidency pursued a more tolerant line.

The momentum created by Univision's high-profile endorsement of immigration reform not only shored up its bottom line but allowed it to act as a practical example of advocacy journalism, focusing on an issue affecting not only recent immigrants but also Latino citizens who had relatives subject to racial profiling or were simply disturbed by the increasingly anti-immigrant tone adopted by right-wing media like Fox News.

This constellation of events seems to have prompted more sophisticated strategies by media producers and marketers in their approach to the Latino consumer, who at times even embraced strategies suggested by Garcia's ambicultural middle ground. The increasing fragmentation of the media due to proliferating cable channels and the infinite world of the Internet had finally created an investment logic wherein markets previously considered to be unprofitable and niche were seen as opportunities for start-ups. The moment for "ambicultural" Latinx niche markets, networks, and media outlets seemed to have arrived.

With varying success, bilingual networks such as Mun2 and MTV Tres paved the way for youth-oriented websites such as Remezcla .com and even mainstream outlets such as BuzzFeed to focus on an English-speaking Latinx audience made up of emergent, often bilingual and bicultural young Latinx. Advertising strategies began to follow suit: recent ads for wireless cell phone companies and fast food giants depict Latinx less as English-handicapped foreigners and more like multihued families with subtle assimilative tendencies who march to a slightly different bilingual drum.

This "raceless" presentation of Latinx appears to be an attempt to signal to Latinx consumers that they are recognized while avoiding markers such as accented English, music, food references, and, of course, race. As if following a mandate from the brief "post-racial" era that ended around the time of Trayvon Martin's murder and the birth of Black Lives Matter in 2012, Latinx have been appearing in films and television without much to indicate their ethno-racial identity. One analysis by Mary Beltrán observes that the *Fast and the Furious* movie series is the "first that makes Latinos, and Latino culture, central defining elements to the raceless aesthetic."

While reinforcing "Hollywood traditions of white centrism," the

series of films, which began in the late 2000s and are still being produced, emphasizes "cultural mingling and border crossing" while at
the same time avoiding explicit reference to the characters'—many
of whom are played by Latinx—mixed-race or Afro-Latinx identity.
The market motivations are there—as has been noted in Negrón-
Muntaner's "Latino Media Gap" study and elsewhere, Latinx buy
25 percent of all movie tickets despite being only 17 percent of the
population. So there is significant motivation for Hollywood to
somehow target these consumers without alienating the majority of
viewers with content that overly emphasizes ethno-racial themes and
content.

The Fast and the Furious, like some films and many major consumer products, uses English- and Spanish-language campaigns to
reach potential viewers. Latinx actors who star in the films, such
as Michelle Rodriguez, can be used in Spanish-language ads to
provide authenticity for those viewers while remaining neutral for
the general audience. The cast of the film includes "light-skinned"
Latinx, including Rodriguez, Vin Diesel, who is not Latinx but of
mixed race (which makes him symbolically Latinx for marketers and
perhaps viewers alike), and darker-skinned Latinx such as Puerto
Rican reggaetón rapper Tego Calderón, who speaks little English
and provides a race-specific anchor for a generally raceless scenario.
As they cross borders, even the "white" character Brian (played by
the late Paul Walker) becomes Latinized in the context of the multicultural milieu, as he is increasingly surrounded by Latinx and other
characters of color.

Yet by locating the heroism and rationality of the film's plot in
the duo of Paul Walker and Vin Diesel, a hierarchy is established
that retains a white supremacy, albeit a somewhat off-white one, that
ultimately triumphs over darker-skinned villains and hot-headed
darker-skinned collaborators. Walker and Diesel symbolize a newer
idea of whiteness that magnanimously adjusts to the onset of Guy
Garcia's multicultural majority and the honorary whiteness to which

Latinx aspire as they often find their connection to Americanness through Hollywood entertainment.

Elements of the raceless Latinx trend in television are also found in non-specifically Latinx characters played by actors such as Aubrey Plaza (*Parks and Recreation*), whose mixed Puerto Rican/Italian background straddles the line between whiteness and Latinx-ness, Karen Olivo (*Harry's Law*), Oscar Nuñez (*The Office*), and Sarah Ramos (*Parenthood*). This phenomenon includes actors who want to identify as Latinx in their personal lives and publicity promotion, but are happy to play ambiguous roles so as not to be professionally pigeonholed. Another example of the ambiguously Latinx entertainment persona is the now-disgraced Louis C.K., who was brought up partially in Mexico but is of Hungarian descent and is for all purposes a mainstream American, yet because of today's multicultural-tolerant climate, is unconcerned about "coming out" as a Latinx in the entertainment media. Inevitably these actors are fodder for magazines like *Latina* to produce an endless series of clickbait photo galleries about "Actors You Didn't Know Were Latino," subtly underscoring their racelessness.

A Brief Surge in News Websites Targeting US Latinx

In 2011, large media conglomerates launched a surge of new websites and channels targeting the growing number of bilingual, bicultural Latinx. NBC, Huffington Post/AOL, ABC Univision, and Fox (whose Fox and Fox Latino sites have already been accused of duplicity in covering immigration reform from both hard-right and pro-Latinx perspectives) all began new ventures in English with professional journalists, although adhering to the web model of paying writers less than traditional press outlets. The staff at these sites, from assigning editors to reporters, were usually majority Latinx, a situation never before seen at any major English-language media outlets in the United States with the exception of the *Miami Herald*.

While these sites have generated some momentum, NBC Latino was shut down at the end of 2013, its Latinx-themed news folded into the mainstream NBC News site. Yet another experiment, like efforts made in the wake of the late 1990s Latin Pop Explosion, apparently had not passed the test of profitability, and while Latinx stories were still available on the main site, they would not be as prominently featured or directly targeted.

Fox News Latino, which shut down in 2016, used a model similar to that of Hispanic marketing and advertising, providing a Latinx spin on stories—concerning immigration reform, for instance—that on the main Fox news site would have a more conservative perspective. Huffington Post Latino Voices remains a viable site with good coverage of both US Latinx issues and Latin America, but has failed to transcend the main site's pastiche of journalism and clickbait. BuzzFeed has made a major effort to cover Latinx stories on a serious level while maintaining its millennial-oriented clickbait humor pieces that sometimes hit sour notes with stereotypes.

The launch of the Fusion network in September 2013 represented an attempt by ABC/Disney and Univision to create a television network directed at both Latinx and general market millennials. Seduced by the potential of new Latinx media figure Selena Gomez, made famous by the Disney Channel, the network hoped to appeal to millennial, bicultural Latinos and "color-blind" millennial Anglos, but was criticized at the outset for not featuring enough Latinx of color. It also failed to make a commitment to bilingual programming. While largely unexplored by major media, code-switching bilingualism, multiracial awareness, and the subtle impact of America's demographic shift away from white majorities and racial binaries should pave the way for a future that institutionalizes bilingualism along with content in both languages.

After some well-documented financial shortfalls, Fusion continues to exist as a website and cable network increasingly devoted to the general millennial market, with less of a focus on Latinx. By

2016, Disney withdrew from the partnership, leaving the network in Univision's hands. While some new Latinx talent was developed at Fusion, the network failed to establish a strong or influential identity and has for the most part served to expand Univision News anchor Jorge Ramos's profile among English speakers. Univision's subsequent acquisition of millennial favorites such as *The Onion* and the remains of the Gawker sites—Jezebel, Deadspin, Gizmodo, Jalopnik, Lifehacker, and Kotaku—reveal that it is most interested in merging its targeting of young, bilingual, bicultural Latinx with millennials in general.

Social Media, Branding, and Progressive Narcissism

Negrón-Muntaner's Latino Media Gap study ends on a hopeful note by suggesting that Latinx, perhaps in response to their lack of representation in front of and behind the camera, at the editorial desk and as field reporters, were streaming into newly developing digital and social media. After all, with the increasingly indecipherable iterations of Latinx identity, the perfect outlet for Latinx expression may be citizen journalism and DIY media production, whose heavy dose of particularity could approach a universal appeal. According to the study, of the top fifty single-focused YouTube channels with the most subscribers in 2014, 18 percent were produced by and/or featured US Latinx content creators.

Some sites such as Latino Rebels (LR) blatantly adopt the inbound marketing approach, producing content that consists of outrage stories involving either overt racism or racial micro-aggressions and drives data collection and information sharing, ultimately providing a profiling snapshot of millennial Latinx and their friends. Their ethnic-specific approach often falls short of real journalism, but they do provide the important function of rallying the community. LR and sites like it are attempting to gather the myriad Twitter, Instagram, Pinterest, and Snapchat users continuously spewing the minutiae of their existence onto the Internet in order to produce immortal evidence of our endlessly diverse experiences. With movie and television audiences dwindling amid all these myriad distractions, it remains to be seen how important the representation on these sites will be as the century wears on.

Remezcla, a site based in the trend-spattered hinterlands on the border of industrial East Williamsburg and Bushwick, Brooklyn, provides a strong mix of lifestyle stories that encourage a cultural mix between US Latinx and young Latin Americans. The small but capable staff skillfully reflects the quirks in cultural and musical tastes of non-assimilative Latinx, but the site lacks a strong news component. It is an example of a local media group with potential to represent a more authentic view of Latinx in the United States, but is limited by its lack of visibility and threatened by much more powerful corporate media powers.

The problem with Latinx and media going forward is the same one faced by the society at large. Can media be disassociated from its increased relationship with marketing? How can Latinx disrupt social media's encouragement of self-branding at the cost of effective community interaction? How is language being permeated by branding terminology? How much of this manipulative language is controlled by so-called "power users" or people who constantly use social media to reinforce their message and branding?

Throughout my career as a journalist, I have reported on and critiqued many works of Latinx cultural production, as well as the content and function of the media in its representation of Latinx and the statistical data about how many Latinx are involved as the subjects or creators of media. I have usually played the role of activist/advocate in urging that more Latinx become involved in media creation and that those who dominate the mainstream media increasingly represent Latinx in film and television. At one point, in the early 2000s, I wrote a column for the *Nation* using a quotation from a song by Brazilian singer Caetano Veloso that played with the story of Narcissus to argue that video media should become a pool "where Narcissus/Shall be a god who will also know how/To resurrect."

By doing so, I reflected the beliefs of the majority of Latinx activists and other activists of color who have argued for more "inclusion" "in front of and behind the camera" and among the ranks of both writers and editors as well as owners of media production companies, print newspapers, magazines, and even network and cable television stations. There is of course value to a degree of narcissism in the sense that to see oneself positively reflected in the media is empowering and self-affirming and goes a long way towards offsetting the continuing use of negative stereotypes. Sociologists and community activists alike have decried these stereotypes as part of the systemic racism whose effects deny academic opportunities, employment, and even housing to Latinx who may be tainted by a negative perception created by stereotypes.

Yet even as Latinx continue to be portrayed in video entertainment as drug dealers, criminals, and, in the case of women, maids, and as mainstream stories in broadcast and print news continue to overrepresent Latinx as criminals or undocumented immigrants, most of the incremental gains being made don't reflect who Latinx are, culturally and racially. Is our community really making progress by Latinx characters in *Grey's Anatomy*, *Orange Is the New Black*, and *Jane the Virgin*? Does the increased pool of Latinx reporters in trendy web-media outlets such as BuzzFeed and Vox or established media giants such as the *New York Times* really push the envelope?

I've more recently come to feel relief from the fact that, despite so many calls from Latinx advocates that we achieve at least proportional representation in the mainstream entertainment media, almost none of that representation has materialized. While in the past I might have interpreted this as harmful and even hurtful, I think it's significant that Latinx don't readily identify with characters and situations that are ultimately complicit with the myopia of American exceptionalism, an almost total lack of historical analysis, and a lack of critique of the growing inequality that is making the middle class extinct—the same middle class that, through our advocacy, would ostensibly be portrayed by Latinx.

While I have never completely embraced social media and have an aversion to the privacy-invading nature of Facebook, the ownership of media has never been easier, and YouTube, Instagram, and Snapchat stars can be made overnight. While these stars usually reinforce the dominant regressive tendencies of this ascendant period of neoliberalism, they are still largely unfiltered by anyone but themselves. There are times I see young people—Black Lives Matter activists, CopWatch activists, Chicano/Native American activists, Afro-Latino activists, fluid sexual identity activists—expressing aspects of themselves I could never have hoped to express on this scale in an earlier time, working through issues in a way that legitimately resists the dominant discourse.

At the very least, they are putting pressure on the viability of mainstream media. If processing and analyzing this multiplicity of perspectives and insisting on racial and other differences can become a central media activity for Latinx, it could become the most artfully progressive form of new media narcissism of our time. Perhaps, finally, a soul would emerge from the echo chamber.

9

The Latinx Urban Space and Identity

Just as none of us is beyond geography, none of us is completely free from the struggle over geography. That struggle is complex and interesting because it is not only about soldiers and cannons, but also about ideas, about forms, about images and imaginings.

Edward Said, *Culture and Imperialism*

Space is the place.

Sun Ra

Yo no nací en Puerto Rico, Puerto Rico nació en mi.

María Teresa Fernández, a.k.a. Mariposa

María Teresa Fernández's poem "Ode to the Diasporican" has been celebrated in New York Puerto Rican circles as part of the late 1990s refreshing of Nuyorican identity in the wake of the gradual receding of its original generation. Its tagline, "I wasn't born in Puerto Rico/ Puerto Rico was born in me," referred to the way her identity was formed through the transference of Puerto Rican national culture from one island archipelago to another (New York City). In the

poem, the idyllic beaches of Luquillo, Puerto Rico, are transformed
into the gritty urban Orchard Beach off the coast of the Bronx, and the
melodic sounds of the island's coquí tree frogs become "city noise."
The final stanza of the poem is a direct reference to her African-
ness—"my live hair, my black hands," she proclaims, signaling, as
several Nuyorican poets had done before her, that the Urban Latinx
is black, if not exactly African American.

The development of this perspective took place over decades, as
I have described earlier, going back to the early pushback against
racism along the Mexican border and later in Southwestern, Cali-
fornian, and Northeastern cities. The history of Latinx and African
Americans is marked by migrations that in the post–World War II
era made them inheritors of the urban space, where they would form
strong cultural identities forged in their post-migration struggle to
get a taste of the American Dream. In the process, Latinx and African
Americans have experienced deeply personal forms of cultural affiliation and sharing, while at times entering into a forced competition
over dwindling resources and political power. It was the consciousness of a marginalized, excluded people who realized, by virtue of
their own creation and development of an urban culture and of their
identity as colonized people, an irrefutable "right to the city" that
they lived in, to borrow from the terminology of French philosopher
Henri Lefebvre.

The urban identity is shared by Latinx, African Americans, and, to
an extent, Asian Americans. The urban Latinx space is the place where
a new, reconstituted version of hybrid or diasporic Latinx identity
is formed, the site for racial and cultural transformation and where
Latinx created a new urban social practice, partially in response to
urban planning and partially to grapple with exclusion. The hybridity of the Latinx diaspora, combining traditions and culture from the
homeland and the stark alienation of late capitalism, imagined a new
urban identity while our spaces were threatened by their transformation into abstract real estate value, fueled by speculation by outside

investors—spaces that were shaped by the imposition of marginalization and oppression and the people's reaction to it. Ancestral memories from the homeland, from African diasporic and displaced indigenous groups, combined with the experience of a rapidly deindustrializing America.

By claiming the right to the city as living space, urban Latinx are demanding the right to the global center, the center of commercial activity and wealth accumulation, a claim that would logically come from migrants from the periphery. In so much of the American exceptionalist discourse we are told that Latinx want to come to the United States because it is the greatest country on the face of the earth. This doesn't explain why so many migrants are risking their lives in Europe—often by crossing the Strait of Gibraltar into Spain—and facing perhaps even more danger and resistance from Europeans. It's because they, too were colonized and marginalized on the periphery and began seeking the center, not necessarily for its cultural or civilizing aspects but for the "full rights" and economic opportunities accorded to the inhabitants there.

The formation of the urban identity happened over several decades in the twentieth century, the result of interactive sharing and competition between European ethnic groups and people of color. But it emerged in earnest during white flight in the 1960s and 70s, when European ethnics left major US cities for the suburbs, a moment that has come full circle with the phenomenon of gentrification in which suburban capital, personified by the children and grandchildren of white flighters, and global capital—one percenters and investors— attempt to reclaim spaces they abandoned. These are the spaces that incubated urban identity, in many cases the overlapping experiences of blacks and Latinx. It's for this reason that Latinx identity, in whatever form of racial mixture it may exist, lives in shared spaces that, despite clashes and competition, allow Latinx access, in theory and practice, to the collective black.

By the collective black, I'm referring to Eduardo Bonilla-Silva's theorized tripartite racial structure in which "whites" remain dominant, and two new categories are formed including "honorary whites," made up of lighter-skinned Latinx, Arabs, Asians, "mixed-race" Americans (symbolized by the baseball player Derek Jeter), and other "off-whites," and the collective black, which includes African Americans, African and black Caribbean immigrants, Southern Asian Americans, Pacific Islanders, Native Americans, indigenous-identified Latinx, and Afro-Latinx. The use of the term and category "collective black" has the potential to unify those who, whether African American or not, experience exclusion from white privilege and are exposed to the worst ravages of racism and lack of access to social justice. "Collective black" also helps generate an urban Latinx identity that does not restrict itself solely to Afro-Latinx identity or indigenous-focused Xicanx identity and build a common ground between African Americans and Latinx in general, particularly those of the latter who ignore their African or indigenous ancestry.

As described earlier, there was a crucial juncture immediately following the era of national liberation movements where unity began to dissolve on the levels of culture and community politics. After the giddy origins of hip-hop culture in which blacks, Latinx, and other marginalized groups, including Asian Americans and working-class whites (many of the latter staking out a claim to graffiti fame), participated, hip-hop began to consolidate itself around an essential blackness, or a codified urban African American-ness.

Hip-hop culture, as described by writers Tricia Rose, Jeff Chang, and Raquel Z. Rivera, was one of the first responses to the 1970s recession that accelerated white flight and disinvestment in urban areas in the spheres of housing development, infrastructure, education, and small businesses. It was the creation of disenfranchised youth who were so stripped of resources and educational opportunities that they made new forms of music, dance, and visual art that almost entirely reflected the experience of the streets. Yet although this early crystallization of creativity involved a cross section of race, ethnicity, and artistic disciplines, the driving force behind hip-hop culture ultimately became an essentialized representation of black male youth that often excluded other cultural representations. Latinx, Asian Americans, and European ethnics who had contributed mightily to genres such as break dancing, graffiti writing, and DJing were subsumed under the monolithic figure of the rapper, who was necessarily African American and granted the authenticity and authority to become what Chuck D, leader of rap group Public Enemy, called "the CNN of the streets."

For Latinx this process evolved in ambivalent fashion. While break dancing and graffiti writing were marginalized in importance and Latinx rappers obscured their identity in order to be accepted, Latinx in the 90s established different forms of credibility within the hip-hop community. Bobbito García, the son of a Latin jazz musician, joined with partner Stretch Armstrong to produce one of the most influential radio shows about hip-hop, featuring early appearances by rappers including Jay Z. Magazines such as *Stress* and *Urban Latino* chronicled the stories of Latinx rappers, Latinx including Mimi Valdes and Elizabeth Méndez Berry held key positions at *Vibe* magazine, and Kim Osorio had a successful, if controversial tenure at *The Source*. *Nuyorican* rappers such as Big Pun and Fat Joe earned a certain authenticity in the age of the Notorious B.I.G., and West Coast rappers such as Kid Frost and Latin Alliance adapted the conventions and techniques of Los Angeles hip-hop to serve an emerging Chicano need for rap chronicles that reflected life on the boulevards of East Los Angeles.

The distinction between the Chicanx and Nuyorican adaptations of hip-hop is emblematic of different affiliations with blackness. Chicanx MCs tended to emulate black rappers and deliver Chicanx-specific messages; theirs were among the first bodies of hip-hop work with a non–African American focus. As described earlier, Nuyoricans at first obscured their presence, then slowly consolidated their role within New York blackness beginning in the doo-wop era of the

1950s. Nuyorican rappers usually did not address specifically Latinx themes; songs such as "100 Percent" by Big Pun, which used a fair amount of Spanglish and focused on Nuyorican identity, were an aberration. Even the exponents of the late 90s salsa revival—led by musicians such as Marc Anthony, La India, and the band Dark Latin Groove—used R&B affectations to increase their appeal among young people.

There were, however, considerable obstacles to overcome in navigating the black-Latinx divide on the West Coast among Chicanxs, despite the work of several movements, particularly among students and community artists, to recognize new scholarship about the prevalence of Africans in Mexico in the period immediately after the conquest. West Coast neighborhoods are more sharply segregated, and suburban streets less amenable to shared experiences than they are in densely packed Northeastern and Midwestern cities. The prison system's gang-by-race segregation has created powerful disjunctures. Massive immigration from Mexico and Central America has exacerbated wage-differential competition and even resulted in displacement of African Americans from traditional neighborhoods in South Central, some of which have become majority Latinx.

Yet both Nuyoricans and Chicanxs, as well as working-class communities across the United States and the world, are facing the specter of urban gentrification, in which the violence of the market displaces families and communities, deporting them to the urban periphery and gestating an even more anti-democratic urban landscape. The changes can often produce short-term improvement in quality of life and services for a neighborhood that marginalized people enjoy for a limited period before the real estate market eventually displaces them. Just as abandoned factories and storefronts from mid-twentieth-century businesses are reoccupied today by a new creative class of millennial artists, Latinx-owned and -operated bodegas, botánicas, and social clubs have been dwindling to the point that they are sometimes enshrined by locals as informal museums.

Yet while urban neighborhoods could at times be heavily seg-regated, Latinx's mixed-race ambiguity often made them a buffer between African American and white neighborhoods, and the cre-ation of those enclaves involved hybridizing cultural and political activity that was just as important as construction of a national iden-tity. When urban Latinx sometimes say they are part Latinx and part American, this doesn't simply mean part "Anglo-American," but part of the creation of American urban day-to-day life and culture in the second half of the twentieth century. While Latinx and other people of color were dismissed by the city's perception of itself as "white," the creation of urban culture and identity in black and Latinx neigh-borhoods increasingly revealed the neoliberal emptiness of the global city ideal. While writers of the privileged sector bemoaned the global city's emptiness, with its "private" public spaces and corporate con-sumer alienation eviscerating its "working class" or "mom-and-pop store" authenticity, those features never disappeared in barrios and hoods, and were charged there with a new, vibrant authenticity revealing neoliberal America's endemic racism.

As Gareth Millington writes in *"Race," Culture and the Right to the City: Centres, Peripheries, Margins*, the "white city fantasy" is one shared by both "white racists and 'tolerant white multiculturalists' alike"—a line of reasoning that underpins a kind of double prob-lematic facing Latinx who continue to try to hold on to their barrios. The overt racism of redlining has evolved into one that denies living space to Latinx on the basis of race either through informal personal encounters or, more insidiously, through escalating rents that effectively eliminate most Latinx from the neighborhoods in which they grew up. And while there is a long history of progres-sive whites involved in the arts or social work who authentically enmesh themselves into these neighborhood spaces, "tolerant multi-culturalists" often pave the way for accelerated gentrification by not fully committing themselves to preserving the neighborhood's ethno-racial character once they move there. These are the sort that will sometimes express themselves in pioneering colonial settler codes like "I was the first to move into that neighborhood; no one was living there," fail to engage with members of the community despite their general liberal leanings, and adhere to the white city fantasy that "conceives of the city as a space structured around white culture, where non-white 'ethnics' are merely objects to be moved or removed according to will." The pioneering of urban hoods gives way to a displacement—something caused not just by rent fluctuations but also by the deteriorating situation for people of color in the United States that can result in homelessness—which, as Millington observes, creates a fragmentation of cities characterized by a chain of hierarchical ghettoes in varying degrees of proximity to the utopian urban "center," where privileged fragments of the public transit infrastructure are preserved and newly constructed bike lanes and pedestrian malls proliferate.

Urban spaces can be analyzed through Lefebvre's three-leveled structure. Barrios are, in practical terms, spaces with a plentitude of low-cost or affordable housing units occupied by lower rungs of the social order. They often contain dense clusters of public housing and serve as a zone where service economy and marginalized workers— those that make up the necessary 5 percent unemployed reserve labor force that keeps a capitalist economy working—live. They are also acted on by outside forces seeking to "plan" and "redevelop" them. Planners—influenced in New York by the early to mid-twentieth-century tyrannical agenda of Robert Moses—originally constructed modern high-rise buildings to act as public housing with park-like areas surrounding them, disrupting the oppressive rectangular grid of streets that dominate Manhattan and large swaths of the outer boroughs. Now planners and their partners, government technocrats, seek to re-zone the remaining low-rise structures in barrios so that market rate housing can be erected and new spaces dominated by big-box corporate chains can operate. Finally barrio spaces are imagined spaces, where difficult lives, resulting sometimes in success but often in tragedy, become part of the cultural memory of the area through neighborhood rituals, traditional folkloric cultural practices, and the invention of modern and postmodern music such as salsa and hip-hop, canonized through written poetry and the spoken word. This is the partially lived-in, partially imagined space that is facing the bulldozers of real estate speculation.

These spaces were constructed with the intention of reflecting the essence of the people who lived in them. Luis Aponte-Parés's 1998 essay "Lessons from El Barrio—The East Harlem Real Great Society/Urban Planning Studio: A Puerto Rican Chapter in the Fight for Urban Self-Determination" begins with a discussion of how legendary community activist Antonia Pantoja locates the forming of "community consciousness" in a constructed political-cultural environment called El Barrio. "Puerto Ricans, like other ethnic groups before them, began reshaping and appropriating the otherwise ordinary industrial city landscapes by building and claiming enclaves that *looked like them,*" notes Aponte-Parés about the period between 1945 and 1960. El Barrio, he continues, became a paradigmatic "representational space" for the place where New York Puerto Ricans and other Latino migrants construct their lived experience.

Arlene Dávila's important book *Barrio Dreams* identifies how the conception of El Barrio as a representational space intersects with the gentrification of East Harlem. The neighborhood has the most concentrated tracts of public housing in Manhattan and has served as a receptacle for surplus labor during the period of disinvestment in urban areas and safety net programs for the poor. It is also one of many barrios that have been central in the formation of the so-called urban underclass. It has since become the focus of rezoning and been penetrated by big box drug stores and a major shopping mall, as well as several neoliberal charter schools. It has also been targeted as an area for tourism, specifically because of its Latinx-dominated population that was key to the creation of salsa music and political activism in the 1970s (one street is named after Tito Puente; a sign celebrates the church that was taken over by the Young Lords in 1969). Yet there has been a strong reaction against this agenda by not only the community that forms East Harlem but also the larger Nuyorican community from all over the metropolitan area, who feel the need to protect the space as a way of preserving their own culture.

Latinx communities are being threatened by gentrification in every major US city, and although the resistance involves nationalist calls for protecting the representational space, the issue is strongly affected by class. One of the best predictors of the gentrification of a neighborhood is a decrease in the black population—even in Latinx neighborhoods. The displacement of the black poor is not usually mitigated by black gentry in barrios—though in Latinx neighborhoods, gentrifiers can often be Latinx from a higher social class, part of the creative or professional class, or from privileged sectors in Latin America. Some writers have described this as "*gente*-fication," a pun on the Spanish word for "people." In general, however, drops in the Latinx population in East Harlem, Williamsburg, Bushwick, the Mission District in San Francisco, and Boyle Heights in Los Angeles have been accompanied by an increase in the Latinx population of peripheral areas further away from urban centers.

Neoliberal urban redevelopment is the logical conclusion of a twenty to thirty-year period of depopulation and disinvestment, which purportedly can be remedied by private reinvestment, without regard to the idea that an ethno-racial group's "well-being" can be affected by the evisceration of its core neighborhoods. This reinvestment, however, was preceded by an identifiable "stage" pattern of gentrification based on "risk-taking" involving artists, students, and sometimes gay people, ultimately resulting in the creation of a youth-oriented lifestyle often completely disassociated with the neighborhoods within which it was incubated. These developments did not follow a linear path to an exploitative agenda, as they also coincided with several well-meaning attempts to integrate artists, young activists, and barrio residents.

The community group CHARAS, founded by the activist Chino García on the Lower East Side, was an attempt to combine Latinx and Latin American activism with progressive white artist groups. This contrasted with the work of a space a few blocks downtown called ABC No Rio, which celebrated anarchist and leftist artwork and hardcore punk and argued that the neighborhood needed to be protected against real estate forces that would disrupt some of the productive, if relatively isolated interactions between local Latinx and downtown artists. The East Village Art Explosion that made the edgy neighborhood popular in the early to mid-1980s was originally fueled by leftist, politically committed artists—whose guerrilla-style art show, The Real Estate Show, ultimately gave birth to the ABC No Rio space. In the South Bronx, brothers Charlie and John Ahearn and Jane Dickson used the Fashion Moda space to form a welcoming intersection between visual artists and local black and Latinx youth. Yet the proliferation of galleries inevitably led to more apolitical spaces that sought to capitalize on the celebrity of the moment, and Wall Street money from the birth of the finance capital era of the mid-1980s paved the way for the marginalization of political art and the neighborhood's Latinx residents.

Ironically, many Lower East Side artists alienated by this glitz moved across the East River to Williamsburg in the late 80s and early 90s, with the resulting community segregating itself from the traditionally Puerto Rican area Los Sures and ultimately pioneering the Greenpoint/Bushwick scenes that serve as a backdrop for the HBO series *Girls*, a pop culture phenomenon criticized for its dearth of people of color. On the Lower East Side and in the East Village there were brief periods of "mixed community" utopias in which the racial/class mix of the neighborhoods became very diverse, and longtime residents enjoyed the benefits of reduced crime rates and better services. But those periods were short-lived and doomed to extinction by forces that would create the mid-2000s real estate bubble and 2008 financial crash.

The contradictions of the seeming benefits of "mixed communities" are clear. While they are promoted by both the government and commercial sectors as panaceas for the uncomfortable segregation of major cities, majority-white communities are not encouraged to be "mixed." Many academic studies have shown that outside of some productive exchanges, the gentrification process rarely achieves sustained meaningful social mixing between whites and people of color.

Clara Irazabal Zurita, professor of urban planning at Columbia University, writes that urban planning elites engage in "a top-down approach that has shifted resources and attention from the areas that would benefit Latinos the most, like education, housing, and job creation." Neoliberal projects to address these issues often entail the creation of charter schools that take away resources from public education while eroding the power of teachers' unions, the creation of affordable housing policies that favor large real estate developers while keeping the number of affordable housing units static; and public projects that encourage job development through the use of big box chain stores that pay minimum wages and lack long-term job security.

Acting from the top down, Mayor Michael Bloomberg's administration, which governed New York from 2002 to 2011, rezoned about 23 percent of the city. Rezoning a neighborhood can have different effects: "upzoning" a neighborhood allows for larger buildings to be built, usually resulting in high-rise development, while "downzoning" limits development to preserve the architectural or historical quality of a neighborhood. Neighborhoods where blacks and Latinos live have been upzoned, while fashionable Greenwich Village has been downzoned. While rezoning and policies like it on a national scale go back to the 1970s, the Bloomberg administration aggressively implemented this policy on a large scale as a result of the immediate aftermath of the 9/11 attacks. For Latinx—the vast majority of whom rent in New York City—this has had significant consequences.

Another planning policy that has been championed by Mayor de Blasio's administration is called inclusionary zoning, in which the development of neighborhoods is organized around the rewarding of city lands to large-scale real estate developers who are in turn compelled to "include" a small percentage of affordable apartments in their massive projects. The implementation of inclusionary zoning has created far less affordable housing than promised, and many community advocates say the resulting increase in property values in the neighborhood has accelerated displacement. The effect of inclusionary housing in Williamsburg, for instance, has been to transform it from a working-class neighborhood into a playground for young bohemians, some of whom are raising families, while 40 percent of the Latinx population, by some estimates, has left.

East Harlem: A Case Study

My personal interest in El Barrio/Spanish Harlem has been forged by the fact that it was the site of my parents' arrival from Puerto Rico during the postwar Great Migration. In what is a typical "immigrant" story, they migrated—as they were both born US citizens —separately and lived just a few blocks apart until they were introduced by members of my father's family. There are times when I go to Jefferson Park on 114th Street and First Avenue—a place now deeply entrenched in the nascent Mexican community in the neighborhood—and imagine my father navigating the streets leading to the walkup where he lived with my grandmother and aunt, his lightish skin allowing him to dodge the threat of Italian street gangs bent on stemming the tide of Puerto Rican migrants.

Yet as a journalist I began to pick up on several cues I'd received during my residence in and witnessing of the gentrification of the Lower East Side in the 80s and 90s. I had been hearing from acquaintances that students and artists were trickling into the neighborhood, prowling streets that had been steeped in barrio ways since the 1950s.

But because New York was in the throes of a wild period of real estate speculation it was happening faster, and without the period of "mixed community" that made the Lower East Side briefly paradisaical in the 1990s.

When I first began to investigate El Barrio/Spanish Harlem, it was still considered by some an escape from downtown for those newer residents made skittish by the World Trade Center attacks. A middle-school student of Mexican origin voiced the concern that "ever since 9/11 there's all these people from downtown around here." Artist and El Barrio/Spanish Harlem native James De La Vega, who would abandon his artist storefront owned by low-income housing developer Hope Community a couple of years later, expressed the point of view of many of the new cadre of young "right to stay" types with a painting consisting of this scrawled, graffiti-style legend, "Don't think for a moment that we haven't noticed that the 96th Street boundary has moved further north."

In the early 2000s, East Harlem was the focus of something called the Uptown New York project, part of a "river to river" development initiative, which would include a "Latino-themed mini-city featuring performance spaces, recording studios, entertainment spaces, and … housing for artists." The problem with this project is that it was intended to be designed by a Los Angeles–based firm and amounted to a kind of Disneyfication of the neighborhood that would not include any input from residents. The form and function of the plan was directed by the Bloomberg-founded Latin Media & Entertainment Commission, which followed from the mayor's fixation on tourist development and large-scale events, as with his failed attempt to stage the Olympic Games in New York.

A sizable and vocal opposition arose, particularly at a meeting held at what was becoming the community space with the most authenticity, the Julia De Burgos Center on 106th Street and Lexington Avenue. A number of emerging voices spoke out in opposition to the project, including activist Marina Ortiz, architect and community board member Gary Anthony Johnson, the African American Community Association of the East Harlem Triangle, and an activist who would eventually run for city council, Melissa Mark-Viverito, who was born in Puerto Rico. In the end, the $1 billion Uptown New York project was canceled in May 2006 because of "community opposition that included concerns that the project would aggravate the area's high asthma rate."

Many contemporary studies of El Barrio/Spanish Harlem have drawn attention to the subliminal conflict between recent Mexican immigrants, who appear to many to have "taken over" the 116th Street commercial strip, and Puerto Ricans who want to stake nationalist claims to the neighborhood. In a documentary called *Whose Barrio?*, which I co-directed with Laura Rivera in 2008, we contrasted two forms of confronting gentrification that seemed to fall along ethnic lines. The first was adopted by Puerto Ricans and African Americans, who worked through connections with local politicians and community boards. The other was exemplified by the efforts of a group called Movement for Justice in El Barrio (MJB), a Zapatista-style direct-action group that primarily concerned itself with advocating for primarily Mexican tenants of a wide swath of buildings owned by an infamous slumlord named Steven Kessner.

MJB has a radical working-class agenda that does not trust established political channels to effect change. Their main concession to working within the system has been connecting tenants with lawyers who then have sued Kessner for various violations, including allowing apartments to deteriorate to unsafe conditions and the use of subtle and unsubtle practices to encourage tenants to move out. But besides this, they often take to the streets to protest, and one of their main targets was City Councilwoman Melissa Mark-Viverito; in the film they even went as far as to demonstrate in front of the house she owns in the neighborhood. Mark-Viverito has long been associated with progressive causes, particularly because of her time as a union leader at local 1199 and in the student- and worker-led movement to force the US Navy out of an island off the coast of Puerto Rico called Vieques, which had long been used for target practice. During the time we filmed our documentary, she alluded to the desirability of a mixed-income neighborhood while staunchly defending the existence of public housing and the "right to stay put" and vitality created by the nationalist movement to defend the Latino character of the neighborhood.

With much chagrin, she accused Movement for Justice in El Barrio of being outside agitators who refuse to work within the established channels set up through her work with Hope Community and their tenant advocacy—an accusation in conflict with one of her early acts as city councilwoman, which had been to set up the East Harlem Anti-displacement Task Force. This task force was made up of constituencies loyal to her, such as Hope Community and various tenant associations in local public and Mitchell-Lama housing. Another important partner, Picture the Homeless, would stage public events to try to highlight the warehousing of apartments, revealing row upon row of empty apartments held by absentee landlords. The use of "East Harlem" rather than "Spanish Harlem/El Barrio" and "anti-displacement" rather than "anti-gentrification" seem, through interviews with Mark-Viverito and a representative of Hope Community in *Whose Barrio?*, to have been concessions to the inevitable change represented by insatiable real estate capital.

The final sequence of *Whose Barrio?* focuses on a town meeting called by Mark-Viverito to discuss a new development project called the East 125th Street Project at a Spanish Harlem school auditorium during which she allowed input from the community. The new project was a scaled-down version of Uptown New York, involving the construction of some high-rise buildings, a modest shopping center, and space for community organizations. City Councilwoman Melinda Katz delivered a presentation about the availability of affordable housing, but without any critical analysis of its affordability based on the larger area's average median income (AMI), instead relying on the AMI of the entire metropolitan area—2.5 times that of local neighborhood residents.

It doesn't take long before the meeting devolves into a shouting match between opponents of the project—a coalition of tenants, members of Community Board 11, small business owners threatened with eminent domain takeovers of the land on which their businesses sit, the Harlem Tenant Council, and the Harlem Triangle Association—and Mark-Viverito. In one of the more dramatic confrontations, CB 11 member Gary Anthony Johnson, who is African American, addresses Mark-Viverito:

> This project is not going to create the level of affordable housing that we as a community envisioned. This project has been structured so that only large-scale developers can compete and get this. There is no way this project—three blocks—should have gone to one major developer.

Mark-Viverito responds that Johnson is being disingenuous about his objections, that the measures in the project "had been agreed to every step of the way," and that he is grandstanding for political purposes. Eerily enough, Arlene Dávila had opened the "Times Squaring of El Barrio" chapter of her 2008 book *Latino Spin: Public Image and the Whitewashing of Race* with this quotation from Johnson during the hearings for the Uptown New York project two years earlier:

> We want a project, but a project that's planned by us, designed by us, and programmed for us ... Don't let this massive project be predetermined and solely given to one developer.

The sequence ends as the town hall audience continues to insist that they don't want the East 125th Street Project, yet Mark-Viverito joins the majority in the city council and votes it through. "These are actions which move the public policy further along," said Mark-Viverito, explaining her vote. "It's not going to get to the point where everybody is 100 percent happy. My job now as a public official is to balance those interests."

But catastrophic events in the US economy in general had the effect of completely undermining this logic. Months after the vote, the main partner in the project, General Growth Properties, a firm that overextended itself by buying up massive malls around the country, lost 90 percent of its value and became an early victim of the quickly evolving recession of 2008. The ambitious goals of the project have since been suspended or scaled back.

Several years later, after Mark-Viverito was appointed speaker of the city council, the city's second most powerful position behind the mayor, several elements of the failed East 125th Street Project drama reemerged. By that time, Mark-Viverito appeared to have absorbed elements from "Participatory Budgeting," a concept whereby residents participate in choosing how the district spends money, and used them to give the mayor's upzoning agenda a streamlined feel of neighborhood participation. By partnering with several community groups that have received considerable amounts of funding from her ability to determine the recipients of the city budget's discretionary funds, she created something called "The East Harlem Neighborhood Plan."

The plan produced an elaborate brochure that earmarked money for specific redevelopment projects, outlined concerns of local residents about possible threats from development to public spaces, and called for robust commitments to local small businesses and, of course, affordable housing. Yet local activists such as Josmar Trujillo, a journalist, and Andrew J. Padilla, a filmmaker, were strongly critical of the procedure. As Trujillo wrote, "Padilla believes de Blasio is strategically trying make the impression that working-class communities of color are leading the zoning process (i.e. Viverito's meeting), in contrast to the famously autocratic style of former mayor Mike Bloomberg." Padilla also characterized the process of upzoning as one that favored the agenda of real estate developers, and argued that the East Harlem Neighborhood Plan was designed to manufacture community consent for their eventual displacement. The East Harlem compromise has the earmarks of progressive neoliberalism at the expense of the collective black.

The story of East Harlem is instructive since it involves blacks and Latinx of different social classes and national origin grappling with what are ultimately issues of class struggle. In five to ten years, East Harlem may very well still have a considerable number of Latinx residents—some upwardly mobile, others the impoverished lucky enough to win a lottery for one of the few affordable housing units— and a fairly well-developed, tourist-friendly circuit of cultural institutions, ranging from El Museo del Barrio to some restaurants or music venues, but with an AMI closer to $75–$80,000 a year, the median for the metropolitan area as a whole. This means that the vast majority of the people who gave the space meaning and intangible spirit will be gone. Will it still be a Latinx neighborhood? Possibly. But what does that mean for Latinx, and how could the idea of that space survive without strong cultural underpinnings?

This is a problem that is being confronted, or will be at some point if urban redevelopment according to the neoliberal framework continues in the future, by many Latinx neighborhoods in the United States, although there are some neighborhoods where the fight may already be over. The extraordinary conditions in San Francisco, for instance, combined with a desirable housing stock and majority of Latinx, who comprised about 50 percent of the neighborhood's population, being renters, created conditions for a turnover at a much higher pace of acceleration than many other Latinx threatened areas. Gentrifiers in that area come from the Bay Area's sprawling tech sector, one of the most cash-flush micro-economies in the United States. The killing of Alex Nieto in that city's Bernal Heights neighborhood took place after new residents connected to the tech sector had racially profiled him by perceiving his red San Francisco 49ers jacket as a sign of possible gang affiliation.

The Mission had long been in a process of gentrification begun by an influx of young people affiliated with music and the visual arts, intensifying during a period of increasing influx of immigrants from El Salvador, a group that has been moving into areas previously dominated by Mexicans in cities all over California and the Southwest. A 1986 California law called the Ellis Act allowed owners to evict a tenant if the owner resided in the building for thirty-six months following the eviction; the owner would be allowed to remove the building from the real estate market and sell it as a single-family home or condominiums. By the early 2000s, the Mission had the highest eviction rates in the United States. The telltale signs of gentrification's systematic process included a flood of shops and restaurants that local residents could not afford to patronize, and an increase in street-level policing that had the effect of making young Latinx uncomfortable just being outside in the neighborhood.

Latinx-flavored businesses have closed, legendary murals have been whitewashed by new owners, and neighborhood schools, having abandoned bilingualism to a large extent due to late 90s legislation, have jettisoned curricula that focused on Mexican culture and history. Yet it's important to remember that the Mission and neighborhoods like it have always been more diverse than their apparent affiliation with Latin-ness would suggest. African Americans and Asian Americans, including Pacific Islanders and Filipinos, played roles in the Mission, just as African Americans and other Latinx groups helped create the history of East Harlem. Joe Bataan, one of East Harlem's most beloved proponents of the Afro-Latinx Cuban/soul music called bugalú, was from an African American Filipino mixed marriage, but had been such an integral part of East Harlem's social fabric that his band was one of the genre's two or three most celebrated acts.

Recent studies suggest that in a kind of twist, the importation of Latinx immigrant labor, which is often undocumented, is associated with the gentrification of rural areas from Wyoming and Colorado to the exurbs of Atlanta and upstate New York. The importation of such labor allows real estate developers to turn an even higher profit in the sales and maintenance of such properties, in the same way that the exploitation of such labor makes high-end restaurants in gentrifying urban areas profitable. The remote nature of these locations can also enhance the potential for exploitation of these workers, as their relative isolation resembles the conditions of a plantation.

Although Latinx immigration to the South dates back to the Spanish incursions in Western Florida and along the Gulf Coast in the eighteenth and nineteenth centuries, as well as Mexican workers in New Orleans and Mississippi in the early 1920s, there is a renewed focus on Latinx in the South because of the immigration explosion of the late twentieth century. While some workers were directly imported into certain Southern cities and towns by labor contractors or ties to previously settled families, much of the migration resulted from Latinx who had a history in cities such as Houston and moved on to areas in Georgia when the Houston labor market became competitive. By 2010, there were almost 3 million Latinx in eight Southern states, a tenfold increase since 1980. While Latinx may be subject to gentrification pressure in Atlanta, their dispersal through smaller cities in the South puts off that problem.

Yet it is important to consider the possibilities for Latinx in the South vis-à-vis their ability to interact with the urban Latinx framework or engage in coalitions with African Americans. While the lessening of immigration in the last few years due to the decline in the US economy and increased border enforcement may have the effect of making African Americans less threatened in the labor market, other factors may inhibit Southern Latinx's ability to join the "collective black." In most of the South's urban areas Latinx and African Americans are highly segregated, and the atmosphere of increased deportations may inhibit Latinx even further from making alliances. While there are trendy stories of crosscultural connections represented by the likes of Kap G, an Atlanta-area rapper who has collaborated with African American rappers including T.I. and Wiz Khalifa, his adaptation to urban Latinx via bilingual lyrics and descriptions of the Latinx Southern experience are unusual. The post-industrial service economy does not provide the conditions that made the creation of urban identity possible: manufacturing jobs, a dense population of working people of color, neighborhoods that defy current levels of segregation.

Black or Brown? The Ambiguous Shades of Coalition Politics

One of the things complicating urban identity, potential coalition building between people of color, and the possibility of Latinx taking their place in the collective black is the nomenclature of colorized identity. Many Latinx have become comfortable with the use of "brown" to describe themselves, and the phrase *black and brown community* is often used to refer to African Americans and Latinx. The notion of brown as a label is obvious enough, and it seems to adhere to the notion that Latinx can proactively choose to identify with racial difference as a path to productive gathering of political power.

Yet in many ways this label is problematic, because it can be used by Latinx to exclude blackness from their identity as the failed Latin American mestizaje ideology did. In some ways brown represents a step forward in reinterpreting or reconfiguring the idealism of mestizaje, when it was used by Chicanxs in the 1970s as a way to describe their new idea of *raza* that strongly identified with the working class, indigenous roots, and defiance in the face of racialization by Anglo-America. Thirty years later in *Brown*, what he describes as his "little Caliban book," Richard Rodriguez made the case that brown, mixture, and homoerotic desire come together to point America to its post-racial future.

This perspective is merely an updating of Vasconcelos's cosmic superiority myth of futurism and mixture, using gender and sex-preference ambiguity as metaphors for a brown hegemony. In one of his most condescending moments, Rodriguez wonders when African Americans will admit that they are mixed, and implies that choosing blackness keeps them from accessing the transcendent race-lessness of whiteness. "What I want for African Americans is white freedom. The same as I wanted for myself," he writes, assuming that whiteness is not belabored by prejudgment and that it acts as the standard discourse for the post-racial individual.

I've already pointed to the real question in the Latinx race debate: when we will be able to fully own up to and understand our blackness, whether it is through direct ancestral ties with African DNA or the societally imposed status of structural racism that enforces collective blackness. In effective political terms, brownness signifies a one-way ticket to obscurity in the face of a still pervasive racial binary. Brown asks racial discourse to observe that there is another, complicating layer of race discrimination that will ultimately be deprioritized, given whites' inability to reckon with racism towards blacks.

Even worse, brown can tend to drag Latinx down the road of competing with blacks in degrees of suffering. This struggle will never be intelligible or logical and would produce only fruitless bitterness and further diminution of political power if Latinx convince America that their suffering should be prioritized over black suffering. This kind of logic began to appear around the early 2000s in response to predictions that Latinx would surpass African Americans as the country's largest minority, indicating that the importance of Latinx suffering is assured only because of its swelling demographic clout.

It also turns out that *brown* is a word that African Americans, often in a very loving sense, use to refer to themselves in casual conversation and on the Internet, which is burgeoning with blogs devoted to brown girls and hashtags such as #smartbrowngirls. Is this a different brown from mestizos who fancy themselves descended from Aztecs, Yaquis, or Mayans? There is also a sizable number of college student groups who use brown to identify themselves as being of South Asian ancestry.

I spent some years as a journalist covering an outbreak of police brutality in New York against Latinx, mostly Puerto Rican, and a movement to combat it led by ex-member of the Young Lords Richie Pérez. While not completely aligned with Al Sharpton, he went about his organizing in a style reminiscent of Sharpton's tactics and helped to create the sense of an urban Latinx community motivated to protect themselves from racial discrimination by the police. I marched alongside families and examined autopsy photos of victims beaten so badly that eyes were displaced from sockets, skulls crushed, thoraxes smashed.

By odd coincidence, soon after these cases peaked, accompanied by a couple of summers of rioting by Dominican residents of Washington Heights objecting to police brutality, the prominent victims of police overzealousness became African Americans again. High-profile cases such as those of Kevin Cedeno, Patrick Dorismond, Abner Louima, and Amadou Diallo, who were actually not so much African American but rather black Caribbean and African immigrants, took over the headlines and seemingly diminished Pérez's movement. Yet the families in that movement joined with ranks led by Sharpton instead, and that synergy helped lead to Sharpton himself being arrested in an act of civil disobedience against the US Navy's base in Puerto Rico's offshore island of Vieques, something that resulted in him serving six months in prison. It did not result in a competition between Latinx and African Americans over who had suffered more casualties.

It is therefore vital that Latinx remain cautious of competing with African Americans about deaths at the hands of police. Some articles in the mainstream press have in fact alluded to the lack of press coverage of Latinx deaths at the hands of police during the week that the horrific deaths of Philando Castile and Alton Sterling were streamed over the Internet (likely an effect simply of the spectacle-driven nature of the media, which soaked up the visceral video footage available). Rather than continue to speculate about whether they have a role in movements such as Black Lives Matter, Latinx should understand that BLM can't help but include them as long as they claim racial difference from whiteness.

Even the founding of Black Lives Matter has two interesting Latinx connections. The group started as a response to the tragic death of Trayvon Martin at the hands of George Zimmerman, who, as half-Peruvian, is a visible symbol of the unresolved racism of Latin Americans. One of the founders of BLM, Alicia Garza, who is dedicated to speaking out against police abuse of African Americans and blacks, is married to a man of Mexican descent. And one of the main organizers of the Movement for Justice in New York, a key player in BLM demonstrations as well as movements for criminal justice reform, is Carmen Perez, a Chicana from California.

Afro-Latinidad and Urban Resistance

The emergence of the Afro-Latinx identity in the United States is a significant factor in cementing the importance of urban Latinx identity. With its origins rooted in the early experiences of Piri Thomas, Julia de Burgos, Mario Bauzá, and Jesús Colón, the Nuyorican movement, and the unique immigration of Panamanians to Brooklyn neighborhoods such as Bedford Stuyvesant, Afro-Latinidad has spawned several organizations, such as the Afro Latino Project and the Afro-Latino Forum, and a major anthology, *The Afro-Latina Reader*, edited by the late Juan Flores and his surviving partner Miriam Jiménez Román. The space created by these organizations helps to mitigate the difficult contradictions for Afro-Latinx who are often judged as being too black to be Latinx and too Latinx to be black.

One of the most significant roles these movements play is pointing out the unsustainable idea that Latinidad is clearly distinct from

African American-ness. They also bring a renewed awareness that Latin America's mestizaje idealism is an exclusionary form of racism that may be even worse than US racism. Also included in the discourse of Afro-Latinidad is the understanding of how urban and African American culture has reverberated in Latin America itself, and that Latin American cities, whose youth culture is forming its own hip-hop and reggaetón music groups, are creating constituencies that identify with US-based urban Latinx identity.

This universality of urban culture that one finds in a city such as New York has a definite impact on new immigrant groups, even if they had previously distanced themselves from blackness. While many young Mexican immigrants in New York forge a loyalty to Mexican traditions from the homeland, they increasingly form part of a generalized hip-hop youth culture that is taking a central place in their identity. Students I've interviewed from Brooklyn to Staten Island, like many immigrant youth before them, have a distinct loyalty to their American-ness, and that American-ness is strongly shaped by urban Latinx culture.

Marketers tend to view this growing urban multiculturalism with the spin originally developed by Guy Garcia. Young, hip people of color, whose very existence seems to question racial and sexual binaries, have formed a melting pot of consumption that will ultimately be the driving force of the consumer-based economy. But is it the new mainstream, or the new resistance?

As street demonstrations and online chatter seem to demonstrate a new urban flow of black, brown, yellow, red, queer, and white voices of struggle coming out of the gentrifying border-spaces of Bushwick, where working-class blacks and Latinx critique and at times check the unbridled intrusion of the elite creative class into their neighborhoods, a different dialogue is developing. They are giving voice to what was once called the irrational political correctness of the 1994 Whitney Biennial, where white lives were target practice for an emerging class of creative people of color. As Lefebvre might have said, the reclaiming and disruption of the white fantasy of the urban center by a politically aware throng of urban multiculturalists is the key to any revolutionary moment. The question is, will they take over the public square or be undercut by a silent, passive consumerist majority that is increasingly made up of people of color?

10

Dismantling the Master's House

The Latinx Imaginary and
Neoliberal Multiculturalism

Prospero, you are the master of illusion.
Lying is your trademark.
And you have lied so much to me
(Lied about the world, lied about me)
that you have ended by imposing on me
an image of myself.

Caliban, from Shakespeare's *The Tempest*

You don't have to have white skin anymore to become white.

Eric Liu, *The Accidental Asian*

The process of racialization in the United States is a double-edged sword. An ever-shifting set of codes and stereotypes is imposed on us, and then there is who we think we are, and how we are actively constructing ourselves. Yet despite the explosion of negative imagery and overt racism unleashed by the white nationalist Trump presidency, the mainstream United States remains on a path towards racelessness that was predicted by Latin America's own race discourse. The challenge for Latinx is how to define themselves within that context. One of the central goals of this book is to provide a set of discursive tools to allow Latinx to escape the neoliberal branding foisted upon them and engage in a productive conversation not only with Anglo-America but with the rest of the American hemisphere, and the world, too.

Latinx in the twenty-first century are still an enigma, a relatively impenetrable target group growing in size and potential force, but we have already discussed at length that the kind of force it will be remains to be seen. The sleeping giant metaphor is nebulous, as the extent of our interconnectedness and common ground remains undefined. Yet there is a strong sense that Latinx are an oppositional force, an outside voice of a counter-discourse that, like African Americans, knows the inside of American culture all too well, and has the potential to transform the idea of Anglo-America. But will we provoke change, or are we destined, as is often suggested by many of our contemporary Latinx leaders, to simply seek a way to fit in?

The ideological reach of neoliberalism—disrupted as it may be by Trumpian neofascism—is crucial to the discussion of the Latinx future because foreign-born Latinx have become an increasingly larger percentage of the total Latinx population. In 1960 only 16 percent of Latinx were foreign born, but by 2014 that figure was up to 54 percent. This means that a large percentage, if not a clear majority of Latinx have experienced the United States through a neoliberal lens, largely distanced from the ideological stances and anti-racist and anti-colonial struggles of the civil rights era. Yet the population growth that is rapidly increasing the demographic percentage of Latinx (as consumers and/or voters) in the United States comes by and large from new births, and these children will become hybrid American-Latinx based on their upbringing, physical location, and the historical moment into which they mature—the current moment being almost as tumultuous as the 1960s.

The percentage of Mexicans, Puerto Ricans, and Cubans in the total Latinx population is also declining, meaning that newer groups with fewer or no ties to previous political struggles are emerging. Proficiency in English is also rising, something that may expand Latinx access to "prime" English-language information, freeing them from the telenovelistic parodies from networks such as Univision. But there is also evidence that suggests a decline in bilingualism and the use of Spanish as a second language for Latinx, which may limit their hemispheric and global perspective. Yet most important is the reality that this emerging population group is dominated by youth, with almost half of US-born Latinx younger than eighteen years of age in mid-2016.

The migration of several new national constituencies of Latinx to the United States has created significant changes in how we see Latinx as a group: an imperfect, curiously unstable constellation of ethno-racial realities. These changes are subject to one of neoliberalism's operative contradictions—opening borders to trade provokes a stronger reaction against the free flower of labor across them, making citizenship a major source of contention. A sizable percentage of new Latinx come to the United States profoundly disempowered by their lack of citizenship, which even island-born Puerto Ricans have had since 1917, millions of Mexicans have maintained since the absorption of northern Mexico by the United States in 1848, and Cubans have obtained relatively easily as a reward for defecting from the Castro Revolution.

On the East Coast, one of the most significant new groups are migrants from the Dominican Republic, largely concentrated in New York and other cities on the Northeast Corridor such as Boston and Philadelphia. With a population of about 1.5 million, Dominicans are the fifth-largest Latinx group in the United States, their migration here a direct result of US foreign policy in the Caribbean. After more than thirty years of the onerous dictatorial reign of Rafael Trujillo, instability in the Dominican Republic in the period after his assassination in 1961 provoked an intervention from the United States. Hoping to prevent further unrest that might result in a second Communist revolution in the Caribbean, the United States encouraged the emigration of potentially left-leaning sectors of the middle and upper classes.

Dominicans are now marginally the largest Latinx group in New York City, and their progress has been measured by the literary success of Junot Díaz, a growing number of prominent athletes and actors, and a significant presence in New York City politics. Peggy Levitt's groundbreaking work *The Transnational Villagers* characterizes Dominicans as quintessential examples of a new kind of transnational citizen because of the relatively free movement between East Coast cities and the Dominican Republic, the large amount of remittances sent back to the island by migrants, and the reach of national and local Dominican politics into Dominican communities in the United States, where members of the diaspora are allowed to vote in the island's elections.

East Coast Dominican experience, as research by Ramón Grosfoguel, Chloe Geras, and Jorge Duany has shown, ironically parallels that of East Coast Puerto Ricans. Saddled with non-citizen status, Dominicans often find it useful to pretend to be Puerto Rican so as not to invoke suspicion they might lack citizenship documentation. In this way, they are racialized as Puerto Ricans—perceived as being a dark or mixed-race Caribbean people with limited education and professional skills. Their presence in the United States to create an escape valve during the explosive years after Trujillo's fall was kept so far below the radar that their higher levels of education and class standing were not rewarded. While not quite possessing the social capital of Cuban émigrés, their skills and levels of education were similar, yet professional degrees that were recognized in South Florida for Cuban exiles often were not in New York. Therefore, Dominicans' survival strategies involved moving into Puerto Rican neighborhoods and investing in businesses such as bodegas that Puerto Ricans were increasingly giving up because many had decided to move back to the islands with the profits they made or had raised families that no longer wanted to continue the business.

In addition, Dominicans exist in a parallel universe of racial identification vis-à-vis Nuyoricans. While the experience of New York racism has tended to increase Puerto Ricans' identification with blackness, Dominicans, despite being generally darker than Puerto Ricans, have "for the most part, denied their blackness," according to Dominican scholar Silvio Torres-Saillant's essay "The Tribulations of Blackness: Stages in Dominican Racial Identity." Even though blacks and mulattos make up nearly 90 percent of the Dominican population, "Afro-Dominicans have failed to flaunt their blackness as a collective banner to advance economic, cultural, or political causes."

There are two main reasons for this phenomenon. First, the Haitian revolution and subsequent brief takeover by Haitians of the Dominican Republic, which shares the island of Hispaniola with Haiti, tended to paint blackness as an invading force. Second, the persistent efforts of Trujillo to erase blackness from the consciousness of most Dominicans (by denying African influences on Dominican culture and actively repressing African practices like vodou) convinced them that they were dark because of racial mixing with indigenous people; they therefore identify as "indios." As mentioned earlier, although the Taíno and Arawak tribes of the Greater Antilles were all but disappeared by the Spanish conquistadors, mixed people in the Caribbean, including Puerto Ricans but more so Dominicans, still claim indigenous identity.

Black Behind the Ears: Dominican Identity from Museums to Beauty Shops, a fascinating study by Ginetta Candelario, documents how Dominican women in New York use an idealized mixed-race standard for beauty to deny blackness while elevating the "off-white" or mulatto as superior to light or white skin. Candelario also reveals how women's hairstyles embody a racial performance—the whitened neatness of straightened hair combating the negative stereotypes of undisciplined, nappy hair—to which Dominican men lack equal access. The preference for a "mixed" appearance shows how mestizaje ideology captures the imagination of a national group whose members are 90 percent black or mulatto.

By generally avoiding the harassment from anti-immigrant groups either in the realm of politics or through actual enforcement efforts by ICE, Dominicans have an untapped potential to move towards an anti-racist, progressive political position and join the collective black of Anglo-America. Junot Díaz has been an outspoken opponent of internalized Dominican racism and demonstrated solidarity across many marginalized interests, while actress Zoe Saldana has drawn criticism for her portrayal of the darker, more African-marked jazz singer Nina Simone in an unsuccessful biopic. Longtime New York politico Adriano Espaillat has vacillated between using Latinx nationalism to win elections and making alliances with African Americans, and his actions in African American legend Charles Rangel's Harlem Congressional seat, as the neighborhood is threatened by significant gentrification, will be a defining one for area Dominicans. It's inevitable that as the Afro-Latinx identity grows in stature in the United States, younger Dominicans, particularly in urban environments where crossover movements between Afro Latinx, African Americans, and queer groups are beginning to proliferate, will be pulled toward embracing it.

The surge in Mexican immigration in the last twenty years has resulted in migration to decidedly un-Latinx cities in the South, as well as a sizable increase of Mexicans in New York, which has long been dominated by Caribbean Latinx. Currently at around 13.5 percent of Latinx in New York, Mexicans will become the largest Latinx group in the 2020s if growth continue at the current rate—not a guarantee given that the US economy has not recovered from the 2008 recession and immigration rates from Mexico have remained flat. Like Dominicans, New York Mexicans often escape the anti-immigrant pressure that exists in the Southwest and along the

Mexican border. But their relatively recent presence and difficulty attaining citizenship have meant that they are primarily organized in left-oriented religious groups such as Asociacíon Tepeyac, which uses the syncretic power of La Virgen de Guadalupe to create spaces for Mexicans to pioneer forms of transnational culture in a city that was never deeply defined by a Mexican presence.

The majority of the Mexican population in New York comes from the city of Puebla, which is south of Mexico City, and which makes it characteristically different from many other Mexican American communities in the United States. Researchers including anthropologist Robert Smith have shown how sizable amounts of cash remittances help create a transnational flavor to new immigrant experiences. Sometimes these remittances help reconstruct whole towns in rural Mexico and create an ambivalence about the pursuit of citizenship by many Mexican immigrants. Local Catholic churches have embraced Mexican immigrant groups to provide a crucial context for community and identity construction, occasionally interfacing with African American and other Latinx groups. Increasingly, the levels of violence associated with drug cartels in northern Mexico, or repressive governments in Central American countries such as Guatemala and El Salvador, have driven much of this immigration.

There is a kind of random mix to the Mexican experience in New York and the South, where identity is often created around religious humanism and devotion to La Virgen; the participation of visual and creative artists in the depiction of the immigrant experience or resistance to deportation and detention; and the strong activism in labor movements that advocate for basic rights, minimum wage, state-sponsored IDs, and of course the Dream Act. Despite the concentration of most deportation binges during the Obama administration in the West and Midwest, there is a major ICE detention center in Elizabeth, New Jersey, less than fifteen miles from New York City, and ICE deportation raids in the New York area are increasing under Trump. Many younger Mexicans that I have interviewed have expressed a desire to keep a low profile, whether it's due to shame or just survival. Some have engaged with African American, Puerto Rican, and Dominican subcultures. Others evoke the middle-class striver air of European or South Asian immigrants.

There is a wide range of new Mexican adaptation to the United States. Some, like Mexico City native rapper Bocafloja, have remained firm devotees to leftist activism and even the recapturing of Afro-Mexican identity. Some belong to cult groups that emulate New Wave (there is a widespread affection for the British group The Cure), goth, and emo subcultures, as well as hardcore punk. When Joey Ramone, lead singer of the seminal punk rock group the Ramones, died in the early 2000s, the makeshift altar at his vigil counted on an unexpectedly large Mexican presence. More recently, Mexican immigrant activism in New York has increased, around not only the DREAM act, but also the mysterious murder of forty-three university students in the small town of Ayotzinapa, Mexico, which has come to symbolize the impunity doled out on poor and working-class Mexicans by a bureaucratic state that is difficult to entangle from the corruption of local politicians, law enforcement, militias, and drug traffickers.

Perhaps because the migration of both groups has simultaneously increased, Central Americans, who have been significantly affected by recent US foreign policy, share many characteristics with recent Mexican immigrants. While Guatemalans have successfully staked out a significant community in Houston, Salvadorans have carved out a proto-Nuyorican presence in South Central Los Angeles and Washington, DC. Salvadorans played a major role in the accumulation of arrest statistics during the Rodney King riots of 1992 and persevered through similar disturbances in the Mount Pleasant neighborhood of the nation's capital a year earlier.

Yet the experiences of Salvadorans and other Central Americans reveal that the phenomenon of transnationalism has different effects

on different social classes. Those who achieve the entrepreneurial
ideal posited by sociologist Alejandro Portes find routes to capital
accumulation that allow for benign movement between nations.
But poor immigrants, who make up the majority of the neoliberal-
imposed mobility of labor, often find themselves in wrenchingly
difficult movement back and forth across the border. America's race
crisis also moves southward with transnational Latinx. Sometimes
it does so in positive ways, as when heightened racial awareness
acquired by Latinx in the United States spurs racial awareness in
Latin America. Other times, it results in transnational gangs like El
Salvador's Mara Salvatrucha gang, which rose to power in part by
marrying Los Angeles street gang activity to the lawlessness typically
exhibited in El Salvador by out-of-control police and military as they
crack down on young people.

While maintaining a relatively low profile, migrants from countries including Honduras and Guatemala can potentially become
identified with race-conscious identity construction because of the
severe effects of US policy that resulted in the creation of death
squads in their respective countries. Much of the indigenous population in the Guatemalan countryside was subject to genocide by the
policies of General Ríos Montt in the 1980s and even though truth
commissions have revealed his role, the development of Guatemalan
indigenous awareness remains in its early stages. Honduras, recently
victimized by a US-tolerated coup, has become one of the most dangerous places in Central America and its children, who have been
fleeing north to cross the border, subjected to a callous policy of
deportation in 2015.

Immigrants from South America have available to them a variety
of paths toward identity construction and participation in Anglo-
America. Several South American countries, such as Venezuela,
Colombia, and even Brazil, have extensive Caribbean coasts whose
cities have cultures parallel to those of Puerto Rico, Cuba, and the
Dominican Republic. But they also have vast interiors with both

intensely populated urban areas and remote rural areas where the ideal of mestizo assimilation is still not fulfilled. Particularly in Northern cities, South Florida, and the Southern region, Colombians, Venezuelans, Peruvians, Argentineans, and Ecuadoreans have created sizable, viable communities with varying strategies for assimilation. In general their obscurity and avoidance of demonization have allowed them to escape the racializing experiences of Puerto Ricans and Mexicans.

In New York City, radicals such as Rebel Diaz, a radical DJ duo who are the sons of a Peruvian activist, have adopted the black/ Puerto Rican approach to radical politics through hip-hop. In Florida, on the other hand, a growing Venezuelan diaspora that opposes the late president Hugo Chávez and his successor Maduro's left government is at times recruited by Miami's remaining base of anti-Castro Cubans, though Venezuela's new expatriates have far more diverse class backgrounds than the Cubans. The same is partially true about that sector of Colombians who identified most strongly with the pro-paramilitary goals of former president Álvaro Uribe, although its diaspora is so diverse and the people have fled from so many different enemies that it is impossible to isolate a general tendency. Perhaps the most well known US-born Colombian is John Leguizamo, an actor whose affect is so much like a Nuyorican's that he has even claimed Puerto Rican lineage. Argentines and Chileans are less of a factor in Latinx race politics, as many Argentineans have a relatively undeveloped racial consciousness that makes them most likely to be "white Latinx." This is true for Chileans to an extent, although some have a stronger identification with indigenous communities and are drawn to racially conscious leftism because of the severe aftershock of the US intervention in Chile in 1973, which not only saddled them with the Pinochet dictatorship but turned their economy into a workshop for neoliberal austerity policies.

Nuestra América in the Twenty-First Century

Clearly there is some tension between the Latinx identity that has been established by Mexicans, Puerto Ricans, and Cubans, and the newer paradigms being constructed right now by more recent waves of immigration. Whereas the older archetypes were shaped by reactions to direct US involvement, newer forms of Latinx identity tend to align themselves with the ideals of individual achievement, consumerism, and entrepreneurship that mark the neoliberal era. The ambiguity or, if taken to its logical extreme, shame surrounding citizenship status for newer immigrants can make national liberation politics dangerous, inaccessible, or irrelevant.

Yet as Trumpism creates an obvious organizing target, US policy towards and interventions in Mexico, Puerto Rico, and Cuba will potentially create a new era of activism and identity construction that critiques America's role in the world beyond its borders and foregrounds the importance of race and racialization in that process. The interaction or joining of causes such as the militarization of Mexico, the re-colonization of Puerto Rico, and new Caribbean and South American free trade zones is key in creating a new level of Latinx awareness as the civil rights era fades from memory. Closer to home, responses to the practices of residential segregation, aggressive policing techniques, mass incarceration, and institutionalized racism can also be central elements in reaffirming and retooling Latinx identity and politics. The new interventions all involve the repercussions of globalization and free trade, with elements of security/surveillance and the drug war in play.

In Mexico, more than twenty years of NAFTA have caused convulsions in Mexico's economy, displacing agricultural workers and subjecting them first to border-zone maquiladoras and then to dangerous border crossings to pursue low-wage employment in California, the Southwest, and beyond. While there have been some economic gains in privileged sectors (the business class and skilled workers), there has also been mass impoverishment and ecological damage. In this context, US military influence, through border security efforts and under the pretense of the War on Drugs, has subjected Mexicans to increasing levels of violence, with the murder of the forty-three students in Ayotzinapa and military repression of teachers' strikes in Oaxaca the most obvious flashpoints of conflict.

The need to open new markets to investment from the corporate and finance sectors was decisive in President Obama's decision to renew diplomatic relations with Cuba. The advent of Obamapertura, the great "opening" that the US neoliberal narrative holds as a form of liberation for the Cuban people, is also a technique for its internal corporate and banking sectors to recapture a lost market. While there is much to celebrate as a victory for the Cuban people—the release of the remaining members of the Cuban Five, for example—the opening creates the possibility of a sudden windfall through selling American products to previously unexploited consumers and exploiting a workforce accustomed to even lower wages than are paid in Mexico, India, and Vietnam.

For an American economy that has been largely stagnant, the opening of Cuba is a last-ditch opportunity to stave off looming worldwide economic disaster. Clearly, the Cuban revolution is far from perfect. A different kind of class system based around party membership rather than material wealth is as ossified as ever, and a new minority class of those who have prospered through outsized remittances and involvement in licensed small business has intensified resentment from below and eroded the social contract of Cuba's socialist egalitarianism. Dissidents have been persecuted, political prisoners have been taken, and Black Cubans have not benefitted as much as lighter-skinned Cubans.

While it's not clear yet how much control the United States and multinational investors can gain in Cuba, the anticipated rush to invest will be exploitative in nature and triumph over the humanist goal of allowing average Cubans access to the Internet and a

degree of capital accumulation if outside interests are allowed unfet-
tered access. The importance of opening up this market—which is
now likely to be delayed or abandoned by the Trump administration—was illustrated by the intense involvement of Obama and the
attendant publicity during his 2016 visit, while several hundred miles
to the east, Puerto Rico, the United States' obscured, unincorporated
territory, was allowed to twist in the wind as vulture and hedge fund
owners began to sue for payment of a debt that grew to about $72
billion. When the island's government—ruled by the party that had
reigned since the 1952 constitution, which granted it limited autonomy to run its own affairs—announced in the summer of 2015 that
it could no longer pay back the debt, President Obama was largely
silent as Congress dragged its heels on a rescue plan for almost a
year. Obama refused to push the Treasury Department to lend the
island money to repay the debt on more reasonable terms, fearing the
perception that he would be bailing the island out.

   This came after over a hundred years of exploitation of an island
that had outlived its purpose as a military and naval base and propaganda tool to combat any conceivable success of a Communist
Cuba during the Cold War. Puerto Rico and Cuba also represent two
widely divergent historical points on the free trade timeline. Puerto
Rico—whose agricultural economy was gutted to create an industrial
manufacturing model in the 1950s that featured a hefty dose of external
investment capital—was a dry run for free trade policies like NAFTA.
US corporations experimented with offshore operations using a non-
English-speaking, lower-wage workforce in Puerto Rico long before
Burger Kings and Walmarts invaded Mexico. It was the vastly lower
wages that US corporations found in Mexico after NAFTA that caused
them to pull out of Puerto Rico and spin it into its current debilitating
fiscal crisis, one immeasurably worsened by a toxic package of credit
default swaps cleverly manipulated by Wall Street banks.

   The events in Cuba are already having the effect of moderating
the rightist politics of South Florida Cubans, who hope that the slow

rapprochement will allow them to reestablish a connection with the island they rejected. Still, it may have been latent anti-Castro tendencies that pushed so many Latinx in South Florida to vote for Trump, whose policy toward Cuba appears to be returning to Cold War protocols. If the penetration of unregulated investment and capital projects are shown to be even worse for Cuban residents than Castro's hardline Communism, it might completely reverse the Cuban American position to one of advocacy for their homeland. Miami Cuban politics will veer toward the neoliberal center as the hard right ages and loses their raison d'être.

Meanwhile the advent of the imposed fiscal oversight board to restructure Puerto Rico's debt that was signed into law in June 2016 has already created a fierce backlash among island residents, as well as many of the diaspora in the United States. Even rightist Puerto Ricans are chafing under the new arrangement, and the prospect of millions of US citizens enraged over the clear reimposition of colonial status by a country that prides itself on its revolutionary war having liberated the thirteen colonies is not a pretty picture. The glaring contradiction of Puerto Rico's subjugated status is a major Achilles' heel for American exceptionalism, not only among Latinx but potentially the broader landscape of the American left as well.

As these three "original" US Latinx groups—the homies of Cuba, Mexico, and Puerto Rico—grapple with the new colonial excess being imposed on their home countries, it will likely become clear that a central reason for these injustices is race, or what Walter Mignolo calls the "colonial difference." Cuba and Puerto Rico were long desired for conquest by US presidents going back to James Madison, but were left on the back burner because of doubts about how to absorb these islands' "mongrel" racial makeup. The fact that Cuba and Puerto Rico were not put on the path towards statehood after becoming US possessions as a result of the war with Spain was also indicative of the racial discomfort their populations aroused in American military personnel and politicians.

We recall, then, that José Martí's conception of Nuestra América was accompanied by the idea that there was no race in Cuba, because race was something used by the colonialists to divide the white and black members of the Cuban independence army. While his message of unity was understandable and admirable and served as a bulwark against the onset of scientific racism that was in its beginning stages, it is most useful now for Mexicans, Cubans, and Puerto Ricans to reassert an identification with racial difference—to subvert and critique not only the racist role of US foreign policy in Latin American and the Caribbean, but also their colonial and neo-colonial collaborators in the elite sectors of Latin America.

Mestizaje and Neoliberal Multiculturalism

The neoliberal moment has not changed much for Latinx, who are faced with three familiar racial options. The first is striving for or attaining assimilation, or whiteness, as either a "White Latino" or a White American. The second is identifying as either "mixed race," or as a "race" comprised of mixed-race people with a generally identifiable phenotypic appearance of brownness. The third option is for Latinx to strongly identify with their indigenous, African, or Asian identities, deprioritizing affiliation with Europe and whiteness.

The third option has the most liberating potential, but there are limitations. There is a beauty to solidarity with those who have suffered the violence of conquest and the ravages imposed on people of color after the abolition of slavery in the form of peonage and Jim Crow laws. Yet the objective reality is that everyone is mixed, even those of us who exhibit such strong phenotypical characteristics that we seem indisputably African or indigenous-descended. Even the objective and subjective realities of race oppression through phenotypical appearance and culture are not entirely indicative of the historical reality of a particular individual—while the majority of black and indigenous people may correctly claim that whatever

European DNA they carry was the result of rape or the confinement of slavery or indentured servitude, they may be related to a dark Moor or a white abolitionist too.

It is indisputable that the ideology of mestizaje, or mixed-race idealism, is unavoidably attached to a whitening process. Mestizaje has been used to silence the black and indigenous and impose a color-blind order to white-dominated societies. Yet as flawed as José Vasconcelos's musings on la raza cósmica were, they were still designed to make an argument against US imperialism and the binary ideologies of purity. The translation of mestizaje into the social sphere of Anglo-America holds enormous potential for how Latinx can affect race and politics in the United States, as well as the contesting discourses of class and identity politics in the wake of Trump's election.

Peter Wade points out in his essay "Rethinking Mestizaje" that there are elements of negotiation and contestation involved in the construction of a mixed-race society in which African-descended people and indigenous people are on some level present, particularly on the level of culture and lived experience. In some senses we can imagine that there is nothing inherently wrong with conceiving societies through the lens of mestizaje, and that Latin America has simply been missing a language that doesn't privilege whiteness. This new language that privileges racial and sexual difference and is open to critiques of capitalism and class oppression is coalescing with the evolution of Latinx identity in Anglo-America.

The imbalance created by privileging the dominant half of a binary opposition is part of an argument that could invoke the unwieldy and rarefied process of what philosophers call deconstruction. Why is the dominant half of binaries—say, white, male, heterosexual—privileged at the expense of the other? In the case of Latinx, this process involved privileging whiteness in Spain and then Latin America, but it remains to be seen what side of the equation will be privileged in twenty-first-century America, or whether the binary itself can be expanded to multiple positions. Mestizaje's process of cultural synthesis has largely favored heterosexual white males, and in the current rhetoric of American exceptionalism, straight white male democracy still stands to be the ultimate winner, the devourer of otherness.

The historical narrative thread that runs through Latin America and is carried, consciously or not, into the United States by Latinx who construct their new hybrid identity in the global center does not happen in a hermetically sealed chamber of racial identity experimentation. It has been intersecting with the changes in US racial ideology prompted by what sociologist Howard Winant calls the "racial break," or what I have been referring to as the era of national liberation movements. While the late twentieth-century confluence of Anglo- and Latin America has often been analyzed at the level of cultural exchange and free trade, two opposing dynamics are evident in the overlooked matters of race.

With the election of Trump, the reemergence of white nationalism in the United States and Europe is a response to the loss of white privilege and may pose a serious challenge to the consolidation of power in global neoliberal regimes that favor multiculturalism. But it seems inevitable that for every Brexit will come a determined resistance pushing gradual acceptance of racial minorities forward. That's why it's important to keep in mind that just as America's original social contract involved extending democratic rights and liberties to white men at the expense of people of color, women, and sexual minorities, a central goal of the new neoliberal order is to include previously marginalized minorities, at least symbolically, in elite circles, at the expense of the world's impoverished majorities of marginalized people. It may not seem obvious as the Trump era begins—his appointment of token African and Asian Americans notwithstanding —but Anglo-America is trying to proceed with moving toward a post-racial society, making a display of absorbing people of color into the idea of American exceptionalism in order to justify its imposition of neocolonial exploitation on countries filled with people of color.

This project, which Jodi Melamed calls "neoliberal multicultur-alism," is a twenty-first-century version of the way race dynamics were created at the beginning of modernism, whether one dates it to the Age of Discovery or the Enlightenment. Rather than base the unequal distribution of wealth on race per se, neoliberalism seeks to include people of color who reside within their cultural boundaries or sociopolitical covenant through a developing discourse of multicul-turalism. At the same time, the disenfranchised poor of the majority of non-Western countries are marginalized by a narrative that paints them as monocultural and intolerant of the "democratic way of life."

It's easy to see, therefore, why the evolution of racial identity among Latinx in the United States, as well as other marginalized groups, is so important as a counter-discourse to neoliberal multicul-turalism. While mestizaje ideology has reinforced white supremacy, it contains, within cultural memory and social practice, the seeds of its dissolution—a presence of blacks and indigenous people that is not as easily folded into the neoliberal multiculturalist project.

On the level of the barrio, this means the prevalence of different races and different colors of people within the same families. It means the use of different languages and mixtures of languages, and the conception of multiple subjectivities in neighborhoods, on streets, in barbershops and beauty parlors. It means the retention of social, cul-tural, and political ties to Latin America, which is part of that world targeted by neocolonialism and free trade acts. It means, if people choose to insist on it and perform it, thinking differently.

A Cautionary Tale: *Hamilton* as a Neoliberal Multiculturalist Syncretism

Neoliberal multiculturalism also revises racial liberalism's model of race as culture. In this new version, "culture" no longer replaces older, biolog-ical conceptions of race; it displaces racial reference altogether. Detached from the history of racial conflict and antiracist struggle, "culture," as the displacement of racial reference, nonetheless remains associated with ideas of "diversity," "representation," and "fairness."

Jodi Melamed, "From Racial Liberalism to

Neoliberal Multiculturalism"

I am not throwing away my shot.

I am not throwing away my shot.

Hey yo, I'm just like my country,

I'm young, scrappy and hungry

and I'm not throwing away my shot.

Lin-Manuel Miranda's *Hamilton*, spoken by Alexander Hamilton

The overwhelming success story of *Hamilton*, a Broadway musical written by Lin-Manuel Miranda, who grew up in New York City as the son of Puerto Rican migrants, is not only about its astonishing levels of profit—currently estimated at $600 million per week, on the way to a multibillion-dollar payday. The play's short-term impact, which includes a troubling synergy with the Democratic Party and national politics such that it has been used to raise large donations for candidates, most notably Hillary Clinton, only hints at its long-term value. *Hamilton* is a quintessential work of neoliberal multiculturalism, one that threatens to have a lasting impact in the way Anglo-America rewrites its race narrative into one of racelessness, where wealth inequality becomes irrelevant and "diversity" rules.

Melamed locates the origins of neoliberal multiculturalism in something she calls racial liberalism, whose founding text is Gunnar Myrdal's *An American Dilemma: The Negro Problem and Modern Democracy*. Myrdal's book pathologizes the black experience and asserts that resolving the "negro problem" will create an anti-racist discourse that will allow the United States to achieve its goals in the postwar scenario of transnational capital accumulation. The epiphany achieved by Americans in finally accepting "the fundamental equality" of African Americans creates a privileged postwar liberal identity to justify American exceptionalism and moral authority over the rest of the world.

In this process—which eventually evolves first into liberal multiculturalism, then into the neoliberal version mentioned above—the "privilege/stigma opposition," or binary, is altered so that, as Melamed writes, it no longer

> mesh[es] perfectly with a color line. Instead, new categories of privilege and stigma determined by ideological, economic, and cultural criteria overlay older, conventional racial categories, so that traditionally recognized racial identities—black, Asian, white, or Arab/Muslim—can now occupy both sides of the privilege/stigma opposition.

This blurring of the racial border results in transitioning away from the established dynamics of exclusion so that exclusion is based on culture and not race, per se. In Melamed's model, deviations from the ideal national culture—one based on a neoliberal ideal of individual entrepreneurialism, the denial inherent in American exceptionalism that systemic racism is inherent to American history—are the new grounds for exclusion not entirely defined by race or phenotypic appearance.

Racial identity can be affected by performance in such a way as to at least partially block forms of overt racism. For instance, the premise of neoliberal multiculturalism makes it more understandable why, in a turn of phrase that shocks and discomforts so many race-conscious white liberals, many African Americans resort to criticizing their peers for "acting white." By acting white, blacks and other people of color are perceived to be engaged in a deliberate strategy to shift from stigmatized to privileged, even while their race is still defined as black. In the process, they are abandoning a way of being in the world that condemns most people of color to exclusion from life, liberty, and the pursuit of happiness, something that creates a kind of class solidarity. But, as certain aspects of what we have come to know as urban culture are sanitized, acting white becomes a less important strategy.

In a sense, *Hamilton* turns acting white on its head, since what Miranda has done is take patterns and practices of "authentic" urban and hip-hop culture, and by a remarkable alchemy for which he should be recognized as either a genius or a charlatan, drag the identification with black/Latinx urban culture across the line between stigma and privilege. The success of *Hamilton* is in this way particularly striking because it opened on Broadway just weeks after a play loosely based on the life of Tupac Shakur, one of hip-hop's most authentically political figures, flopped miserably. *Hamilton*'s triumph proves that Broadway audiences were not so much seeking a musical about hip-hop per se, but a version of hip-hop that was somehow transformed to at once glorify the founding myth of the United States and privilege a white liberal audience by allowing them to embrace blackness on their own terms.

Miranda achieved this by engaging in what in theater circles is called "non-traditional casting," something most often used in Shakespeare productions, in which people of color or women assume white male roles. While it's true that Shakespeare is not hip-hop, there are occasional characters of color in *Othello* and *The Tempest*. Yet outside of a brief appearance by Sally Hemings, a mulata slave owned and used as a vessel for procreation by Thomas Jefferson, there are no people of color who appear as characters in *Hamilton*. Slavery is almost never mentioned, and the actions and thoughts of founding fathers including Hamilton, Aaron Burr, George Washington, and Jefferson are transposed entirely into hip-hop parlance replete with knowing references to rappers such as Mobb Deep, the Notorious B.I.G., DMX, and Eminem. The play's success is measured by how seamlessly the founding fathers take on the voices of street authenticity and allow people of color to "own" a history that was administered by people who actively enslaved and marginalized them.

By adapting passages taken from existing archives of statements made by the founding fathers in testimony, speeches, and letters and transforming them into a work of musical theater driven by the aesthetic form of hip-hop and the cultural feel and ambience of R&B, Miranda is erasing the fact that most of the founding fathers were either slave owners or tolerant of slavery, even if some of them participated in abolitionist societies. Hamilton himself married into one of New York's largest slave-owning families, the Schuylers—who were also members of the New York Abolition Society—and some scholarship asserts that he handled slave transactions for the family in his capacity as an accountant, unsurprising given that the "trading charter" referred to in one of the songs as one of his earliest accounting jobs in Saint Croix was a company that shipped molasses to the north in the triangular trade generated by profits from the slave trade.

Another disingenuous narrative in *Hamilton* is his casting of the protagonist as a Horatio Alger–like striver, a paradigm for the contemporary immigrant experience. Because Hamilton was born on a Caribbean island of dubious (possibly mixed-race) parentage, his story is framed as parallel to that of many Latinx immigrants, and his ascent to the top levels of American government as a success story to which all immigrants should aspire. Hamilton never faced the race discrimination and threats of deportation that contemporary immigrants do, and an infinitesimally small percentage of Latinx immigrants are able to enroll directly in an Ivy League school, as Hamilton did in King's College, Columbia's predecessor. Of course the neoliberal government that so favors *Hamilton*—in 2016, Barack Obama warmly received Miranda and cast members for a private performance at the White House—presided over a deteriorating situation for immigrants increasingly subject to deportation and for the most part not skilled enough to entertain the idea of anything close to Hamilton's position. Finally Hamilton—despite being the "son of a whore"—was white, perhaps more analogous to William Carlos Williams, the medical doctor and poet who emigrated to Paterson, New Jersey, from Puerto Rico with his white Caribbean wife.

Hamilton was not at all racialized in any way that the written record shows, and expressed many condescending opinions toward blacks as well as members of the working class. He even authored a letter of complaint addressed to England after the Revolutionary War, complaining that some of the blacks whom the Tory Army "stole" from Americans should be returned to their rightful owners.

The fact that Miranda is New York Puerto Rican is not insignificant in analyzing *Hamilton*'s success. He has famously described combining his love for Broadway musical theater with hip-hop, the kind of hybrid cultural upbringing that is so strongly characteristic of US Latinx identity construction. He is tightly connected to his father, Luis Miranda, the co-founder of the Hispanic Federation, a large and fast-growing philanthropic organization that channels money to a myriad of Latinx advocacy groups and nonprofits, and also the co-director of MirRam Group, which receives a $8,000 a month retainer from the Hispanic Federation, and is a high-powered lobbying and consultancy group that works with Latinx elected officials, some of whom acted as key fundraisers for the Hillary Clinton campaign.

One of the fascinating subtexts to *Hamilton* is how Miranda fuses different guises of possible Nuyorican identities—the knowing references to hardcore hip-hop, the blackness of hip-hop culture, the whiteness of the Founding Fathers, the nerdy love of musicals—with his own persona, which includes an elite educational background: he went to Hunter College High School, where MSNBC's Chris Hayes was a classmate, and holds an undergraduate degree from the elite millennial creative class factory Wesleyan University. His synthesis of styles is similar to fellow MacArthur Genius Grant recipient Junot Díaz, but the effect, from the text of *Hamilton* as well as its intellectual impact, is largely superficial, particularly when compared to Díaz's decolonial masterpiece, *The Brief Wondrous Life of Oscar Wao*.

Even as pure political theory, *Hamilton* aligns itself with the neoliberal presidency of Barack Obama. In the recent past, or the period of Winant's "racial break," the New Left adopted Thomas Jefferson as their hero for his resistance to metropolitan elites in favor of his agrarian utopia of Virginia. The emerging pro-ecology counterculture movement of the 1960s, and even urban radicals such as Abbie Hoffman, praised Jefferson for promoting the true ideals of democracy, calling him the predecessor of a back-to-the-land utopian socialism. In the age of Obama, whose cabinet and high-level administration posts were inhabited by a revolving door of financial sector employees, the center-left liberalism of the early twenty-first century gravitated more easily to Hamilton, the father of the US banking system, a self-made elitist who professed a loyalty to abolition while tolerating slave ownership in his own family. This banking system was the repository of the expanding base of capitalist production in the South, which allowed abolitionist Northerners to at once look down their noses at slave economy bulwarks such as Virginia and South Carolina while pocketing their share of the profits. This arrangement makes clear how the three-fifths compromise, which allowed Southern states to count their slaves as three-fifths of a person and enhance their representation in Congress, got into the Constitution.

Yet despite the disingenuousness of its racial turn, the musical has received much praise from people of color, from influential hip-hop-associated musicians such as The Roots' drummer Questlove and politically conscious rapper Talib Kweli, because of what they perceive as its formal authenticity in terms of rap performance and R&B aesthetic. It is also almost universally praised by Nuyorican poets and musicians who see some of themselves reflected in the musical's assertive posturing and spiritual centering, its allusion to gospel and faith as the ultimate tradition of resistance. Yet while all these meanings and references are present, it is troubling how all this race-affirmation seems to ultimately serve as race erasure.

The artifice of *Hamilton*'s false narrative began to show when Miranda began stumping for the austerity-imposing restructuring plan Congress was devising for Puerto Rico's overwhelming $72 billion debt, of which a significant percentage came to be owned by Wall Street hedge and vulture funds. During the crucial period in 2016 when Democratic Party leaders were negotiating a Congressional deal to renegotiate Puerto Rico's debt, Miranda shamelessly offered conservative Republicans tickets to *Hamilton* in exchange for a deal—any deal, regardless of what the provisions would be. When the bill that passed, ironically called PROMESA, it required the creation of a proto-colonial fiscal oversight board, and Miranda praised it as a not-perfect rescue, the best deal that could be hoped for. His letter to the New York Spanish-language newspaper *El Diario* explaining this drew much derision from nationalist Puerto Ricans and caused a small backlash.

Journalist David Dayen, writing in the *Fiscal Times*, even observed that when arguing over how the United States should pay off bonds used to finance the Revolutionary War, Hamilton wanted to pay off the creditors at face value; Madison wanted to pay them at only the rate the creditors had paid, so as not to reward speculators. Hamilton eventually won out. "Hamilton would be proud of his protégé's support for rewarding financiers for taking advantage of a government in trouble," wrote Dayen. "But if Miranda looked closer at what this bill would mean for friends and family suffering on the island, maybe he wouldn't endorse something so, well, Hamiltonian."

The flack Miranda got from his own community, even some who had previously admired his achievement through *Hamilton*, demonstrates how a conscious Puerto Rican constituency, even while attempting solidarity with a wider US Latinx community, can immediately understand the negative implications of US foreign policy and still-extant colonialism. In the case of Puerto Rico, the United States' presence is not obscured behind the military planners of drug-war-fueled Plan Mérida or Plan Colombia, or the coup that Hillary Clinton tolerated in Honduras, or the tacit approval of US-friendly destabilization attempts in Venezuela. The PROMESA fiscal oversight board will be constituted by US bureaucrats and members of the

Puerto Rican financial elite and directly impose economic austerity on Puerto Rico, outraging almost all of the island's residents and sympathizers in the United States diaspora. Yet little outrage emanated from the US Latinx and progressive liberal community that so faithfully backed Hillary Clinton when PROMESA was signed into law in the summer of 2016.

How can we measure the ultimate legacy of a work like *Hamilton?* Let me return briefly to the story recounted by María Elena Martínez, which described the disruption of a 1612 coup attempt by blacks and mulatos to seize power from Spanish authorities and replace them with their own rule of impunity. The rebels wanted to impose their own authoritarian rule that would subjugate Spaniards and their women as they themselves had been subjugated, complete with the same racial and gender hierarchies under which they had suffered. "Indeed," writes Martínez, "the rebels did not seek fundamentally to alter society; they sought to rule it and to appropriate the sexual and racial prerogatives of their masters."

Of course *Hamilton* does not depict a murderous plot to bring vengeance on white supremacy and its defenders. The inhabiting of Hamilton's ephemeral body by Nuyorican Lin-Manuel Miranda actually bears more resemblance to the syncretic process that created Mexico's Virgen de Guadalupe. When Mexican mestizos and indigenous people saw the Virgen, they saw the goddess Tonantzín, despite the fact that she had been co-opted by Roman Catholic symbolism. While white liberals see Hamilton as a cool guy like them, a white guy who could rap and dance, people of color see Hamilton as one of their own, despite the fact that he was spouting a "religion"—the trappings of a financed-based central government making deals with slave-trade money—under which they were historically oppressed.

It can be argued that, in the guise of a bloodless revolution, *Hamilton* does not "seek to fundamentally alter society," especially when the values and triumphs it celebrates are drawn entirely from founding fathers who did not consider people of color to be human. It

is first and foremost a project to justify, through neoliberal multiculturalism, the new order of American exceptionalism, which since
9/11 has become more and more central to the political narrative of
the country, whether it's through unwavering support of the armed
forces or the militarization of police in the homeland. The narrative
developed by many people of color who have become mainstream
politicians and political leaders is in lockstep with this—they feel it
represents their best chance at long-term political empowerment. But
if it is true that "others"—previously excluded blacks and Latinx—
have become included in the American ideal of white universalism
that means less about race and more about culture, turning a dying
white America into "multicultural America," is this form of survival
a justification for what is lost? If a multicolored, multicultural self
arises as the central vision of Americanness without changing what
America is, are we really progressing?

My critique here is linked to perspectives voiced by Marxist and
otherwise leftist thinkers who insist on the primacy of class struggle
and the pitfalls of identity politics, as well as to those who feel that
questioning the universalism of the Enlightenment, which holds that
we all share certain natural similarities and moral dilemmas, is a dangerously neofascist project, particularly when you look at how the
alt-right has appropriated the logic of victimization. But what I'm
trying to advance is not a condemnation of identity politics in favor
of class politics, holding to one side of the binary over the other, but
an insistence that the two must be fused. As Hardt and Negri said in
Commonwealth, "Revolutionary thought … should not shun identity
politics, but instead must work through it and learn from it." It's my
feeling that because border thinking or Latinx thinking is already
practiced in such multipositional, dialectical logic, we are uniquely
equipped to do so.

Class and race are so deeply entwined as to enable Latinx to see
their complexity and interrelations. Rather than a black-white binary
and class divide, we see gradations of social standing through race,

or see how class standing and race hierarchies are not strictly defined by the black-white binary. The notion of a strict separation between social class and race-identified politics can be subverted by our potential for seeing how perceived racial or class standing can be arbitrary or in flux. In this way, Latinx argue from race toward class, and can see that the universal has always been in bed with the particular.

Even now, the dynamic at work in exploding the myth of mestizaje in the United States has already started to have repercussions back in our ancestral homelands. At the same time it has become evident that Anglo-America's racial discourse is in the throes of change. A hundred years after José Martí's declaration that being Cuban was more than just being black, mulatto, or indio, Latin America is slowly being forced, through a series of popular movements in Colombia, Cuba, Mexico, Brazil, Ecuador, and elsewhere, to engage with its people of color, acknowledge the separateness of their identities, and address the denial of their human rights. The question is whether Latin Americans can effectively interact with US Latinx movements and create solidarity between oppressed racial groups in both Latin America and the US, as well as sympathetic whites. In this way, Latin America is both ahead of the curve and behind the times in terms of hemispheric race relations.

Still there is the argument that David Roediger discusses in his introduction to *Class, Race, and Marxism* about David Harvey's separation between capitalism, which is "permeated with race and gender oppression," and capital, whose systemic logic can be considered abstractly. I've often felt fascinated with the idea of capital having a life of its own, lurking as the logic of a viral movement that infects the bodies to which it is subjected. The idea of self-expanding capital should always be considered as a kind of unerring logic outside of the particularities of human behavior, even as we acknowledge its grounding in human experience and its inevitably lasting impact on our lives.

But what about Marx himself, who, as a representative of a

nineteenth-century peak in European thinking, seems to represent that universalist project, albeit with his ineluctable historical materialist component? What if there were something about the racialized body of Marx himself that allowed him to engage in the cerebral gymnastics necessary to turn Hegel on his head? In a *Monthly Review* article written at the dawn of Reaganism, Herbert Vilakazi, a black South African teaching at a community college in Newark, New Jersey, argued precisely that. The article, called "Was Karl Marx a Black Man?," cites several descriptions of Marx: he is described as having "a complexion as dark as it is generally possible for a Southern European to be" and a "big wooly head." He was given a nickname by the Young Hegelians he fell in with at Berlin University: Der Mohr, or the Moor.

Vilakazi goes on to cite the self-taught scholar J. Rogers, who compiled a vast array of tracts that found African traces in several European countries, and who wrote that "most of the Negro strain in Northern Europe and Russia were taken in by the Jews. So dark were the Jews, especially of Portugal and Southern Spain, that many whites thought all Jews were black or dark." So Marx, whose otherness has mainly been attributed to his Jewishness though he may have been whitened by the fact that his family were successful members of Bavaria's bourgeoisie, would most likely have been considered black in the binary ethos of nineteenth-century America.

Not only was Marx "black," says Vilakazi, but so was "the principal founder and organizer of the German working-class party, Ferdinand Lassalle, and the principal founder of French Marxism ... Paul Lafargue." Did any of these men live blackness in the sense that we know in Anglo- and Latin America? That is not clear, but something about the bodily existence that they lived may be surmisable—particularly that of Marx, who, after this suggestion, begins to look more and more like his contemporary Frederick Douglass, and whose racial experience may have been crucial to his being able to devise a theory of class consciousness.

There are so many contradictions to resolve, so many wounds

to heal. What Latinx bring to the US racial debate is a decidedly outsider perspective, one that can offer much insight into the way America deals with race, even as it seems threatened by the chaos of confronting it. It is as if a long-lost relative has visited your house, and the visit, rather than acting as a temporary distraction, changes your life forever by turning everything you think you know upside-down. The merging of the hemispheres is not just a globalist economic project—it is perhaps our last and best chance to reckon with the buried truths of the racist colonial conquest and construction of an empire.

Epilogue

The Latin-X Factor

The prolonged interaction between Anglo-America's binary racial narrative and Latin America's mestizo logic has produced some notable results, mostly in cultural production. The US census has recently considered adding Hispanic/Latino as a racial category, making the choice between a three-tiered conception of race and a more ambiguous, spectrum-like perspective possible. Whether the United States develops a formal conception of something analogous to South Africa's "coloured" class or simply an informal notion of honorary whiteness with an unspoken hierarchy signaled through subtle variations of language and codes, remains to be seen. But as racial borders become more permeable, with certain people of color allowed to pass into zones of diminished segregation and marginalization, the concept of race may be vanishing, although not quite in the way that has long been imagined.

This of course does not mean that I am reformulating the misguided notion that we are entering a post-racial world, or that racelessness and color blindness are about to be instituted in a more efficient fashion than through the awkward liberalism of the 80s and 90s. I mean that a new form of exclusion may be about to take its place;

long-standing notions of "race" may no longer define the "other" or determine class standing and access to wealth accumulation.

Regardless of whatever category emerges as the receptacle for the exploited, efforts by marginalized groups to dismantle the racial binary implicate how we conceive of self and other, subject and object. This binary has come to be viewed as symptomatic of the faulty thinking that also produced oppressive binaries such as male/ female, straight/gay, and good/evil. These binaries are considered structural, a part of the way language works, locked in a yin/yang symmetry in which one concept cannot exist without the other.

Binary thinking has been deployed in many pre-Western societies, including, for example, among indigenous people in Mexico. In the West, however, one side of the binary becomes dominant, which is the mechanism that sets oppression into motion (Derrida attributes this to the Western fixation on the dominance of presence over absence). While this could easily be traced to a patriarchal imperative, Latinx are often exhorted to change the rigidity of the US racial binary by drawing on Latin America's tradition of more ambiguously codify- ing race. By blurring the dividing line, more truth becomes known about both sides. And despite earlier support in Anglo-America's gay movement for strict separation between straight and gay, there is evidence that Anglo-America is moving toward more fluid ideas of gender and sexuality that already existed not only in Latin America but in indigenous and African societies as well.

Yet as much as we might revel in the death of binaries, they seem to be with us for the time being at least. It turns out that the core of digital information in the current technological age is digital binary codes. German philosopher Gottfried Leibniz, considered to have discovered modern binary code, was fascinated by the I Ching, a text for divining the future. Binary codes are systems of symbolic representation that try to make sense out of or simplify endless com- binations or possibilities, with roots in alchemical practices such as the use of divining rods to find water—a utilitarian prophecy.

Leibniz wanted to make sense of binary divination as a way to fit the creation myth that best suited the birth of rationalism. He called it creatio ex nihilo, Latin for "creation out of nothing," which was a way of elevating the Western consciousness, defined as male and European, over the material forces of the earth.

Leibniz's binaries were part of a movement of Western thinking away from the Greek ideas of creation that theorized that the world was created out of a prima materia, or a previously existing substance or mass of substances that in the Greek language was known as "chaos." Through the ideas presented by Martin Bernal's controversial *Black Athena*, in which he argues that many of the defining myths and religious and philosophical paradigms of the Enlightenment were actually transmitted to Western thinking from Egypt through Greece, one can make connections to African and other non-Western traditions, including women's and other polytheistic religions, that revere the earth as either the remains or the origins of that original chaotic prima materia.

Another pre-Western predecessor to Leibniz's binary codes were the Ifá divination charts used by Yoruban priests, the purveyors of the religion that eventually evolved into Santería in the Caribbean. Popular images of Santería that many Latinx might recall are the tossing of cowrie shells by a priest, or babalawo—essentially the use of binary numerical codes to predict the future. Clearly the binaries themselves were not limiting or enslaving aspects of Western patriarchal thinking, but reductive equations that granted one side or voice unequal, hegemonic power. This facilitates a set of easily discernible truths for all possible interpretations. America's "truth," for instance, is that it is the greatest country on the face of the earth, and that the rest of the world, being "outside the text," as Derrida would put it, does not really exist. I Ching and Ifá were spontaneous, ritualistic practices intending to reveal not only truth but also the fact that truth itself is slippery and mostly definable by chance. The rationalism of the West ultimately generated binaries

1	2	3	4
Ogbe / Gbe	Oyeku / Yeku	Iwoli / Woli	Odi / Di
I	II	II	I
I	II	I	II
I	II	I	II
I	II	II	I

5	6	7	8
Obara / Abla	Okanran / Akia	Irosun / Loso	Iwonrin / Wele
I	II	I	II
II	II	I	II
II	II	II	I
II	I	II	I

9	10	11	12
Ogunda / Guda	Osa / Sa	Irete / Lete	Otura / Tula
I	II	I	I
I	I	I	II
I	I	II	I
II	I	I	I

13	14	15	16
Oturupon / Turukpe	Ika / Ka	Ọsẹ / Ce	Ofun / Fu
II	II	I	II
II	i	II	I
I	II	I	II
II	II	II	I

Odu Ifé divination system

and binary codes that formed what we recognize today as machine logic, a system of yesses and nos, opens and closeds, the benevolent corporation and the targeted consumer—or something you might recognize from watching Congressional sessions on CSPAN, the up or down vote.

What happens, then, when, in neoliberal multiculturalism, black, Latinx, Asian, and queer bodies are absorbed into American exceptionalist machine logic or even the dreaded advent of artificial intelligence as a force that shapes society and human existence?

When marginalized groups become "included" through a change of perception of their bodies, allowing them to pass from stigma to privilege, the change is merely one that changes the brand on their bodies. I say this acknowledging that there is a level of relief through admittance of the body or gradual acceptance of the phenotype or appearance. After all, the colonial wound has wreaked so much suffering on this body that the temporary benefits are considerable.

But will all marginalized bodies be able to pass through this new re-segregation? When I suggest that Latinx and other marginalized groups join the collective black out of solidarity with the deepest instance of oppression, or venerate the bodies of women as the violated source of life, I am recognizing the importance of the somatic essence of history's injustice. But what Latinx, and by extension, all of those who possess what Chicana feminist Chela Sandoval calls "differential consciousness" have to offer is something deeper and equally essential to social change. It's a change at the level of thinking.

This change is analogous to what Cornel West calls prophetic love and the indispensability of regard and deep caring for the other that resists the binary logic of inside and outside. What I'm suggesting is something that has survived the long process of mestizaje, that doesn't require poring through ancient codices, trying to resuscitate authentic, so-called pre-Western thought. Latinx and other subjugated groups have developed a consciousness resulting from a tortured, unstable yet hopeful mix of identities, for several centuries.

It can be something as simple as "In Lak'ech," a Mayan proverb unearthed by the Chicano playwright Luis Valdez in the 1990s that has been adopted in Chicano ethnic studies curricula, like the one banned by Arizona officials in public schools in 2012.

> In Lak'ech
> Tú eres mi otro yo

Si te amo y te respeto

Me amo y me respeto yo

Si te hago daño a ti

Me hago daño a yo

Luis Valdez, *Pensamiento Serpentino*

"You are my other me," says Valdez's text, quoting proverbial indigenous knowledge. "If I love and respect you, I love and respect myself. If I harm you, I harm myself." In this reflection, Valdez is drawing on what he perceives is the Mayan consciousness able to conceive of more than one position within itself. The idea of multipositional consciousness is, again, not confined to a particular racial or ethnic group— one fairly obscure reference to it was made by Earl Lewis in an essay called "Connecting Memory, Self, and the Power of Place in African American Urban History," in which he described a sense of self constructed through a "notion of multipositionality that allows us to add, subtract, multiply, and divide parts of identities at the same time. Such a perspective allows us to examine how race is shaped by other aspects of the self and in turn, how race shapes those aspects."

Multipositionality in consciousness is also clearly related to Du Bois's double consciousness, and again stems from the idea of an individual well versed in a dominant narrative—universal whiteness —as well as that of one's particular experience, which is marginalized. The late Juan Flores argued that Afro-Latinx, for example, had a triple consciousness because of the added layer of their Latinx identity. Yet rather than engage in strict limits about how many strands might exist, this line of reasoning can open itself up to the broad intersections of color, race, religion, queerness, gender identification, and the unstable lines between race, gender, and sexual preference and identity.

The growing awareness of affect, or the importance of emotional responses to colonial wounds, disappearances, subjugations, and shaming, theorized in one case by José Muñoz's liminal evocation of "feeling down, feeling brown," is among several new ways of conceiving a "differential" consciousness that acknowledges the practical activity of Gramscian wars of position. It is a self-love and a revolutionary shared love with a maternal cloak that envelops all living beings. These levels of awareness allow different ideas, memories, and emotions to exist on parallel planes, the rhizomatic structures of trees in a vineyard sharing common roots.

Yet the seduction of allowing one's self or selves to venture into this world of ambiguity seems to stray from the political intent of constructing identity and embracing race. The nation, despite its patriarchal roots, is a source of protection for marginalized people, and is one of the principal forms of social organization that is under attack by the fragmentary consciousness of globalization. When under the spell of imaginary Puerto Rican nationhood, which is not even verifiable in objective terms, I find a profound sense of community that ascends to a spiritual level that fulfills the promise of collective memory of all people.

Latinx was coined so as not to privilege gender, and is perhaps the first time an ethno-racial group has chosen to rename itself for such a reason. This is inextricably tied to the nature of the Spanish language, which designates all nouns as either male or female—arbitrary distinctions that were perhaps suggested by the church or handed down or even debated over centuries. Its accepted use is emblematic of the nature of Latinx identity construction, which is—theoretically at least—constantly open to redefinition as different constituencies stake their claim in the broader mass of subjects.

The Latin X factor—the product of a race made up of all races, genders, sensibilities, proclivities—is something that remains partially untapped and has the ability to draw from multiple human traditions and work between them. Doing so in the creation of song, poetry, dance, and casual conversation creates analogies that valorize multiple subjects. The multilingual mind must draw analogies to process multiple meanings just as a multipositional consciousness works full-time to resolve the ambiguities of race. Perhaps Piper was too harsh when she claimed that whiteness is defined by an inability to imagine the other's behavior, but to the extent that there is any degree of truth in that statement, what Latinx can claim is the ability to imagine multiple others within one awareness, allowing otherness to fade as it becomes part of an internal conversation.

These combinations, tangled and extending back to Spain, North and sub-Saharan Africa, migrations northward to a new plane of meaning, and the fusing of languages and religion, include substantial chunks of human matter drawn from materia prima, the earth, and a myriad of undiscovered truths. The Latin X factor shares a space with a universe of justice seekers. It's where mourning for the dead students of Ayotzinapa intersects with Black Lives Matter. It is a continuing, eternal process of translation, in which the next analogy is fruit for a new conversation, a new beginning.

Acknowledgements

The conception of this book goes back to 2011, when I began teaching a seminar at Columbia University's Center for the Study of Ethnicity and Race. The seminar, "US Latino Cultural Production," was based on work I began in my previous book *Living in Spanglish*, but sought to expand on areas I'd neglected as well as to revise missteps. Preparing for this seminar compelled me to dig deeper into ideas about race and identity, and engaging with the work of my many students helped shape the tone and tenor of seminars as the years passed, as well as to develop new ways to focus my work.

While it has long been the default state of Latin Americans is to avoid speaking about or engaging with matters of race, the sharply unpleasant edges of the race debate in the US have re-emerged, provoking new Latinx narratives and sustaining marginalized ones. This book is essentially about the interplay between static ideas about race—black, white, brown—and the in-between border space that acknowledges the potential for shifts in racial identity. In many ways it is a dialog between the Afro-nationalist sense of black pioneered by W. E. B. Du Bois and the feminist/queer/indigenous mestiza narrative of Gloria Anzaldúa.

The book, *Latinx*, then does not intend to argue for either essentialized notions of race or the primacy of the in-between or liminal space of mestizo/a utopia, but instead follows the movement and negotiated exchanges between the two. Just as I tried, with some success, to argue for the spirit of a people as expressed through constant shifts in language in a code-switching manifesto of Spanglish, I seek to embrace the healing notions of black/brown body-identity while simultaneously alluding to their ephemerality.

In that spirit I would like to thank Frances Negrón Muntaner, who hired me to teach the seminar, CSER staff Teresa Aguayo and Josefina Caputo, and the current director, Neferti Tadiar, as well as the many faculty members at Columbia and the greater community of Latinx scholars who engaged with me about my ideas. For their various insights and feedback about my ideas and the text itself, I would like to thank all of those who took the time to read various parts of this manuscript or merely listen to me as I worked out ways to approach the task: Ula Berg, Arlene Dávila, Arcadio Díaz Quiñones, Rebio Díaz, the late Angelo Falcón, the late Juan Flores, Alyshia Gálvez, Libertad Guerra, Gabriel Haslip-Viera, Miriam Jiménez Román, Linda Martín Alcoff, Yasmín Ramírez, Uruyoán Noel, Ian Seda-Irizarry, Monxo López, Cristina Pérez Jiménez, Colette Perold, Andrés Torres, and Melissa Valle.

In addition to the editorial crew at Verso, I'd like to thank my editor Andrew Hsiao for believing in and acquiring this project and for our many years of friendship dating back to our time at the *Village Voice*. My own trajectory as a thinker and writer has inhabited the in-between space on the border between journalism and academia. In alternative journalism, I found a platform where I could fuse a more creative style with the discipline and ethics of journalism.

Over the years I've experienced much support from colleagues in journalism, such as Roane Carey, Mandalit del Barco, Karen Durbin, Ángel Franco, Todd Gitlin, Mike Kamber, Lisa Jones, Enrique Lavin,

Jeff Z. Klein, Julie Lobbia, Evelyn McDonnell, Evette Porter, Elaine Rivera, Karen Rothmyer, and Matt Rothschild.

The revolution in thinking and cultural production of the 1970s that defined the Nuyorican experience is in many ways the home base of my writing. I would like to acknowledge the profound impact of Young Lords Felipe Luciano, Miguel Meléndez, Iris Morales, Juan González, and the late Richie Pérez and Eddie Figueroa; Nuyorican poets Miguel Algarín, Miguel Piñero, Sandra Esteves, and Pedro Pietri, and the poets I shared the stage with during the Nuyorican Poets Café revival in the 1990s: Paul Beatty, Reg E. Gaines, Tracie Morris, Willie Perdomo, Mike Tyler, Dael Orleander Smith, Edwin Torres, Dana Bryant, Mike Tyler, the late Maggie Estep, and so many others.

Among the many friends and supporters that have blessed me in recent years I thank Lara Bello, Héctor Matos, Mariana Reyes, Rubén Blades, Ismael Cancel, Esperanza Cortés, Esperanza León, Michael Pribich, Felipe Luciano, Miguel Luciano, Macdara Vallely, Miguel Meléndez, Adal Maldonado, Marusa Reyes, Marta Moreno Vega, Cristina Tufiño, William Ramírez, Rubén Reyes, Adriana Hurtado, Joseph Rodríguez, Ray Santisteban, Draco Rosa, Juan Sánchez, Carina del Valle Schorske, Bryan Vargas, Isabelia Herrera, Lidia Hernández Tapia, Bill Lipton, Jorge Matos, Efraín Molina, Greyzia Baptista, Camila Gelpí.

Finally, I want to thank my mother, María Rijos Fuentes, my sister Marisa, and my father, Zoilo Morales Figueroa, who passed away in 2012.

A Note on Sources

Introduction

The conceptual framework for this book has evolved over the several years I've been teaching a seminar at Columbia University's Center for the Study of Ethnicity and Race. In some ways it was inspired by my 2002 book *Living in Spanglish* (St. Martin's Press), but using race instead of language as a lens through which to view a loosely constructed idea of Latinx identity.

I've been influenced in many ways by Eduardo Bonilla-Silva's sociological investigations, particularly "Rethinking Racism: Toward a Structural Interpretation," *American Sociological Review* 62, no. 3 (June 1997), and also *Racism Without Racists: Color-Blind Racism and the Persistence of Racial Inequality in America*, 4th ed. (New York: Rowman & Littlefield, 2014). Bonilla-Silva's work pioneered studies in color-blind racism that eventually toppled the myth of a post-racial America.

By setting up a dichotomy between the mestizaje ideologies of Latin America and the US racial binary, I depict hemispheric convergence as a kind of dialectical activity. David A. Hollinger offers a brief explanation of the US construction of hypodescent as a guiding principle for the racial binary in "The One Drop Rule & the One Hate Rule," *Daedalus* 134, no. 1 (Winter 2005). There has been much discussion about the difference between the construction of racial hierarchy in the US and Latin America, often prompted by Frank Tannenbaum's *Slave and Citizen*, but I wanted to get away from the idea of those hierarchies as static and tried to show how they interacted to bring about something new.

Bonilla-Silva's "The Latin Americanization of Racial Stratification in the U.S.," coauthored with David R. Dietrich, also addresses post-racial and color-blind views of race, in *Racism in the 21ˢᵗ Century: An Empirical Analysis of Skin Color*, ed. Ronald E. Hall (New York: Springer, 2008).

Ivan Hannaford traces racism back to antiquity, providing an excellent view of Spain's more original and nuanced view of race and racism, in "The Idiocy of Race," *The Wilson Quarterly* 18, no. 2 (Spring 1994) and *Race: The History of an Idea in the West* (Baltimore: Woodrow Wilson Center Press with The Johns Hopkins University Press, 1996). Race in antiquity scholar David M. Goldenberg's review of Hannaford's book, "The Development of the Idea of Race: Classical Paradigms and Medieval Elaborations," *International Journal of the Classical Tradition* 5 (1999), praises Hannaford while criticizing what he sees as an overreliance on kabbalistic text in the construction of European ideas about race.

Enrique Dussel's investigations of the philosophical underpinnings of Latin American thought and the case he makes for a new Latin American culture and politics have strongly influenced me. "'Being-in-the-World-Hispanically': A World on the 'Border' of Many Worlds," *Comparative Literature* 61, no. 3 (2009), is a good introduction to Dussel's view of the Hispanic subject as containing multiple subject positions. His work contains a good balance between scholarly wrangling about abstract philosophy and practical political thinking.

The uses of the term *raza* to transmit ideas about race, mixed-race, colonialism, and social class are nicely detailed in Lorena Oropeza, *Raza Sí! Guerra No!* (Berkeley: University of California Press, 2005).

Chapter 1. The Spanish Triangle

In this chapter I explore the roots of the construction of race in Latin America through Spain's interactions with and at times domination by a series of Islamic caliphates between the eighth and fifteenth centuries.

Stuart Hall's idea of transnational Caribbean identity is a basic building block for my work at the intersection of Latinx and African diasporic identity. See his "The Local and the Global: Globalization and Ethnicity," in *Culture, Globalization and the World-System: Contemporary Conditions for the Representation of Identity*, ed. Anthony D. King (Minneapolis: University of Minnesota Press, 1997). See also Stuart Hall, David Held, Don Hubert, and Kenneth Thompson, eds., *Modernity; An Introduction to Modern Societies* (Cambridge, MA: Blackwell, 1996).

For a nuanced and well-researched view of the controversial concept of *convivencia* in Spain, see Jerrilynn Dodds, María Rosa Menocal, and Abigail Krasner Dalbalc, *The Arts of Intimacy: Christians, Jews, and Muslims in the Making of Castilian Culture* (New Haven, CT: Yale University Press, 2009).

Historian David Nirenberg's chapter "Race in the Middle Ages: The Case of Spain and Its Jews" is one of many insightful essays on the racial history of Spain in *Rereading the Black Legend: The Discourses of Religious and Racial Difference in the Renaissance Empires*, ed. Margaret R. Greer and Walter Mignolo (Chicago: University of Chicago Press, 2008). Also see Nirenberg, "Enmity and Assimilation: Jews, Christians, and Converts in Medieval Spain," *Common Knowledge* 9, no. 1 (Winter 2003) and his chapter "Mediterranean Exemplarities: The Case of Medieval Iberia" in *Iberian Modalities: A Relational Approach to the Study of Culture in the Iberian Peninsula*, ed. Joan Ramón Resina (Liverpool, UK: Liverpool University Press, 2013).

Ramón Grosfoguel and Nelson Maldonado-Torres are key Puerto Rican scholars and part of the decolonial school. See Grosfoguel's "The Epistemic Decolonial Turn: Beyond Political-Economic Paradigms," *Cultural Studies* 21, nos. 2–3 (March/May 2007) and "Transmodernity, Border Thinking, and Global Coloniality: Decolonizing Political Economy and Postcolonial Studies," *Eurozine*, July 4, 2008 (available at eurozine.com). Maldonado-Torres's "Religion, Conquest and Race in the Foundations of the Modern/Colonial World," *Journal of the American Academy of Religion* 82, no. 3 (September 2014); "On the Coloniality of Being," *Cultural Studies* 21, nos. 2–3 (March/May 2007); and *Against War: Views from the Underside of Modernity* (Durham, NC: Duke University Press, 2008) have greatly informed my views of the role of medieval Spain in the Enlightenment and of the colonial-era development of the world economy and Western philosophy in the sixteenth to eighteenth centuries.

Jalil Sued-Badillo has produced important and nuanced portraits of the encounter between Columbus (Cristobal Colón for Spanish speakers) and the Caribbean as an extension of Immanuel Wallerstein's conception of the Mediterranean world-system. See "Christopher Columbus and the Enslavement of the Amerindians" in *Displacements and Transformations in Caribbean Cultures*, ed. Lizabeth Paravisini-Gebert and Ivette Romero-Cesareo (Gainesville: University of Florida Press, 2008) and "Facing up to Caribbean History" *American Antiquity* 57, no. 4 (October 1992).

Sylvia Wynter's "Unsettling the Coloniality of Being/Power/Truth/Freedom: Towards the Human, After Man, Its Overrepresentation—An Argument," *CR: The New Centennial Review* 3, no. 3 (Fall 2003) and "1492: A New World View" in *Race, Discourse, and the Origin of the Americas: A New World View*, ed. Vera Lawrence Hyatt and Rex M. Nettleford (Washington, DC: Smithsonian Institution Press, 1995) are classic decolonial school texts.

Enrique Dussel's "Anti-Cartesian Meditations: On the Origin of the Philosophical Anti-Discourse of Modernity," trans. George Ciccariello-Maher, *Journal for Culture and Religious Theory* 13, no. 1 (Winter 2014), makes a convincing argument that René Descartes's formulation of the Western subject was at least partially founded on seventeenth-century Spanish philosophy and the de las Casas–Sepulveda debate.

In many ways we can see how this debate corresponds to the rhetorical difference between neoliberal globalists and right-wing nativist populists. Neoliberals promise inclusion through acculturation without attempting to dismantle entrenched systems of exploitation, while authoritarian nativists are unapologetic in their condemnation of less than human "others," most specifically Latin American, Middle Eastern, and African immigrants. In material terms, neither side seriously addresses the problem of white privilege through unequal wealth accumulation and the grinding poverty experienced primarily by the collective black.

Dussel also tries to provide a pre-history of Western rationalism by emphasizing that Spanish philosophers, taking their cue from cultural Golden Age of the thirteenth-century Islamic Almohad dynasty, strongly influenced Descartes's famous declaration of the individual subject: "I think, therefore I am." But with the Sepulveda–de las Casas debates, the Spanish confronted the first dilemma of colonialism and its treatment of foreign others, and however imperfectly, resolved the problem of "I conquer, therefore I am." Dussel argues that post-Descartes the white, European male "I" necessarily assumed a century or so of erasure of black and indigenous others, what Frantz Fanon might call a dispatching to the "zone of non-being."

By the time of the English colonization of the Americas, the argument over the inferiority of others was settled, and the world economy and the birth of capitalism had already taken off, and there was less significant debate over effectively erased others, who were clearly seen as objects of labor exploitation. Whatever selfish love the Spaniards had toward their colonial subjects was turned inwards by the exploding profitability of the slave trade, excluding regard for others absolutely.

The rational subject of the rapidly industrializing economies of Europe would develop a more abstract idea of "self " and "other" that would base rationality itself on an exclusion of subjugated others from individual perception, without a direct reference to "conquest" or "race." This may be the reason why historians find it so difficult to find evidence of codified racism before the nineteenth century. It was only when Western Europe embarked on its nineteenth-century project of colonization of Africa and Asia that it would find the need to produce a "scientific racism" with its certainties about quantifiable data and skull size to replace antiquated notions based on god and morality.

Walter Mignolo's writings on Spain, the Black Legend, decoloniality, and border thinking were greatly influential as I began the process of researching the theories developed in this chapter. See *Rereading the Black Legend*, referenced above, particularly Mignolo's "What Does the Black Legend Have to Do with Race?," as well as Mignolo's "Racism as We Sense It Today," *PMLA* 123, no. 5 (October 2008), the source for the triangle hypothesis, and "Delinking," *Cultural Studies* 21, nos. 2–3 (March/May 2007), among his many other works.

Barbara Fuchs's *Exotic Nation: Maurophilia and the Construction of Early Modern Spain* (Philadelphia: University of Pennsylvania Press, 2011); *Passing for Spain: Cervantes and the Fictions of Identity* (Champaign: University of Illinois Press, 2002); and "A Mirror Across the Water: Mimetic Racism, Hybridity, and Cultural Survival" in *Writing Race Across the Atlantic World: Medieval to Modern*, ed. Philip Beidler and Gary Taylor (New York: Palgrave Macmillan, 2005) provided the basis for my writing on the way Spain's "century of passing" influenced Latinx culture in the United States.

The various ideologies associated with the Spanish nation remained entwined, often obsessively so, with its plural nature up to the twentieth century. The fascist order created by Franco in the wake of a civil war that was arguably one of the twentieth century's broadest fusions of class, race, and sexual politics hinged on the suppression of difference and, its partner in crime, translation. Mandating "zero translation," Franco ordered the burning of books of translated Spanish for a "One, Great, and Free" Spain, ensuring there would be little conversation about the three-sided mixture of Spanish racial identity. The Franco regime was particularly threatened by and later worked to repress a writer named Blas Infante, whose seminal essay *Ideal Andaluz* (1915) argued for the nation's essential multiracial identity centered in the southern province of Andalucía, the last stronghold of the Islamic caliphate, finally reconquered by Ferdinand and Isabella at the end of the fifteenth century. Andalucía, he wrote, was a "middle" space for the fusion of races and cultures, a "bridge between Europe and the Other." But it was not Infante but the Spanish king Alfonso XIII who began the tradition of the Fiesta de la Raza in Spain on October 12, known in the United States as Columbus Day. The meaning of this holiday varies from a validation of Spanish imperialism through an association with the Roman Empire, to the more muted celebrations in Central America that try to valorize multiracialism, to the Día de los Indígenas in Chávez's Venezuela, which purported to reject entirely Columbus and the conquest. La raza in Spain and Latin America can imply anti-Semitism and philo-Semitism; Maurophilia or Islamophobia—leading us again to ponder the combustibility of raza and its multiplicity of meanings.

When considering the hidden history of Afro-descendants in Mexico, it's important to consider that Nueva España, the Spanish colony that eventually became Mexico, had imported large quantities of African slaves in the seventeenth and eighteenth centuries, and that African-descended Mexicans played a major part in its history. Its second president after independence, for instance, was a black mestizo named Vicente Guerrero, and a sizable population of Afro-Mexicans still reside in the Costa Chica region on the Pacific that are not included in José Vasconcelos's vision of raza cósmica. Laura Lewis's book *Chocolate and Corn Flour* observes that the surviving Afro-Mexican culture in that area identify mainly as black Indians, with little retention of African traditions or memory of their practice.

For an original view of José Vasconcelos's life and work—buttressed by her analysis of texts only available in Spanish—see Juliet Hooker, *Theorizing Race in the Americas: Douglass, Sarmiento, Du Bois, and Vasconcelos* (New York: Oxford University Press, 2017). Hooker's readings of some of Vasconcelos's rarer manuscripts, only available in Spanish, mitigate some of the perceived racism of his raza cósmica project.

Fernando Ortiz's *Cuban Counterpoint: Tobacco and Sugar* (Durham: Duke University Press, 2015), originally published in 1940, is the seminal text about transculturation.

Arcadio Díaz Quiñones's *El arte de bregar* (San Juan, PR: Ediciones Callejón, 2000) and *La memoria rota* (Rio Piedras: Ediciones Huracán, 1993) are timeless commentaries on Puerto Rican existentialism.

Anthropologist Peter Wade's writing on mestizaje convinced me not to discard the idea completely and greatly influenced this book. See "Rethinking Mestizaje: Ideology and Lived Experience," *Journal of Latin American Studies* 37, no. 2 (May 2005) and "Images of Latin American *Mestizaje* and the Politics of Comparison," *Bulletin of Latin American Research* 23, no. 3 (July 2004) in particular.

See Christiane Stallaert, "Translation and Conversion as Interconnected 'Modes': A Multidisciplinary Approach to the Study of Ethnicity and Nationalism in Iberian Cultures" in *Iberian Modalities: A Relational Approach to the Study of Culture in the Iberian Peninsula*, ed. Joan Ramón Resina (Liverpool, UK: Liverpool University Press, 2013).

Jesús Colón's *A Puerto Rican in New York, and Other Sketches* (New York: International Publishers, 1982) is a groundbreaking work by an Afro–Puerto Rican about the New York Puerto Rican experience at the intersection of racial identity politics and the socialist movement.

Laura Lomas's *Translating Empire: José Martí, Migrant Latino Subjects, and American Modernities* (Durham: Duke University Press, 2008) is an excellent account of Cuban author, journalist, and freedom fighter José Martí's time living in the United States.

See Frantz Fanon's *Black Skin, White Masks* (New York: Grove Press, 1952) and Gayatri Chakravorty Spivak's *The Spivak Reader*, ed. Donna Landry and Gerald MacLean (New York and London: Routledge, 1996) in reference to her coining and ultimate disavowal of "strategic essentialism."

Chapter 2. Mestizaje vs. the Hypno-American Dream

This chapter attempts to describe the parallel evolution of mestizaje in Latin America and the racial binary in Anglo-America, while noting that there were some attempts at mixed-race discourse in the United States that had roots in settler colonialism and the abolitionist movement, but were summarily written out of the American narrative.

Nell Irvin Painter's *The History of White People* (New York: W.W. Norton, 2011), Michael Banton's *The Idea of Race* (Boulder, CO: Westview Press, 1977), and the work of David Theo Goldberg, including in *The Racial State* (Malden, MA, and Oxford, UK: Wiley-Blackwell 2011) and *The Threat of Race: Reflections on Racial Neoliberalism* (Malden, MA, and Oxford, UK: Wiley-Blackwell, 2008), all examine the historical construction of race in illuminating ways.

Influential theorist Samuel Huntington's last two books, *Who Are We? The Challenges to America's National Identity* (London: Simon & Schuster, 2004) and *The Clash of Civilizations and the Remaking of*

World Order (New York: Simon & Schuster, 2011), identify Latinx and Muslim cultures as major threats to US stability and security, a significant factor in shaping our current politics of fear.

Peggy Levitt's *The Transnational Villagers* (Oakland: University of California Press, 2001) has become a classic ethnographic text defining the transnational reality of Dominicans in the United States and the Caribbean, and is usefully applied to other Latinx experiences.

See Jorge Duany and Patricia Silver's "The 'Puerto Ricanization' of Florida: Historical Background and Current Status," *Centro Journal* XXII, no. 1 (Spring 2010) for a discussion of Puerto Ricans' categorization as a "third race" in Florida.

Latinx critical race theorists such as Ian Haney-López and Richard Delgado, as well as scholars researching legal decisions that established discrimination against Mexicans on the basis of race, have documented the different racial categories assigned to Mexicans at different times and in different places, as well as the assertion of whiteness as a way for Mexican Americans to claim equal protection under the law.

La Última Controversia, a fascinating black-and-white documentary about Cuban *controversias* produced in 1988 by the government film institute ICAIC, is available on YouTube. The Spanish poetic form of controversia, which has been likened to a kind of Ibero-Franco peasant folkloric antecedent to hip-hop rap battles, literally translates as "opposing verse," where agendas between groups or among mixed-race peasants can be negotiated in the form of spontaneously improvised ten-line, octosyllabic poems.

María Elena Martínez's *Genealogical Fictions: Limpieza de Sangre, Religion, and Gender in Colonial Mexico* (Redwood City, CA: Stanford University Press, 2008) and "The Black Blood of New Spain: Limpieza de Sangre, Racial Violence, and Gendered Power in Early Colonial Mexico," *William and Mary Quarterly*, 61, no. 3 (July 2004), include strong research on early constructions of race in colonial Mexico.

See Elizabeth Anne Kuznesof, "Ethnic and Gender Influences on 'Spanish' Creole Society in Colonial Spanish America," *Colonial Latin American Review* 4, no. 1 (1995).

Henry Louis Gates's PBS series *Black in Latin America* provides a digestible introduction to the Afro-Latinx experience, while Herbert S. Klein's *African Slavery in Latin America and the Caribbean* (New York: Oxford University Press, 1986) is a seminal text on the subject.

For accounts of early New York history, see Russell Shorto, *The Island at the Center of the World: The Epic Story of Dutch Manhattan and the Forgotten Colony That Shaped America* (Waterville, ME: Thorndike Press, 2004). For an account specifically of the early Latinx presence in New York, see Mike Wallace, "Nueva York: The Back Story," in *Nueva York: 1613–1945*, ed. Edward J. Sullivan (New York: Scala Publishers, 2010).

See Brewton Berry, "The Mestizos of South Carolina," *American Journal of Sociology* 51, no. 1 (July 1945).

Winthrop D. Jordan's *White Over Black: American Attitudes Toward the Negro, 1550–1812* (Chapel Hill: University of North Carolina Press, 2012) is an excellent account of the formation of racial rhetoric from the colonial period through the Revolutionary War.

See Gilbert C. Din, "The Offices and Functions of the New Orleans Cabildo," *Louisiana History: The Journal of the Louisiana Historical Association* 37, no. 1 (Winter 1996).

For more about the Ariel/Caliban relationship between Latin America and the United States, see Enrique Rodó, *Ariel*, trans. Margaret Sayers Peden (Austin: University of Texas Press, 1988); Roberto Fernández Retamar, *Caliban and Other Essays* (Minneapolis: University of Minnesota Press, 1989); and Elizabeth Millán-Zaibert, "A Great Vanishing Act? The Latin American Philosophical Tradition and How Ariel and Caliban Helped Save It from Oblivion," *CR: The New Centennial Review* 7, no. 3 (Winter 2007).

Chapter 3. The Second Conquista

This chapter describes the effects of proto-mestizaje ideologies on the evolution of nations in Latin America as they declared their independence from Spain in the nineteenth century, as well as strategies used by Anglo-Americans to appropriate aspects of indigenous culture and identity in the formation of the "American" identity.

See Matthew Karp's excellent *This Vast Southern Empire: Slaveholders at the Helm of American Foreign Policy* (Cambridge, MA: Harvard University Press, 2016) for a detailed description of how slaveowners used elected officials as surrogates in order to develop an imperialist foreign policy, as well as Manifest Destiny.

I was inspired to contrast US and Latin American "indigenous cross-dressing" by Francisco A. Scarano's "The Jíbaro Masquerade and the Subaltern Politics of Creole Identity Formation in Puerto Rico, 1745–1823," *American Historical Review* 101, no. 5 (December 1996).

Elizabeth Maddock Dillon's *New World Drama: The Performative Commons in the Atlantic World, 1649–1849* (Durham and London: Duke University Press, 2014) is an innovative and engaging look at how colonialism is constructed through performance.

Philip Joseph Deloria's *Playing Indian* (New Haven: Yale University Press, 1998) is a definitive text on the creation of US "Creole" identity through the adoption of Native American dress and rituals.

See Iris Marion Young's "Hybrid Democracy: Iroquois Federalism and the Postcolonial Project" in *Political Theory and the Rights of Indigenous Peoples*, ed. Duncan Ivison, Paul Patton, and Will Sanders (Cambridge, UK: Cambridge University Press, 2000) for a discussion of the influence of Native American political organization in the Northeast on the architecture of the US Constitution and its government.

Matthew B. Karush's "Blackness in Argentina: Jazz, Tango and Race Before Perón," *Past & Present* 216, no. 1 (August 2012) comments in fascinating detail on the black roots of Argentinean tango, as well as how mixed-race singers maintained the music's "authenticity" as it was whitened for mainstream consumption.

Tanya Katerí Hernández is a prominent researcher and theorist of the legal construction of racism in Latin America. Her seminal work is *Racial Subordination in Latin America: The Role of the State, Customary Law, and the New Civil Rights Response* (New York: Cambridge University Press, 2013).

A very important and inspirational thread of knowledge and scholarship comes through the work of José Luis González and Juan Flores. The spirit of González's essays, short stories, and activism lived after González's death in the work of Flores, who passed away in 2014 and was the preeminent scholar and a passionate educator in Puerto Rican and Latinx studies. See Flores's *Divided Borders: Essays on Puerto Rican Identity* (Houston. Arte Público Press, 1993); *From Bomba to Hip-Hop: Puerto Rican Culture and Latino Identity* (New York: Columbia University Press, 2000); *The Diaspora Strikes Back: Caribeño Tales of Learning and Turning* (New York: Routledge, 2008); as well as the anthology *On Edge: The Crisis of Contemporary Latin American Culture* (Minnesota: University of Minnesota Press, 1992), edited with George Yudice.

Lola Rodríguez de Tío was a pioneering feminist poet as well as abolitionist. Her poem "Cuba y Puerto Rico son de un pájaro las dos alas" ("Cuba and Puerto Rico are two wings of the same bird") describes the unity between the two colonies at the end of the nineteenth century in their collective fight for liberation from Spain. Her ideas may have influenced the design of the flags of the two islands, which are the same, with the colors blue and red reversed. The poem's refrain was revived by legendary nueva trova singer Pablo Milanés in his "Son de Cuba a Puerto Rico."

See Antonio Cornejo Polar, *Sobre literatura y crítica latinoamericanas* (Caracas, Venezuela: Ediciones de la Facultad de Humanidades y Educación, Universidad Central de Venezuela, 1982) and Alberto

Moreiras, "Hybridity and Double Consciousness," *Cultural Studies* 13, no. 3 (1999).

Immanuel Wallerstein's works, initiated by his four-volume study *The Modern World-System*, are highly influential rejoinders to orthodox Marxist analyses that stress the primacy of the development of capitalist formations in Western Europe. Wallerstein's world-system theories are more consonant with current ideas about globalization and the foundations of global economic exploitation that began with the Dutch East India Company and the Iberian conquest of the New World.

See Alejo Carpentier, *Music in Cuba,* trans. Alan West-Durán (Minneapolis: University of Minnesota Press, 2002) for a discussion of the origins of Afro-Cuban music.

See Ned Sublette, *Cuba and Its Music: From the First Drums to the Mambo* (Chicago: Chicago Review Press, 2004) for a tireless historical recounting of the evolution of Afro-Cuban music.

Ruth Glaser's *My Music Is My Flag: Puerto Rican Musicians and Their New York Communities, 1917–1940* (Berkeley: University of California Press, 1995) is a pioneering work that unearths important histories of under-acknowledged Puerto Rican musicians in New York.

See Urayoán Noel, "In the Decimated City: Symptom, Translation, and the Performance of a New York Jíbaro from Ladí to Luciano to Lavoe," *Centro: Journal of the Center for Puerto Rican Studies* 19, no. 2 (Fall 2007).

See José Antonio Burciaga, *Drink Cultura: Chicanismo* (Santa Barbara, CA: Joshua Odell Editions, 1992) and Mario Suárez, *Chicano Sketches: Short Stories by Mario Súarez* (Tucson: University of Arizona Press, 2004) for lucid descriptions of the origins of Chicano culture in the Southwest.

The current surge of Afro-Mexican advocacy in the United States includes Miguel, an alternative pop/R&B singer and USC graduate student, and *New York Times* journalist Walter Thompson

Hernández, who are both part Mexican, part African American. Thompson Hernández assembled a photography project documenting the lives of "Blaxicans" in Southern California. "You have relatives that are being deported and you have relatives that are being gunned down on the street because they are Black," he says.

Latin Music USA, a four-part PBS series that debuted in 2007, contains many stories about the connection between Mexican American rock and American "roots rock," as does Tom Waldman and David Reyes's *Land of a Thousand Dances: Chicano Rock 'n Roll from Southern California* (Albuquerque: University of New Mexico Press, 1998). These connections and more are the subject of Deborah Pacini Hernández's excellent *Oye Como Va! Hybridity and Identity in Latino Popular Music* (Philadelphia: Temple University Press, 2010).

Chapter 4. Raza Interrupted

In this chapter I undertake the complicated task of describing how Latin American ideas about race begin to intersect with the Anglo-American racial binary. The essence of this interaction is the potential of latent racial identities in Latin America to manifest themselves more strongly as the result of racialization in Anglo-America and to play a significant role in the civil rights era.

Latinx groups made initial contact with the United States as a result of two wars: the US-Mexican War and the Spanish-American War, which resulted in the absorption of thousands of Mexicans, followed by early twentieth-century migration from Puerto Rico and Cuba. Those early contact zones and the resulting cyclical waves of immigration have given the Latinx presence in the United States a dynamic character in contrast to the experience of European immigrants—whose migrating activity waned after World War II—and African Americans, who cannot be compared to immigrants given the horrors of the middle passage, slavery, and Jim Crow.

While Latinx in the United States were constantly engaged in a negotiation with America's social mores that impelled them to shift racial identities strategically or keep their true ethno-racial identity private, advocacy organizations geared their early efforts towards assimilation through whiteness, if merely to escape either the possibility of being enslaved or subsequent Jim Crow legislation and pseudo–Jim Crow policies of the North and West. Certain Latinx were able to gain the status of whiteness and succeed by passing, class mobility, and success in professional sports or entertainment, yet what evolved into Latinx identity crystallized around those who were not granted this status. Latinx identity would not exist without an assertion of racial difference.

The poet Victor Hernández Cruz was one of the first to coin the term *tropicalization*, using it as the title of an anthology of his poems (New York: Reed, Cannon & Johnson Communications, 1976).

See Shorto, *The Island at the Center of the World*, and Wallace, "Nueva York," for descriptions of New York's early history as New Amsterdam and the Latinx presence there.

Cuban author Antonio Benítez Rojo's *The Repeating Island: The Caribbean and the Postmodern Perspective* (Durham: Duke University Press, 1996) was one of the most influential works about the Caribbean of its time.

Colón's *A Puerto Rican in New York, and Other Sketches*, and Piri Thomas's *Down These Mean Streets* (New York: Knopf, 1967) are two major classics of Nuyorican literature.

Venezuelan critic César Miguel Rondón's *The Book of Salsa: A Chronicle of Urban Music from the Caribbean to New York City*, trans. Frances R. Aparicio with Jackie White (Chapel Hill: University of North Carolina Press, 2008) offers insightful observations about New York's 1970s salsa scene. See also Juan Flores, *Salsa Rising: New York Latin Music of the Sixties Generation* (New York: Oxford University Press, 2016).

There are several recent books about the Young Lords, most notably Darrel Wanzer-Serrano's *The New York Young Lords and the Struggle for Liberation* (Philadelphia: Temple University Press, 2015) and his edited compilation *The Young Lords: A Reader* (New York: New York University Press, 2010), the latter as Darrel Enck-Wanzer; Miguel "Mickey" Meléndez's firsthand account *We Took the Streets: Fighting for Latino Rights with the Young Lords* (New York: St. Martin's Press, 2003); *Palante: The Young Lords Party* (Chicago: Haymarket Books, 2011), a collection of excerpts from the party's newspaper; and Iris Morales's *Through the Eyes of Rebel Women: The Young Lords: 1969–1976* (New York: Red Sugarcane Press, 2016).

See Miguel Algarín and Miguel Piñero, eds., *Nuyorican Poetry: An Anthology of Puerto Rican Words and Feelings* (New York: William Morrow, 1975) and Miguel Algarín and Bob Holman, eds., *Aloud: Voices from the Nuyorican Poets Cafe* (New York: Henry Holt, 1994).

For more on the New Rican Village, see Marina Roseman, "The New Rican Village: Artists in Control of the Image-Making Machinery," *Latin American Music Review/Revista de Música Latinoamericana* 4, no. 1 (Spring–Summer 1983).

Homi Bhabha's *The Location of Culture* (New York: Routledge, 1994) offers an indispensable analysis of mimicry and colonialism.

See Lee Bebout, "The Nativist Aztlán: Fantasies and Anxieties of Whiteness on the Border," *Latino Studies* 10, no. 3 (September 2012), and "Hero Making in El Movimiento: Reies López Tijerina and the Chicano National Imaginary," *Aztlán: A Journal of Chicano Studies* 32, no. 2 (Fall 2007).

F. Arturo Rosales's *Chicano! The History of the Mexican American Civil Rights Movement* (Houston: Arte Público Press, 1996) is a very useful book version of the informative, workmanlike PBS special of the same name.

Gloria Anzaldúa's *Borderlands/La Frontera: The New Mestiza* (San Francisco, CA: Aunt Lute Books, 1987) is an unparalleled classic of "border thinking" and Chicanx feminist studies.

See Jeff Chang, *Can't Stop Won't Stop: A History of the Hip-Hop*

Generation (New York: St. Martin's Press, 2005) for definitive story-telling about the origins of hip-hop.

See Marta Moreno Vega's *The Altar of My Soul: The Living Traditions of Santería* (New York: Ballantine, 2000); "Espiritismo in the Puerto Rican Community: A New World Recreation with the Elements of Kongo Ancestor Worship," *Journal of Black Studies* 29, no. 3 (January 1999); and "The Yoruba Orisha Tradition Comes to New York City," *African American Review* 29, no. 2 (Summer 1995).

For an extraordinary account of the Latinx impact on New York's art scene in the 1960s, 1970s, and 1980s, see Yasmín Ramírez, *Nuyorican Vanguards, Political Actions, Poetic Visions: A History of Puerto Rican Artists in New York 1964–1984*, PhD diss. (New York: CUNY Graduate Center, 2005).

Chapter 5. Border Thinking 101

The phrase *border thinking* was coined in reference to hybrid cultures that formed in the border areas of the American Southwest and northern Mexico. Yet the gradual migration of Latinx people to the North, as well as African Americans fleeing the Jim Crow South, created variations of border thinking that serve as an oppositional force to American exceptionalism and standard American discourse about identity.

Pedro Pietri's "Puerto Rican Obituary" appears in his first book, *Puerto Rican Obituary* (New York: Monthly Review Press, 1973).

The original use of the phrase *double consciousness* is attributed to W. E. B. Du Bois's signature auto-ethnography, *The Souls of Black Folk* (Mineola, NY: Dover, 1994).

A useful dissection of Du Bois's theory of double consciousness appears in José Itzigsohn and Karida Brown's "Sociology and the Theory of Double Consciousness: W. E. B. Du Bois' Phenomenology of Racialized Subjectivity," *Du Bois Review* 12, no. 2 (2015).

See Ta-Nehisi Coates, "Why Precisely Is Bernie Sanders Against

Reparations?," *The Atlantic*, January 19, 2016 (available at theatlantic .com).

For a discussion of double consciousness and mestiza consciousness, see Teresa A. Martínez, "The Double Consciousness of Du Bois & the 'Mestiza Consciousness' of Anzaldúa," *Race, Gender & Class* 9, no. 4 (2002).

See Ana Louise Keating, "From Borderlands and New Mestizas to Nepantlas and Nepantleras: Anzaldúan Theories for Social Change," *Human Architecture: Journal of the Sociology of Self-Knowledge* 4, no. 3 (Summer 2006).

See Gloria Anzaldúa, "How to Tame a Wild Tongue," in *Borderlands/La Frontera*, and Frances R. Aparicio, "Whose Spanish, Whose Language, Whose Power? An Ethnographic Inquiry into Differential Bilingualism," *Indiana Journal of Hispanic Literatures* 12 (1998).

See Flores, "'Qué Assimilated, Brother, Yo Soy Asimilao': The Structuring of Puerto Rican Identity in the U.S.," in *Divided Borders*, and Tato Laviera, *AmeRícan*, 2nd ed. (Houston: Arte Público Press, 2003).

See Paula M. L. Moya, "Dismantling the Master's House: The Decolonial Literary Imaginations of Audre Lorde and Junot Díaz," in *Junot Díaz and the Decolonial Imagination*, ed. Monica Hanna, Jennifer Harford Vargas, and José David Saldívar (Durham: Duke University Press, 2016).

For more on constraint and creativity, see Patricia D. Stokes, "Crossing Disciplines: A Constraint-Based Model of the Creative/ Innovative Process," *Journal of Product Innovation Management* 31, no. 2 (March 2014). Interestingly, Stokes describes jazz pianist Thelonious Monk's creative process as one designed to escape constraints. "By precluding specific features of bebop, often borrowing their substitutes from earlier jazz styles," Monk tried to reformulate bebop by being both more and less complex in his approach. He excised Charlie Parker–style virtuoso soloing with

"New Orleans–style paraphrase improvisation." He replaced the "harmonic densities of bop" with "spare, calculated melodies and carefully chosen notes, graced with silences." New Orleans jazz had already been encoded with Afro-Cuban influences, particularly the separation between left- and right-hand playing. So Monk was in a sense reprising much of the history of the development of Afro-Cuban music by taking a contemporary development, bebop, back a notch to recover some of its ancestral past.

For a discussion of the Chicana influence on punk music in California, see Michelle Habell-Pallán, "'Soy Punkera, Y Que?': Sexuality, Translocality, and Punk in Los Angeles and Beyond" in *Loca Motion: The Travels of Chicana and Latina Popular Culture* (New York: New York University Press, 2005).

See Yudhijit Bhattacharjee, "Why Bilinguals Are Smarter," *New York Times*, March 17, 2012 (available at nytimes.com).

Chapter 6. Our Raza, Ourselves

This chapter is a discussion of how Latinx view ourselves and our racial identity. While this view is often fluid, it can be highly influenced by the Anglo-American racial binary, which tends to make clearer the latent binary in Latin American racial attitudes.

For a discussion of the mirror in child psychology, see Jacques Lacan, "Aggressiveness in Psychoanalysis" in *Écrits*, trans. Bruce Fink (New York: W. W. Norton, 2002).

For more on the Bronx and Robert Moses, see Marshall Berman, *All That Is Solid Melts into Air: The Experience of Modernity* (New York and London: Verso, 1983), and Robert Caro, *The Power Broker: Robert Moses and the Fall of New York* (New York: Vintage, 1975).

The Taíno elements in Puerto Rican culture are examined in depth in Antonio M. Stevens-Arroyo, *Cave of the Jagua: The Mythological World of the Taínos*, rev. ed. (Scranton, PA: University of Scranton Press, 2006).

See Gabriel Haslip-Viera, ed., *Taíno Revival: Critical Perspectives on Puerto Rican Identity and Cultural Politics* (Princeton, NJ: Markus Wiener Publishers, 2001), particularly its introduction, "Competing Identities: Taíno Revivalism and Other Ethno-racial Identity Movements Among Puerto Ricans and Other Caribbean Latinos in the United States, 1980–Present," and the chapter by Miriam Jiménez Román, "The Indians Are Coming! The Indians Are Coming! The Taíno and Puerto Rican Identity."

For more about the term *moreno* in Brazilian racial identity, see Stanley R. Bailey and Edward E. Telles, "Multiracial Versus Collective Black Categories: Examining Census Classification Debates in Brazil," *Ethnicities* 6, no. 1 (March 2006).

For further discussion of new immigrant-demonizing and anti-Latinx stereotypes, see Leo R. Chávez, *The Latino Threat: Constructing Immigrants, Citizens, and the Nation* (Redwood City: Stanford University Press, 2008).

A discussion of genomes and the DNA test fad can be found in Peter Wade, Carlos López Beltrán, Eduardo Restrepo, and Ricardo Ventura Santos, eds., *Mestizo Genomics: Race Mixture, Nation, and Science in Latin America* (Durham: Duke University Press, 2014), and Alondra Nelson, *The Social Life of DNA: Race, Reparations, and Reconciliation After the Genome* (Boston: Beacon Press, 2016).

See Richard Delgado, Juan F. Perea, and Jean Stefancic, eds., *Latinos and the Law: Cases and Materials* (St. Paul, MN: Thomson/West, 2008), and Ignacio M. García, *White but Not Equal: Mexican Americans, Jury Discrimination, and the Supreme Court* (Tucson: University of Arizona Press, 2008).

See Adrian Piper, "Xenophobia and Kantian Rationalism," *Philosophical Forum* XXIV, nos. 1–3 (Fall–Spring 1992–3).

For the definitive discussion of racialization in *Mendez v. Westminster*, see Jennifer McCormick and César Ayala, "Felicita, 'La Prieta' Méndez (1916–1998) and the End of Latino School Segregation in California," *Centro Journal* XIX, no. 2 (Fall 2007).

See Nicholas Vargas, "Latina/o Whitening? Which Latina/os Self-Classify as White and Report Being Perceived as White by Other Americans?," *Du Bois Review* 12, no. 1 (2015).

See Bonilla-Silva and Dietrich, "The Latin Americanization of Racial Stratification in the U.S."

Chapter 7. Towards a New Raza Politics

What kind of politics should Latinx pursue when identity politics and class-based politics are often considered mutually exclusive? How can Latinx, with our ability to maintain strong connections with political and economic struggles in our origin countries, reveal the continual myopia of US foreign policy? In this chapter I make a case for how Latinx, by virtue of our racial and national identities, can pursue an anti-neoliberal perspective that is harmonious with global working class interests.

See José Martí, *Nuestra América* (Barcelona: Editorial Ariel, 1973).

See David Hayes-Bautista and Jorge Chapa, "Latino Terminology: Conceptual Bases for Standardized Terminology," *American Journal of Public Health* 77, no. 1 (January 1987).

See Roberto Suro, "Whatever Happened to Latino Political Power?," *New York Times*, January 2, 2016 (available at nytimes .com).

See Matt Barreto and Gary M. Segura, *Latino America: How America's Most Dynamic Population Is Poised to Transform the Politics of the Nation* (New York: PublicAffairs, 2014).

For a discussion of Marco Rubio and Ted Cruz as Latino politicians, see Lizette Álvarez and Manny Fernández, "Marco Rubio and Ted Cruz Diverge in Approach to Their Hispanic Identity," *New York Times*, December 16, 2015 (available at nytimes.com).

See Ed Morales, "Koch Front Group: The Libre Initiative," *The Progressive*, 2014, for a discussion of how the Koch Brothers have attempted to co-opt Latinx voters.

The Herbalife controversy demonstrates the ties between financiers and lobbyists that are largely responsible for eroding democracy. See Michael S. Schmidt, Eric Lipton, and Alexandra Stevenson, "After Big Bet, Hedge Fund Pulls the Levers of Power," *New York Times*, March 9, 2014 (available at nytimes.com), and Chris Bragg, "Charity Tied to Council Speaker Quadruples Its Funding," *Crain's New York Business*, June 30, 2014 (available at crainsnewyork.com).

For more on Univision radio's role in organizing immigration reform demonstrations in the mid-2000s, see Ed Morales, "The Media Is the Mensaje," *The Nation*, April 27, 2006 (available at thenation .com).

Louis A. Pérez Jr.'s work on Cuba is excellent, particularly *On Becoming Cuban: Identity, Nationality and Culture* (Chapel Hill: University of North Carolina Press, 1999) and *The Structure of Cuban History: Meanings and Purpose of the Past* (Chapel Hill: University of North Carolina Press, 2013).

For a fascinating discussion of aspects of the Dream Act not often discussed in the mainstream media, see Cristina Beltrán's "No Papers, No Fear: DREAM Activism, New Social Media, and the Queering of Immigrant Rights," in *Contemporary Latina/o Media: Production, Circulation, Politics*, ed. Arlene Dávila and Yeidy M. Rivero (New York: New York University Press, 2014).

Chapter 8. Media, Marketing, and the Invisible Soul of Latinidad

In this chapter I demonstrate how Latinx are elided in Anglo-American media conventions. The fluid nature of Latinx identity is a starting point for critiquing the media's alleged objectivity and encouraging effective use of twenty-first-century de-centered media formats and practices.

For an authoritative commentary on Latinx stereotypes, see Clara E. Rodríguez, ed., *Latin Looks: Images of Latinas and Latinos in the*

U.S. Media (Boulder: Westview Press, 1997), particularly Charles Ramírez Berg's chapter "Stereotyping in Films in General and of the Hispanic in Particular."

Frances Negrón-Muntaner headed up a team of researchers for two studies on Latinx in the media: "The Latino Media Gap: A Report on the State of Latinos in U.S. Media" in 2014 and "The Latino Disconnect: Latinos in the Age of Media Mergers" in 2016. Both were commissioned by Columbia University's Center for the Study of Ethnicity and Race, the National Hispanic Foundation of the Arts, and the National Association of Latino Independent Producers, and are definitive in this field of study.

See Linda Martín Alcoff, "Is Latina/o Identity a Racial Identity?" in *Hispanics/Latinos in the United States: Ethnicity, Race, and Rights,* ed. Jorge J. E. Gracia and Pablo de Greiff (New York: Routledge, 2000) for a discussion of Latinx as an ethnoracial group.

Alejandro Portes and Rubén G. Rumbaut demonstrate, through data, Latinx's tendency towards downward mobility in their book, *Immigrant America: A Portrait* (Oakland: University of California Press, 2001) and in their edited compilation, *Ethnicities: Children of Immigrants in America* (Berkeley and Los Angeles: University of California Press, 2001).

Miriam Jiménez Román and Juan Flores, eds., *The Afro-Latin@ Reader: History and Culture in the United States* (Durham: Duke University Press, 2010) is an indispensable volume on the subject.

For an original discussion of racelessness, see Naomi Zack, *Race and Mixed Race* (Philadelphia: Temple University Press, 1993).

Arlene Dávila's *Latinos, Inc.: The Marketing and Making of a People*, rev. ed. (Berkeley and Los Angeles: University of California Press, 2012) is a landmark work, and initiates a discussion of "reverse assimilation."

In *Life on the Hyphen: The Cuban-American Way*, rev. ed. (Austin: University of Texas Press, 2012), Gustavo Pérez Firmat coins the term *1.5 generation.*

See Ginetta E. B. Candelario, *Black Behind the Ears: Dominican Racial Identity from Museums to Beauty Shops* (Durham: Duke University Press, 2007) for a discussion of how women express racial identity through hair styling.

See Ed Morales, "'Mega' Mania," *Village Voice*, August 18, 1998 (available at villagevoice.com).

For a discussion of the vacillating attempts by broadcast media to incorporate English/Spanish bilingualism into their programming, see Viviana Rojas and Juan Piñon, "Spanish, English or Spanglish? Media Strategies and Corporate Struggles to Reach the Second and Later Generations of Latinos," *International Journal of Hispanic Media* 7 (August 2014).

See Mary C. Beltrán, "The New Hollywood Racelessness: Only the Fast, Furious (and Multiracial) Will Survive," *Cinema Journal* 44, no. 2 (Winter 2005) and "Fast and Bilingual: *Fast & Furious* and the Latinization of Racelessness," *Cinema Journal* 53, no. 1 (Fall 2013).

See Ed Morales, "We Ought to Be in Pictures," *The Nation*, September 27, 1999.

Chapter 9. The Latinx Urban Space and Identity

Latinx identity is a key reference point for dismantling the marginalizing myth of the White City. The urban space is essential for Latinx to share lived experience with the collective black and create a nexus for political power.

Henri Lefebvre's contributions are many, but for his work relating to the points made here, see *Writings on Cities* (Oxford, UK: Wiley-Blackwell, 1995).

See Ed Morales, "How Ya Like Nosotros Now?," *Village Voice*, November 26, 1991, for a discussion of East Coast versus West Coast Latinx rap.

An early mention of "gentefication" in the mainstream press appeared in Jennifer Medina, "Gentrification Protesters in Los

Angeles Target Art Galleries," *New York Times*, November 5, 2016 (available at nytimes.com).

Alan Moore and Marc Miller, eds., *ABC No Rio Dinero: The Story of a Lower East Side Art Gallery* (New York: ABC No Rio with Collaborative Projects, 1985), is an excellent anthology of materials, essays, and reminiscences about political art on the Lower East Side.

See Gary Bridge, Tim Butler, and Loretta Lees, eds., *Mixed Communities: Gentrification by Stealth?* (Chicago: Policy Press / University of Chicago Press, 2012) for more on the debate about "mixed communities."

The central elements of Mayor Michael Bloomberg's rezoning strategy are laid out in Alex Garvin & Associates, Inc., "Visions for New York City: Housing and the Public Realm," report prepared for the Economic Development Corporation of New York City (New York: Alex Garvin & Associates, 2006).

An early discussion of inclusionary zoning can be found in Alyssa Katz, "Inclusionary Zoning's Big Moment," *City Limits*, December 15, 2004 (available at citylimits.org).

This chapter's section on East Harlem grows directly out of three sources: a story I wrote for the City Section of the *New York Times* called "Spanish Harlem on His Mind," February 23, 2003 (available at nytimes.com); the documentary *Whose Barrio?*, codirected with Laura G. Rivera (Nuyo-Isla Films, 2008); and a chapter I contributed to *Latinos in New York: Communities in Transition*, ed. Sherrie Baver, Angelo Falcón, and Gabriel Haslip-Viera, 2nd ed. (Notre Dame, IN: University of Notre Dame Press, 2017), called "Latino Core Communities in Transition: The Erasing of an Imaginary Nation."

See Rebecca Solnit, "Death by Gentrification: The Killing That Shamed San Francisco," *The Guardian*, March 21, 2016 (available at theguardian.com).

See Ed Morales, "Brown Like Me?," *The Nation*, February 19, 2004 (available at thenation.com).

For more on reggaetón as an expression of Afro-Latinx culture, see Wayne Marshall, Deborah Pacini Hernández, and Raquel Z. Rivera, eds., *Reggaetón* (Durham: Duke University Press, 2009), and Petra R. Rivera-Rideau, *Remixing Reggaetón: The Cultural Politics of Race in Puerto Rico* (Durham: Duke University Press, 2015).

Chapter 10. Dismantling the Master's House

This chapter describes the emergence of vital new national groups of Latinx and cautions against a neoliberal multiculturalist discourse that tries to erase border thinking in favor of nuanced assimilation into future neoliberal globalist projects.

See Jorge Duany, "Dominican Migration to Puerto Rico: A Transnational Perspective," *Centro Journal* 17, no. 1 (Spring 2005) and Ramón Grosfoguel and Chloe Georas, "The Racialization of Latino Caribbean Migrants in the NY Metro Area," *Centro Journal* 1 and 2 (1996).

See also Silvio Torres-Saillant, "The Indian in the Latino: Genealogies of Ethnicity," *Latino Studies* 10, no. 4 (December 2012).

In "Latinos and the Mayoralty: Who Will Be First?," a four-part series for *City Limits*, November–December 2012 (available at citylimits.org), I discuss the attempts of Adriano Espaillat to unseat longtime US representative Charles Rangel in Harlem.

See Mark Weisbrot, Stephan Lefebvre, and Joseph Sammut, "Did NAFTA Help Mexico? An Assessment After 20 Years," Center for Economic Policy and Research, February 2014.

For an excellent social, economic, and political history of Puerto Rico, see César Ayala and Rafael Bernabe, *Puerto Rico in the American Century: A History Since 1898* (Chapel Hill: University of North Carolina Press, 2007).

See Walter Mignolo, *Local Histories/Global Designs: Coloniality, Subaltern Knowledges, and Border Thinking* (Princeton, NJ: Princeton University Press, 2000), and *The Darker Side of the Renaissance:*

Literacy, Territoriality, and Colonization (Ann Arbor: University of Michigan Press, 1995).

Howard Winant discusses his conception of the "racial break" in "The Modern World Racial System," in *Transnational Blackness: Navigating the Global Color Line*, ed. Manning Marable and Vanessa Asgard-Jones (New York: Palgrave-MacMillan, 2008).

See Jodi Melamed, "The Spirit of Neoliberalism: From Racial Liberalism to Neoliberal Multiculturalism," *Social Text* 23, no. 4, issue 89 (Winter 2006).

For an excellent discussion of the contradictions inherent in Lin-Manuel Miranda's *Hamilton*, see Lyra D. Monteiro, "Race-Conscious Casting and the Erasure of the Black Past in Lin-Manuel Miranda's Hamilton," *The Public Historian* 38, no. 1 (February 2016); Ishmael Reed, "'Hamilton: The Musical': Black Actors Dress Up Like Slave Traders … and It's Not Halloween," *CounterPunch*, August 21, 2015 (available at counterpunch.org); and Matt Stoller, "The Hamilton Hustle: Why Liberals Have Embraced Our Most Dangerously Reactionary Founder," *The Baffler*, no. 34 (March 2017).

See also Alana Semuels, "How *Hamilton* Recasts Thomas Jefferson as a Villain," *The Atlantic*, August 19, 2015 (available at theatlantic.com).

See Michael Hardt and Antonio Negri, *Commonwealth* (Cambridge, MA: Harvard University Press, 2009).

Herbert W. Vilakazi's "Was Karl Marx a Black Man?," *Monthly Review* 32, no. 2 (June 1980), which I discovered after watching a BBC *Genius of the Modern World* episode on the life of Marx, alerted me to the fact that his nickname among his Young Hegelian friends at Berlin University was "the Moor."

Index